THE COMPOSER
IN HOLLYWOOD

By the Same Author

Impressionism in Music

Miklós Rózsa: a sketch of his life and work

Delius: Portrait of a Cosmopolitan

Ravel (Novello short biography series)

Herbert Howells: a study

Szymanowski (BBC Music Guide)

George Dyson: a centenary appreciation

Dyson's Delight: a selection of essays, lectures and broadcasts (editor)

The Britten Companion (editor and contributor)

Spring Returning: a selection from the works of James Farrar (editor)

The Collected Arthur Machen (editor)

Prokofiev (in preparation)

Published Arrangements and Transcriptions

Serge Prokofiev	Flute Concerto (transcription of Sonata for Flute & Piano, Op. 44)
	War and Peace — suite from the opera
William Walton	Troilus and Cressida — symphonic suite from the opera
	Henry V — a Shakespeare scenario, for chorus and orchestra
	Hamlet — a Shakespeare scenario, for orchestra
	Richard III — a Shakespeare scenario, for orchestra
	A Wartime Sketchbook, for orchestra
George Gershwin	An American in Paris — orchestral suite in 4 movements, from the movie
Claude Debussy	Printemps (reconstruction of the original version for wordless chorus and orchestra)

Christopher Palmer

THE COMPOSER
IN HOLLYWOOD

Marion Boyars
London · New York

Published in Great Britain and the United States in 1990 by
Marion Boyars Publishers
24 Lacy Road, London SW15 1NL
26 East 33rd Street, New York, NY 10016

Distributed in the United States and in Canada by
Rizzoli International Publications Inc,
New York

Distributed in Australia by
Wild & Woolley Pty Ltd, Glebe, NSW

British Library Cataloguing in Publication Data

Palmer, Christopher
   The composer in Hollywood.
   1. American cinema films. Music, Composers
   I. Title
   782.8'5028

Library of Congress Cataloging-in-Publication Data
Palmer, Christopher.
   The composer in Hollywood/ Christopher Palmer.
   Includes bibliographical references.
   1. Motion picture music — History and criticism.   2. Music—
California — Hollywood — 20th century — History and criticism.
I. Title.
ML2075.P28   1990
781.5'42'0979493—dc20   89-22401

ISBN: 0–7145–2885–4 Cloth

Typeset by Ann Buchan (Typesetters) in Baskerville 11/13 pt and Optima
Printed and bound by Biddles Ltd, Guildford and King's Lynn

CONTENTS

ACKNOWLEDGEMENTS

The following people and institutions, listed here in alphabetical order, helped me in the preparation of this book in ways too numerous to describe individually.

Keith Alain, Jeff Atmajian, The Alfred Newman Memorial Library at USC, Juliet Battaglino (née Rózsa), Mr and Mrs Elmer Bernstein, Robert Blackmore, Robert Bornstein (Paramount), The British Film Institute, Jill Burrows, Jeffrey Dane, Ken Darby, John and Mary Fitzpatrick, Dan and Joel Franklin (Warner Bros), Charles Gerhardt, John Green, Judy Green, George Hall, Alan Hamer, the late Bernard Herrmann, Marvel Jensen, the late George Korngold, John Steven Lasher, The Max Steiner Music Society, David Meeker, John Morgan, the late John Munro-Hall (RKO), the late Jerome Moross, Alex North, Frances Palmer, André Previn, Nicholas Raine, David Raksin, Leonard Rosenman, Dr and Mrs Miklós Rózsa, Nick Rózsa, Pat Russ, Fred Steiner, Tony Thomas, the late Dimitri Tiomkin, Olivia Tiomkin, John Waxman, the late Roy and Jean Webb.

I offer sincere thanks to all of them, not only for their helpfulness but also for their patience: for this book was begun in 1970 and finally completed only in the late summer of 1988.

Christopher Palmer

To Elmer
and all the Bernsteins

PROLOGUE

Film music is a notoriously difficult subject to discuss in depth, since (like all musical topics) such discussion presupposes some knowledge of the musical science which the average student of film or the man-in-the-street cannot be expected to possess. So I have restricted technical talk to an absolute minimum.

I have limited myself to the broad outlines of Hollywood music 1930–50 and to its chief representatives. There are many interesting composers who are not discussed, (for instance Daniele Amfitheatrof, David Raksin, Leigh Harline, Victor Young, Hans Salter, John Green, Anthony Collins, Paul Sawtell, Leith Stevens, Bronislau Kaper), nor can I claim to have dealt exhaustively with many of those who are. To write a complete history of Hollywood music would be the work of a lifetime. To contain this book within reasonable bounds I start in the mid-thirties and stop short in the early 'fifties, the twenty-year period which roughly encompasses the Golden Age of Hollywood music, from the end of its beginning to the beginning of its end. I study something of its origins, its character, the life and work of its chief architects, those whose film careers began in the 'thirties and early 'forties. For each composer discussed, my policy has been to place his achievement in overall perspective, and then to analyze a small number of major scores in detail. However, on occasion I have not hesitated to follow certain composers when their work has taken them outside the Hollywood area, for example the Herrmann–Truffaut collaboration.

Selecting the major scores has not been easy; for although few superior films are mated with inferior scores, the converse by no means always applies. In fact, the composer is frequently called in as a first-aid man, morally committed to the restitution of a product unworthy of his best efforts. This is why many composers have produced excellent scores for second- or third-rate pictures. I decided, however, that with one or two exceptions, I should concentrate on films which have won acclaim *per se* and which, therefore, should stand a fair chance of being familiar to the ordinary film-goer to whom — more than to the film-music fanatic or to the professional musician — this book is directed.

Having spent my professional life largely in this field, I am closely involved. I have worked in Hollywood; and as an orchestrator with several of those whose work is discussed here and knew personally others with whom I did not work. An unbiased account is therefore scarcely to be looked for, although I hope there are compensatory virtues. I do, after all, know something of the nature of film music from the inside, so to a degree I can talk *about* it as opposed to *around* it.

I discovered music through film music. In the summer of 1962, as a boy of 15, I first saw *King of Kings*, with the music of Miklós Rózsa. But what music! It came as a revelation, both as music in itself and in terms of the purpose for which it had been designed. Symphonic music: orchestral and evidently the work of a professional composer with his own individual sound, in a *film*? It was a fascinating phenomenon. Then I began regularly to notice film music credits; 'Music *by* . . . .' I knew enough to appreciate all that was implied in that 'by' in a symphonic orchestral score lasting 40–50 minutes and sometimes longer.

Amazingly, I found then — and still find now — that few are struck by the force of that phenomenon. Film music is, and always has been, a minority interest; and like many minority interests, it often seems fated to attract uninformed and unsympathetic critical attention whenever it attracts any at all. The root cause is surely that film music is a hybrid and as such has never gained wholehearted acceptance as a legitimate form of musical creativity. It is not quite film and not quite music. The film maker acknowledges the need for music on the soundtrack, but because of its highly specialized technical nature cannot really understand it in the way he can understand script-writing or camera-work. Music has been described as a universal language, and it is that which renders it so indispensable to the film maker. Yet in the discussion and analysis of music there yawns a tremendous chasm between musician and non-musician. Much well-meaning film-music criticism has been written by people with great enthusiasm but little technical knowledge of music. But musicians both willing and able to expound film music seem scarcely to exist, except in the persons of those few practitioners of the art who are as articulate in words as in music.

This basic problem of communication profoundly affects the relationship between film director and composer. A director may have no *technical* knowledge of music but knows what he wants from it *dramatically*, in which case he can make his wishes known to the composer and all will be well. Frequently, however, directors have a confused idea of what music is and what it can do, and when they have insisted on overruling the composer the results have often been disastrous.

Within the musical fraternity there is a fundamental lack of sympathy for film music. The idea that music should play the subsidiary role it has to play within a cinematic context seems unacceptable. The film composer, whose music is regulated in quantity and essence by the script and camera movement, is regarded as an impoverished relation of the aspiring architect of symphony, concerto or opera. But this is the price the composer has to pay if he wishes to participate in the creation of the composite art form that is film, in which the active presence of music is a basic need. Why? Because music exerts over the audience a manipulative control that is necessary because the motion picture's major drawback, compared with the live theatre, is its complete lack of direct audience communication. The screen and the audience are brought into a closer relationship through music. In Bernard Herrmann's view:

> Music on the screen can seek out and intensify the inner thoughts of the characters. It can invest a scene with terror, grandeur, gaiety or misery. It often lifts mere dialogue into the realm of poetry. It is the communicating link between screen and audience, reaching out and enveloping all into one single experience.

Frequently music's role in film is utilitarian or cosmetic. Where cutting from one shot or scene to another is fast and constant, music has to supply continuity. A good example is the newsreel: a montage in which music acts as a kind of binding veneer. It can ease transitions between one scene and another. It can reinforce action and emotion. As for speeding up action and slowing it down, one has only to experience the interminable time that credit titles played *without* music seem to last to realize the power wielded by music in negating our time sense. This credit title area is musically one of the most important, for in it the audience must be put in a suitably receptive frame of mind for the coming drama. Think of the collective mind of the audience before the movie begins in terms of an empty room awaiting a guest. If the guest arrives to find the room still empty, he will have to spend valuable time furnishing it himself. If, however, the furniture and everything designed to provide for his comfort is installed beforehand, he can immediately proceed with his business. Occasionally a director will purposely leave his main title sequence void of music, the effect of which is disquieting and disorienting (as silence always is), simply because we are not told what to expect. This negatively demonstrates the powerful 'manipulative control' that music exerts over us even before the film has begun. It follows of course that the audience may easily be put on the wrong track if the title music is (intentionally or unintentionally) inappropriate.

The camera is restricted to a two-dimensional representation of what it has to communicate. Music, being by nature fluid, ambiguous and elusive of definition, can set up emotional vibrations in the mind of the audience that may complement, supplement or even contradict the visual image. It supplies an all-important third dimension. Cinema is after all an art of fakery and illusion, and music is a superbly competent illusionist. A composer's job is to interpret and illuminate, rather than gratuitously to illustrate or describe, even if some element of illustration may often be involved in the illuminating.

Ideally a commodity as indispensable as film music would be provided only by composers of the highest responsibility and accomplishment, their sole aim being to enhance the film's stature as a work of art. But film has never viewed itself so exclusively: artistic integrity has always had to compromise with commercial viability (films have to make money), and this holds as good in the musical sphere as in any other. Bernard Herrmann was one of those who regarded film music first and foremost as an art, deserving of the very best a composer has to offer. Nevertheless the music *per se* should never regard itself as more than a single element in an act of corporate creativity. Each film brings with it an individual set of dramatic premises, and the composer has to advance to meet them on their terms, not on his. Colour, style, temper, pacing — all must be determined by the requirements of the films in question, and, as no two films are exactly alike in every respect, no two scores should be. The composer's responsibility is nothing less than the final shaping and rounding off of a perfect dramatic entity or composite, the film. He may be let down badly enough by the film, but that is no reason why the film should be let down by him.

But many films *have* been let down, and when one takes a bird's-eye view of the history of film music and sees the age-old conflict between art and commerce renewed in each successive generation, there is little cause for wonder. From the earliest silent films, music was deemed to be necessary both as a means of illustrating and sustaining the action and for covering the sound of the projection machine. A pianist with a gift for improvisation was invaluable, but there were also orchestras whose size and quality depended on the prosperity of the movie theatres that employed them. The classics were ransacked, re-scored, re-edited and put into utilitarian categories, often with scant regard for dramatic propriety. Someone decided, for instance, that Valentino's *The Son of the Sheik* should have Tchaikovsky's Fifth Symphony as music wherever he went. Libraries of classified 'mood' music did the rounds of theatres large and small. Some bigger films, such as *Birth of a Nation* (1914), had special scores (mostly quotations) fitted to them, and groups of musicians travelled with the film to play the music.

Movie orchestras began to attract good players; the hours were longer and the salaries therefore better than in the theatre. The music director studied the film with his librarian, selecting the music and arranging the cues for changes of scene. He was helped by a suggestion list sent with the film: the pieces recommended were obtainable in arrangements for all sizes of orchestra from fifty players (in the larger theatres) down to five, the usual size of the band that relieved the orchestra for brief intervals. The silent film thus acquainted millions of people with classical music — even if in a modified form — and created lucrative employment for many performing musicians. But this was not the whole story. As long ago as 1908 Saint-Saëns had written a small-orchestra original score for *The Death of the Duke of Guise*, and the silent era witnessed the birth of film scores by such established artists as Darius Milhaud, Paul Hindemith and Arthur Honegger. The German composer Edmund Meisel (now forgotten but for his film work) made a number of signal contributions with his music for the Sergei Eisenstein productions *Battleship Potemkin* (1925) and *October* (1927), and for Walter Ruttmann's documentary *Berlin* (1927).

The coming of talkies in 1929, bringing with it the chance of much closer correlation between sight and sound, stimulated interest on the part of 'serious' composers all over the world. By the mid-1930s Prokofiev, Shostakovich, Kabalevsky and Shaporin had written scores for Russian films; Milhaud, Auric, Honegger and Maurice Jaubert were composing for the French cinema; and in England Walter Leigh had contributed a celebrated score to *Song of Ceylon* (1934). In the late 1930s Benjamin Britten, Arthur Bliss, William Alwyn, Arthur Benjamin, William Walton, Hanns Eisler, Erich Wolfgang Korngold and George Antheil were all writing film scores and formulating a variety of techniques. By 1940 film music was recognized as a highly specialized compositional form. However, it should not be thought that music on the soundtrack was in its earliest days immediately the highly evolved and sophisticated affair it has since become. At first music (and dialogue) was used sparingly. In some cases the greater part of an entire picture would be silent, and then suddenly in the fourth or fifth reel someone would burst into song, as in *Pagan Love Song*. The theatre orchestra would play up to the moment when the soundtrack was due to enter and would finish in the appropriate key; then, after the recorded intermezzo was over, the band would strike up again and accompany the film to the end.

Early resistance to the dramatic use of music on the soundtrack was generally grounded in a fear that audiences would wonder where the music was coming from. Nor did directors always appreciate the necessity of a specially composed score for a film; as late as 1936 *Camille* could still be tricked out with a silent-movie-like hodgepodge of a score derived from the classics. Gradually it was realized that scores of unoriginal material were harmful to a picture, inasmuch as they drew unwanted attention to themselves by virtue of their familiarity: the music was noticed rather than being allowed to register subliminally. This practice still persists — examples are *2001 — A Space Odyssey*, *Elvira Madigan*, *10*, *The Sting* and *Manhattan* — and basically the same objection holds good. Acknowledging the need for an original, specially conceived dramatic musical support for each picture was a major breakthrough. It was also a challenge of the first magnitude, for it offered musicians the opportunity to develop what was in effect a completely new and untried medium.

MAX STEINER: BIRTH OF AN ERA

On Christmas Eve 1914 a 24-year-old Austrian Jew called Max(imilian Raoul Walter) Steiner docked in New York looking for a job in the music 'business'. Born in Vienna, he had up to then spent all his working-life in the musical theatre, and had abandoned a promising career as musical director in London to avoid being interned as an enemy alien when war broke out. His conspicuous talents as light-music composer, orchestrator, conductor and all-purpose musician quickly won him recognition on Broadway, where he was uninterruptedly active for the next 15 years of his life:

When I left my home in Austria as a very young man, it was the Viennese Operetta that ruled the entertainment world. Now in the New World I was to be in on the formative years of the American Musical Comedy. During my lifetime I was a witness to the evolution of this art-form to its present pinnacle as represented by such shows as *My Fair Lady, South Pacific, Oklahoma!, Brigadoon* and others. It was my privilege to know and sometimes to work with many of the great talents which were then emerging in the musical comedy world: Victor Herbert, George Gershwin, Jerome Kern, Vincent Youmans, Sigmund Romberg, as well as impresarios and theatrical producers like Ziegfeld, the Shuberts, George White and many others who played a large part in the development of musical comedy. Later on, I was also to be in on the very beginning of the art of scoring a motion picture.[1]

Steiner made this decisive move in 1929, once again at Christmastide.

Nineteen twenty-nine was, of course, the year of the Wall Street Crash and the beginning of the Depression. Two years earlier, the coming of sound to films with the Al Jolson vehicle *The Jazz Singer* had marked the beginning of a swift decline in the fortunes of theatres and consequently theatre musicians. Vaudeville theatres were soon closing all over the country, and by 1931 45% of Broadway was shut. This was the background to Steiner's move, but the irony was that the use of sound in pictures did not at first provide the opportunities for the development of the film score that might have been expected:

The economic distress in which musicians found themselves after the advent of talking pictures was somewhat counteracted by a miniature gold rush to California. Well-known musicians and orchestra leaders were brought to Hollywood, and the march of recorded pictures began in earnest.

. . . There was very little underscoring (background music) in those days, but chiefly main and end titles (opening and closing music). Recorded music was deemed necessary only for musical productions, such as *Rio Rita, The Street Singer, The Rogue Song* and *Vagabond Lover*.

Almost insurmountable difficulties confronted musicians in those days in successfully transferring even a small part of the actual sound on to the sound track. The reasons were numerous: producers and directors did not know how to handle music; sound men and musicians were inexperienced; the microphone was in its infancy; and, therefore, the entire technical staff went into contortions to reproduce, even in part, what was actually heard on the set. . . .

. . . Music for dramatic pictures was only used when it

was actually required by the script. A constant fear prevailed among producers, directors and musicians, that they would be asked: where does the music come from? Therefore they never used music unless it could be explained by the presence of a source like an orchestra, piano player, phonograph or radio, which was specified in the script.[2]

The opportunities for work for musicians were obviously greatest in musicals, and a number — *Broadway Melody, Rio Rita* and *The Street Singer* — were great successes. But this vein was to run quickly dry:

> Through lack of sufficient good material and the ever changing taste of a fickle public, musical picture after musical picture failed, and the studios decided to call it a day and go back to dramatic pictures. It therefore became unnecessary to maintain a large staff of musicians, and so in September 1930 I received a letter telling me that the studios would not require our services any longer and to dismiss everyone not under contract. In most instances the studios even tried to buy up existing contracts. Musical activity in Hollywood was almost at a standstill.
>
> But in the spring of 1931, due to the rapid development of sound technique, producers and directors began to realize that an art which had existed for thousands of years could not be ruled out by 'the stroke of a pen'. They began to add a little music here and there to support love scenes or silent sequences. But they felt it necessary to explain the music pictorially. For example, if they wanted music for a street scene, an organ grinder was shown. It was easy to use music in night club, ballroom or theater scenes, as here the orchestras played a necessary part in the picture.
>
> Many strange devices were used to introduce the music. For example, a love scene might take place in the woods, and in order to justify the music thought necessary to accompany it, a wandering violinist would be brought in for no reason at all. Or, again, a shepherd would be seen herding his sheep and playing his flute to the accompaniment of a fifty-piece symphony orchestra.

Half of this music was still recorded on the set, causing a great deal of inconvenience and expense. Whenever the director, after the completion of his picture, made any changes, or recut his film, the score was usually ruined as it was obviously impossible to cut the sound track without harming the underlying continuity of the music. Occasionally we were able to make cuts that were not too noticeable.

At this time the process of re-recording was slowly being perfected, and we soon learned to score music *after* the completion of a picture. This had two advantages. It left the director free to cut his picture any way he pleased without hurting our work, and we were able to control the respective levels between dialogue and music, thereby clearing the dialogue.[3]

When Steiner arrived in Hollywood he had been taken on by RKO simply as an orchestrator, and his first job was on the Bebe Daniels/Ben Lyon film *Dixiana*. But as the slump continued the studio had less and less use for him and eventually he was given notice. His agent managed to find him a job as musical director on a new Rudolf Friml operetta opening in Atlantic City, but just before he was to leave RKO asked him to stay on a month-to-month basis without contract as head of the Music Department, with a promise of interesting things in the offing. Steiner agreed, and stayed in California forever.

First came *Cimarron* (1931), starring Irene Dunne and Richard Dix. Steiner had so far done no original composition for films, but as all of the few recognized composers in Hollywood were unavailable he was offered the job. Steiner's twenty-five minute contribution to this ninety-minute film was much admired and given substantial credit for the film's success. An important breakthrough was made with *Symphony of Six Million* (1931), again starring Irene Dunne, this time with Ricardo Cortez. This David O. Selznick production told the story of a Jewish doctor from Eastside New York moving to Park Avenue and losing some of his cultural identity on the way. Selznick, then a new executive producer brought in from

Paramount, had already glimpsed the potential of Steiner's music and asked him to score one reel — roughly ten minutes — to see whether the use of music outside a realistic context would interfere with or help the dialogue. In the deathbed scene of the doctor's father, accompanied by the 'Kol Nidrei', there was no question but that it helped.

This distinction between *realistic* music — that is to say music that comes from within the action of a scene, like for example, the negro chorus in Steiner's score for *Jezebel* — and *commentative* music which conveys and underscores the film's action, is one I shall be dealing with throughout the book.

In the following year (1932) two pictures were released which contained large quantities of Steiner's original music: *Bird of Paradise* (an exotic South Seas romance with songs and dance sequences choreographed by Busby Berkeley) and *The Most Dangerous Game*, a thriller. Then came *King Kong*, and with it the real beginnings of Hollywood music.

By the time Steiner retired from films in 1965 (he died in 1971 at the age of 84) he had written over 300 scores, his working life having spanned the early growth, climax and watershed of the Golden Age of Hollywood. His achievements were basically twofold: he dictated a stylistic norm which resulted in what we now think of as the characteristic 'sound' of the Golden Years, and he inaugurated many techniques relating to the interplay between dialogue, action and music which subsequently became standard practice in Hollywood.

Steiner the composer was really created by Hollywood. For he was not in the first instance a real composer at all; juvenilia excepted, his main business was arranging and conducting the music of other composers, operettas, light opera and musical comedy: all Tin Pan Alley as opposed to Carnegie Hall. So it was only natural that when Steiner started to compose himself, his chosen idiom was initially a kind of flotsam-and-jetsam of late nineteenth-century mid-European romantic influences, popular and to a lesser extent classical: a dash of Liszt, a dash of Wagner, dashes of any number of Strausses, Lehár, Friml, Romberg, Victor Herbert, with the occasional seasoning of Gershwin, Berlin or Rodgers

King Kong: finale

Max Steiner

The Warner Brothers Fanfare

reflecting Steiner's later years in the American theatre; but, apart from this, almost nothing of true twentieth-century concert music. The same was true of those of Steiner's colleagues who arrived in Hollywood at intervals during the 'thirties and established themselves at one or other of the major studios. They came not from the world of the symphony or the concert hall but from that of the pop song, light orchestra, jazz band, vaudeville and theatre pit. Roy Webb, Herbert Stothart, Alfred Newman and Adolph Deutsch all hailed from Broadway; Victor Young was a popular radio conductor and song and light-music composer; Bronislau Kaper and Frederick Hollander were pianist-songwriters, refugees from an increasingly nazified Europe; Franz Waxman, also a refugee from Nazism, was still comparatively inexperienced as a composer; David Raksin was a jazz instrumentalist and arranger; Dimitri Tiomkin was primarily a concert pianist, originally less of a professional composer even than Steiner; and so the list goes on.

As for the heads of the studio music departments, in the early days some of them were barely even musically literate,[4] and even for those who were, 'Carnegie Hall' was still a term of abuse. Of course, many (in fact most) of these musicians ultimately transcended their origins and attained through their talents, industry and adaptability a high degree of professionalism. But in the main conservatory-bred composers like Miklós Rózsa, Erich Wolfgang Korngold and Bernard Herrmann were the exception rather than the rule: musical theatre was the cradle of Hollywood music, and the musical idiom of the theatre has always been conservative. Hence the fact that in Hollywood's formative years there grew up a deeply-entrenched conservatism which jealously guarded its prerogatives and was quick to suppress any 'progressive' or 'modernistic' tendencies among juniors or novices. Composers like Jerome Moross and Hugo Friedhofer, whose idioms were conservative by any standards of contemporary 'serious' music, were kept busy for years orchestrating the work of 'establishment' composers (Moross was assigned to Waxman, Deutsch and others, Friedhofer to Steiner and

Korngold)[5] because it was considered dangerous to turn them loose on scores of their own. The musical hierarchy was as terrified of 'Carnegie Hall' as its overlords were of Communism, and dissident factions were firmly locked out in the first place or, if they were allowed in, made to toe the party line. Genuine musical progress on the Hollywood soundtrack was all but shackled until the mid-fifties when, significantly, the studio system began to be forced to yield its monopoly.

For it was above all the studio system which established Steiner and his colleagues in their positions of authority, gave the royal imprimatur to their music and actively promoted it. Musically speaking Hollywood has always seemed to be something of an autonomous community, its composers generally cut off from the mainstreams of musical activity in other spheres and (to those on the outside looking in) paddling their own canoes in murky backwaters of varying degrees of disreputableness. It has, after all, always been a Los Angeles speciality to insulate itself from the rest of the world, to create its *own* world, one which in many ways has little enough contact with life's realities as understood elsewhere. This musical isolationism was wholly typical: the 'real' world would have decried the music of Korngold, Newman and Steiner as anachronistic and refused it a place, whereas the 'fantasy-world' of Hollywood not only wanted it but encouraged its procreation in vast quantities. 'Romantic' music, music of romance, of fantasy, dream, illusion: what more logical than that it should find a final refuge in the real world's dream-factory? Nor, perhaps, should we overlook the seductive qualities of the Californian climate, which are far more likely to encourage self-indulgence than austerity. You tune in with rapturous melodies, melting chords and rich colour-textures, not with dissonance and disruptive rhythms. *They* could jolt you back to the here-and-now all too abruptly.

Many allege that there is a stylistic anonymity about much Hollywood film music and a notable absence of top-flight creative talent among the ranks of composers. It is true that whereas other countries have composers who either regularly or irregularly write for films, America has film composers. Whereas in Britain, France and Germany 'serious' composers are (or rather were) to the fore in writing film music, the Hollywood contributions of America's leading composers have been few and far between. And quite often even if a 'highbrow' composer *were* invited to score a Hollywood production, it was more than likely that his work would in the end be 'fixed up' (as the common expression was) by some local genius — as when Aaron Copland had to disclaim responsibility for the main title music of *The Heiress* which was substituted for his own work. Some 'outside' composers came and went with lightning rapidity, e.g. Villa-Lobos (*Green Mansions*), Alexandre Tansman (*Sister Kenny*), Leonard Bernstein (*On the Waterfront*).

Other refugee European composers of note — Ernst Toch, Mario Castelnuovo-Tedesco, Eugene Zador — never properly fitted into the system at all; they were given the occasional (generally insignificant) film of their own to compose, but for the most part their activities were restricted to providing utility sequences for use in whatever picture their studio deemed appropriate, to orchestrating, or to ghosting music for other 'composers' who received all the credit. The piano-conductor scores of a studio like MGM — a more-or-less reliable source as to who exactly did what — could yield some surprising secrets were they to be examined in detail. In extenuation however we should remember that the average output of Hollywood in its prime was 400 films per year. Most of these films had music of one kind or another, and that music had to be provided by someone; and such a productivity rate was incompatible with 'serious' composers taking time off from their 'serious' assignments to work at the studios on a casual basis.[6] The studios needed composers, orchestrators, arrangers, conductors, copyists, musical administrators and performing musicians who, like other technicians and artists, would be under permanent contract to work on any film in production, would ask no questions and be told no lies. And because no composer with a 'serious' career would be prepared to commit himself irrevocably in this way, studio heads were obliged to put under contract the only composers who were available — those versed in a discipline light (in more senses than one) years removed from that of the concert hall.

Of course, Steiner and Young were precisely the kind of musicians studios wanted to have under contract anyway. For the 'front office' was naturally anxious not to alienate its public on any grounds whatsoever, and, as frequently happens, it made the mistake of underrating public taste. They assumed the public would refuse to tolerate any music more modern-sounding than the Liszt symphonic poem or the Lehár operetta. The latter-day progeny of Liszt and Lehár were in plentiful supply in the pop world and in no time at all they had been allowed to permeate the film industry. That is how Max Steiner and his followers became the arbiters of musical fashion in Hollywood for nearly a quarter of a century.

Yet given these unpromising circumstances, the individualism of Hollywood's major composers is remarkable. Nobody familiar with their work could ever mistake Steiner for Newman, Webb for Tiomkin, Herrmann for Rózsa. Of course there are areas where their idioms momentarily converge; but so there are in any wave or community of composers broadly similar in technique and outlook.

It has long been recognized that the phenomenon of Hollywood was almost entirely the creation of European expatriates and that few, if any, indigenous American elements were involved. Even those Hollywood composers actually born in the USA — Webb, Young, Stothart, Newman, Leigh Harline — were totally European in outlook. The *real* Americans — Alex North, Elmer Bernstein, Leonard Rosenman, Leith Stevens — came later.[7] As John Baxter notes in his book *The Hollywood Exiles*:

> Few ideas or institutions in Los Angeles belong to California . . . the film industry we know as 'Hollywood' grew out of foreign ideology. Indigenous American cinema died in the early 1920s, with its best artists destroyed by

their own artistic and business *naïveté* and the growth of a commercial film industry to which they could not adjust — an industry founded and propogated by Europeans.

The case of Hollywood music was no different. The confluence of talent and non-talent to be found there, particularly during the war years, was as unevenly and colourfully productive as it was unlikely and ill-assorted. But there was musical experience and practical knowledge, and a willingness to learn, even if the process of building on precarious foundations — or even on no foundations at all — often led to results of dubious quality. Those who were less rather than more literate quickly learned by doing. And some of the finest musicianship in the world was to be found in Hollywood.[8] In the main these Hollywood composers of the old guard possessed a core of genuine creative talent, much of which they dissipated in over-productiveness. Perhaps the most serious vice inherent in the studio system was the unrelenting pressure it brought to bear on the creative faculties of employees. In return for the handsome salaries they received they had to give a full pound of flesh with every drop of blood. If a composer finished a score at 5pm on a Monday evening, he might easily be expected to start work on another at 9am the following Tuesday morning. He might even be working on more than one at a time. There was no guarantee of a proper breathing space between jobs, since emergencies would always be liable to arise: changes might be made in a just-previewed picture necessitating patches of re-scoring, and if the original composer was not available (because he had already started a new assignment) anybody who happened to be 'between assignments' could be called in to help. Or this same composer, theoretically vacationing, might receive an SOS from a colleague unable to meet his deadline and therefore appealing for help. Any help thus given would be rewarded in terms of royalty payments but not screen credit. This procedure was facilitated by the stylistic uniformity of much studio music, and for every one detected instance we may be sure that many more have never come to light. Many sins can be laid at the door of Hollywood composers, but lack of industry is not one of them. It was a case of those who paid the piper literally calling the tune. No wonder that many of the staff composers (those who preferred the security of a studio contract to the hazards of freelance casual employment) came to regard music not so much as an art but as a commodity; something that was bought and paid for. No money, no goods. This explained why many took little interest in music outside the span of their working hours or after retirement. Those whom the studio closures forced into premature retirement were frequently happy to take up different occupations — just as in the early days there were those who entered the music 'business' because it seemed to promise greater financial returns than whatever 'business' (possibly quite unrelated to music) they were engaged in at the time. Films were entertainment. There was big money in the entertainment business, and for musicians after the coming of sound the biggest money was to be made in the West.

So westward they went, in droves, and the early development of American film music became their responsibility. Many are merely names now, some not even that. Who today has heard of Gerard Carbonara, Alberto Colombo, Louis de Francesco, Mort Glickman, William Lava, David Snell? Yet we should not allow unfamiliarity and the relative oblivion into which most of them have (often deservedly) fallen to blind us to this one basic fact about Hollywood musicians: in one way or another they were or became well-equipped professionals who instinctively gave of their best, often against fairly intimidating odds.[9] Somehow it happened; and in the work of Max Steiner — the father of them all — is contained a fair cross-section of the best and worst of Hollywood music.

King Kong was the 'beginning' of Steiner, who described it as 'a picture made for music — one which allowed you to do anything and everything'. At this stage, of course, Steiner was still finding his feet as a composer. He had had very limited experience of writing in the symphonic manner, since at that time and for several years to come he was still much involved with arranging and composing for musicals rather than feature films.[10] The music of *Kong* is derivative; more important is how it demonstrates, for the first time in the 'talkies', that music has the power to add a dimension of reality to a basically unrealistic situation: in this case the survival of prehistoric monsters (created by Willis O'Brien) in a modern urban civilization.

Before music was added, studio executives feared that O'Brien's creations would provoke mirth in an audience, rather than inspire terror, and this might well have happened but for Steiner's music. Steiner produced a total of about seventy-five minutes of symphonic music in about eight weeks. His sketches are fascinating to study: he is generally content to indicate orchestration in general rather than specific terms, although he obviously had a very clear idea in his mind of the sound he wanted. The sketches are full of little notes and 'asides' to his orchestrator Bernard Kaun: 'The orchestra should go nuts at this point'; 'Bernard! Remember the "Kol Nidrei" in *Symphony of Six Million*'; 'This should sound like the "Miserere" in *Trovatore*'; 'Do this like the dragon' (presumably Fafner in *Siegfried*); and at one point in the finale when the bass instruments have been trilling frantically in imitation of aeroplanes: 'Good bass here! To hell with the airplane effect!'

The score is constructed on the Wagnerian leitmotif principle, with special themes for the leading characters and concepts and whatever other facets of the scenario lend themselves conveniently to this form of labelling. It is worth noting the clever way in which Steiner, by making the theme of the monster a memorable and easily recognizable but also eminently simple descending three-note chromatic motif, greatly facilitates its contrapuntal inclusion in many different contexts. At one point it becomes the motif of Kong's approach. Later it is transformed into the first phrase of the march played in the theatre when Kong is put on public display in New York (doubtless a nostalgic backward look on Steiner's part at his years in the pit on Broadway.) A particular subtlety is the way in which at certain critical moments — notably the finale, in which Kong falls to his death from the Empire State Building after depositing Fay Wray in a place of safety — the Kong theme and the Fay Wray theme (which in its pristine state is a pretty waltz melody with more than a suspicion of *fin-de-siècle* Vienna) actually converge and become one, thus musically underlining the explicitly-stated parallel between the story of King Kong and Ann Darrow and the old fairy-tale of Beauty and the Beast. Here the music is required, perhaps for the first time in an American film, to explain to the audience what is actually happening on the screen, since the camera is unable to articulate Kong's instinctive feelings of tenderness towards his helpless victim. In these last moments the music becomes almost operatic in character as it picks up the speech-rhythm of the last line of dialogue: 'Beauty killed the Beast'.

Inevitably most of the music is heavy and loud, but some is not: particularly well-scored is the ship's fogbound approach to the uncharted Skull Island. Here Steiner holds his dynamics and orchestral colours down for a lengthy period, with just enough movement in the texture (harps) to suggest the ship cautiously edging its way through the mist-wreathed waters.

King Kong is a landmark; it showed the basic power of music to terrorize and to humanise. But in the 1935 *The Informer*, American film music finally comes of age. Steiner won his first Oscar for this film, and many years later said that of all the hundreds he had scored, *The Informer* was the only one whose director, John Ford, sought him out and conferred with him before shooting began. And we need listen only to the first few bars of the main title to realize that one of Steiner's most positive assets is his ability to crystallize the essence of a film in a single theme.[11]

The *Informer* main title is certainly one of Steiner's tersest. Its dramatic relevance is basically threefold: first the heavy march-like tread does duty both for the oppressive military element in the story (the setting is Dublin in the troubled years just after World War I) and for the inevitability of the tragedy which hangs over the head of Gypo (Victor McLaglen). Second, the character of the theme itself is stern, sombre and puts the audience in the correct frame of mind for the story. Third, the theme contains certain melodic and rhythmic intimations of Irish folksong to add the requisite touch of local colour.

Although references to this theme recur at intervals throughout, it does not in itself take a leading role in the drama. Instead it provides a framework for the inter-play of those motivic elements which *are* directly related to persons and events in the screenplay. One such motif is the theme for Gypo's girl Katie. As so often, with a few well-chosen brush strokes Steiner creates a musical picture that tells us all we need to know about the character. In this music the pathos of her love for Gypo — which is genuine — blends with suggestions of a syncopated rhythm, indicating that when circumstances are difficult she is not above turning her natural charms to monetary profit. In fact we witness something of the sort in one of the opening scenes, when the advances of a flashily dressed man are thwarted by the unexpected arrival of Gypo. After the latter has thrown the man into the street Katie calls after him — 'Gypo!' — in a voice of such utter abjection that the music is compelled to echo the falling cadence of her voice on a solo violin. This pathos is recaptured on later occasions — particularly when Gypo, looking longingly at the steamship placard advertising a passage to America, sees in its place a shot of himself, splendidly dressed, holding Katie's hand on the deck of a liner. Distant church bells and organ are momentarily superimposed as we see that Katie is wearing a bride's veil and holding a big bunch of flowers. Later, when Gypo and Terry invade Aunt Betty's, and Gypo, his faculties already fuddled by drink and excitement, sees a beautiful cultured lady sitting aloof from the revellers, the 'Katie' theme tells us at once that he mistakes her for his beloved.

The other leitmotifs are a fragment of an Irish folksong on fanfare-like French horns for Frankie McPhillip; a warm, compassionate string theme for Dan Gallagher and Mary

McPhillip; and a sad theme on cor anglais with throbbing harp accompaniment for the blind man, symbol of Gypo's accusing conscience. All these themes have tiny but telling links with Irish folkmusic.

The most important and pervasive motif, however, is the 'blood-money' motif, relating to the twenty pounds for which Gypo, Judas-like, betrays his friend Frankie. We can hear it in its clearest form as the Captain throws the money down on the table after Frankie has been shot dead: it is a simple four-note descending harp figure, but, significantly, the first interval through which it descends is the tritone, the *diabolus in musica*.[12] When, after Gypo's guilt has been established, Mulholland's men are drawing lots as to who shall be his executioner, this motif is repeated throughout the whispered colloquy unchanged in every respect *ad infinitum*, as if constantly to remind the audience of the justification for their drastic action; it is also synchronized with the dripping of the water in the cell-house. Its last appearance is very different: Gypo, mortally wounded, makes for the little church where Mrs McPhillip is praying. As he staggers up the steps the blood-money motif is built on the full orchestra to a challenging climax, released by a *fortissimo* blow on the cymbals when he staggers in — as if to signify that, having reached the church as a penitent, there is no further need for the fact of his guilt to be insisted upon.

There still remain traces of silent film-music mannerisms, especially the melodramatic device whereby a remark or action of sudden consequence is accentuated by a sharp *sforzato* chord placed a split second before it and followed by silence — as when Frankie accosts Gypo in the lunch-room, just after Gypo has been studying the poster offering £20 for information leading to his arrest; or when Katie says to Gypo in all innocence, 'What d'you take me for — an informer?' — words which understandably have a terrible effect on him. There is also some dispensable 'Mickey-Mousing' — the skirling string figures which follow the gusts of wind as they catch the ripped-down poster of Frankie and tumble it along the street. But these are minor when set beside Steiner's ever-strengthening grasp of the true film-music potential — demonstrated in such matters as the use of music to portray the struggle of dark thoughts within Gypo's confused, almost imbecilic mind as he stands torn between loyalty to Frankie and the lure of the twenty pounds offered by the British; the fish and chip shop scene, where the traditional Irish 'Circassian Circle' depicting the mad ecstasy of the mob won over by Gypo's munificence is criss-crossed by the 'blood-money' and 'Frankie' motifs like an all-seeing, never-resting fate; the moment when Gypo, brought face-to-face with Mulligan, the man he has falsely accused, is suddenly struck by the enormity of his crime; and finally the span of tension when the overwhelming forces of conscience and circumstances drive him to confess before the court of inquiry (the 'blood-money' theme again). Here Steiner's music probes inside Gypo's knotted mind and attempts to clarify the semi-articulate emotions doing battle. The score's only real calamity is the finale, in which, as Gypo falls dead in the church after Mrs McPhillip has assured him of her forgiveness, an unseen chorus soars with a maudlin 'Ave Maria' which is as bereft of any true sense of spiritual ecstasy as is the Stokowskified 'Ave Maria' of Schubert which similarly sabotages the ending of Disney's *Fantasia*.

In general terms the *Informer* music complements well the movie's foggy expressionistic exteriors. Steiner was less successful with the type of later *film noir* — gangster melodramas, semi-documentaries of the metropolis, dark crime-studies, all pictures which demanded a more sophisticated, more 'modernistic' musical treatment than came naturally to him. Roy Webb and Miklós Rózsa both handled this genre better. But Steiner knew little of Stravinsky, Prokofiev, Hindemith, Bartók — all of whom would have met his case better than Liszt or Rachmaninov. Steiner's *oeuvre* nevertheless contains at least two exceptions in this regard, *The Letter* (1940) and *The Big Sleep* (1946).

The Letter, a tale of murder, passion and subterfuge set in Singapore, starred Bette Davis in one of her most powerful roles as Leslie Crosbie, and Steiner's score is one of his most insidiously potent. The main theme, blasting the credits *fortissimo* across the theatre, sets the atmosphere of tropical tension and violence. It underlines Leslie Crosbie's wild, passionate temperament, but also tells us that hers is a tragic passion, not a vicious one.

The full force of this theme is felt in the final showdown between Leslie and Robert when she admits to being still in love with the man she has murdered; and also in the climactic confrontation between Leslie and the dead man's Eurasian wife in the Chinese shop. This extraordinary scene is played throughout to the sinister jangling of wind chimes, which increases in volume as the widow, hideously bangled, chalk-faced and cobra-eyed, approaches through a haze of opium smoke. This jangling continues throughout the confrontation, but as Mrs Hammond asks that Leslie should remove her shawl and draw closer, the main theme suddenly bursts forth as if to stretch to breaking-point the tangled skein of emotions — hate, grief, jealousy, fear — which enwraps the two women. There is only one subsidiary motif: a quivering figure associated with the lace-work through which Leslie continually seeks to steady her raw-edged nerves. There is also a quantity of Hollywoodian pseudo-*chinoiserie*, which does, however, burgeon into some genuinely-felt love-music as Hammond's widow gazes on his dead body and closes her eyes in grief. Apart from this, the whole score is dominated, like the film, by Bette Davis, musically transmogrified into the main theme.

The Big Sleep, one of the most famous of the Bogart-Bacall vehicles, has a score of a tougher fibre than was usual with Steiner. Again there is some instant thematic characterization: the theme for Marlowe (Bogart) is roguish and ironic, with an impish little grace-note towards the end. Usually it remains poised in an ambivalent manner between major and minor. Only in the victorious finale does the full orchestra give it out fairly and squarely in the major before the slashing chord which abruptly terminates the picture.[13] There is another motif, elusive and insidious with a more explicit clash between major and minor, which we hear first of all as Bogart, in the hall of the Sternwood mansion, is forced to catch teenage nymphomaniac Carmen Sternwood in his arms to prevent her falling to the floor. It does not allude specifically to any one person or thing but merely colours the atmosphere. These undocketed but characterful motivic fragments are useful and necessary in films of this kind where people, their commitments, motivations and actions, are shrouded in obscurity. This secondary motif is generally given to the celesta, which can sound either sweet, innocent and ethereal (as in the snow scene of *The Magnificent Ambersons*, see page 264) or sinister, as here.

Bogart's theme opens the film in a bantering scherzo-like mood as Philip Marlowe introduces himself, although there is no reference to it in the main title music. As the shadows lengthen and the atmosphere becomes murkier and more claustrophobic, the mood of the music darkens to match. Three sequences in particular stand out. The first is the murder of Geiger, planned in terms of sound almost as an ABA format: silence — music/action — silence again. Bogart slumbers in his car outside Geiger's house. He is roused by a piercing scream, and for a brief hectic moment all is noise and confusion — running footsteps, slamming doors and hysterical music based on an agitated development of Bogart's theme. This sudden assault on the audience is all the more effective for its brevity. Silence reigns again as Bogart forces his way into the room whence had issued the scream, and, as Chandler picturesquely puts it, 'neither of the two people paid any attention to the way I came in, although only one of them was dead'.

In one of the film's most frightening moments — the unexpected murder of Joe Brody in his apartment — there is a ring at the doorbell, two enormously amplified gunshots, and, as Bogart tears after the gunman, a hair-raising transformation of his theme is sounded on high trumpets. While Bogart and Bacall are still Canino's prisoners, their love theme — one of Steiner's strongest — is allowed to take wing three-quarters of the way through the picture. Its underlying pulse is that of a waltz, just like that of the music which picks up delightedly when Bogart establishes his famous rapport with the sexy proprietress of the bookstore opposite Geiger's. But in this scene, with Bogart and Bacall driving through the blackest night in torrential rain on their way to a final rendezvous with Eddie Mars (40s *film noir* in a nutshell) Steiner superimposes the love theme in long notes over a grinding, trilling *basso ostinato* low down in the orchestra. Timpani, played with snare-drum sticks, and sharp, explosive brass accents create a brutal conflict of rhythm and mood. Bogart's feeling for Bacall (high strings) is pitted rhythmically against the electric savagery of the underworld (low strings and brass). This is fine scoring; and Steiner is writing here an authentic music of the asphalt jungle.

Elsewhere, the lack of sophistication inherent in the Steiner idiom created problems — in *The Treasure of the Sierra Madre* (1948), for instance. John Huston's examination of the corrosive effects of greed on a group of gold prospectors, or rather chiefly on one of them, Fred Dobbs (Humphrey Bogart) in the Mexican mountains is told with a blistering realism, a roughness, rawness and gusto enhanced by some splendidly rugged location shots; and there are two real protagonists — the bleakness and hostility of nature, and the starkness of the conflicts within the group (Bogart, Tim Holt, Walter Huston). Except for isolated moments which are magnificent, none of these elements is convincingly handled by Steiner. The main title music is a piece of routine Spanishry which may superficially suggest a Mexican location but fails to give any intimation of the mood of the film or the true role of the natural background, which is anything but colourful and picturesque. Then Steiner does not attempt to differentiate musically between the three principal characters. Had he given Bogart a theme to himself he would have been able to chart his astonishing moral, physical and mental deterioration into a hideous wreck of humanity with mad eyes and a soulless grin. Instead, Steiner uses a collective theme for the trio and their enterprise, a well-rounded melody admirable enough in its own right, but incongruous and consistently intrusive. In a scherzo-like variant it can suggest something of Walter Huston's goblin-like agility and sly bonhomie, but on only one occasion does it have something really constructive to say.

After discovering gold, Bogart and Holt toil under a brutal sun for hours on end to dig a mine. The music intensifies their anguish, building inexorably on a descending four-note motif earlier associated with the idea of gold and greed; here it assumes the character of a fiercely protesting funeral march. The mine caves in with Bogart inside it, and for the time being the music caves in with it. Then Tim Holt appears on the scene. Momentarily he seems undecided — and the music tells us why; for in the previous scene the three men have been discussing the best way of distributing the gold, and Bogart has been quick to point out that, were one of the partners to meet with an 'accident', his share would revert to the others. Here the music, insistently re-iterating the 'greed' motif, tells us the nature of the thoughts flashing through Holt's mind as he stands outside the ruined mine. But then the warm main theme surges up, telling us that the finer side of his nature has prevailed. He fights his way through the dust and rubble and brings Bogart out alive, and the climax is marked by a *grandioso* statement of the theme on full orchestra.

Otherwise, occasions when this theme is *not* involved give the drama its most purposeful support. The long-shot scenes of the approaching bandits, for instance: the rhythmic drum-figures suggest a distant menace, the piercing wood-winds the bright outline of the hills. The space between low drums and high woodwinds is left unfilled, adding depth to the landscape. The ear links the insect-like figures of the distant marauders with the dim-focused drums while the sharp-etched woodwind forces it to take stock of the hills looming up all around. As so often, the ear helps the eye without either being aware of the fact.

Towards the end Steiner begins to tighten his grip on the drama. He depicts Bogart's madness with a Wagnerian string *tremolando* motif which may well have been suggested by the sound of the wind that has the last ironic word in the film, scattering the gold-dust back to the mountains whence it came. It haunts the scene of Bogart's attempted murder of Holt and the stirrings of conscience which erupt spectacularly in the flames of the camp fire; and, most harrowingly of all, when he returns to bury his partner's body and finds it missing. Here, and in the following scene when Bogart assures himself that a tiger must have found the body and devoured it, Steiner scales a height of dissonance which foreshadows his evocation of the sinister Syon mountain country in *This is Cinerama*.

The best music is the quietest. In one of the early scenes around the camp fire, the men discuss the uses to which they plan to put their riches. Tim Holt — the most sympathetic and straightforward of the three — describes his own conception of Eden: 'I figure on buying some land and growing fruit, peaches maybe . . . one summer when I was a kid I worked as a picker on a peach harvest in the Santa King Valley . . . hundreds of people, old and young, whole families working together . . . at night after a day's work we used to build big bonfires and sit around and sing to guitar music, till morning sometimes. You'd go to sleep, wake up, sing and go to sleep again. Everybody had a wonderful time. Ever since then I've had a hankering to be a fruit grower. Must be grand watching your own trees put on leaves, come into blossom and berry . . . watching the fruit get big and ripe on the boughs, ready for pickin' . . . .' Later, when the unwelcome interloper Cody dies helping to ward off the bandits, the other three search him for identification. They find a letter from his wife in Texas and Tim Holt reads it: 'The country is especially lovely this year. It's been a perfect spring, warm rains and hardly any frost. The fruit trees are all in bloom, the upper orchard looks all aflame and the lower like after a snowstorm. Everybody looks forward to big crops. I do hope you are home for the harvest.' And, at the very end of the film, Huston offers Holt his share of the money realized by the sale of donkeys and hides if he will use it to buy a ticket to Texas to see Cody's widow: 'It's July, and . . . the fruit harvest . . . how about it?' 'It's a deal!' Taking his cue from Tim Holt's mention of guitars in his first monologue, Steiner links these three episodes by a soft rustle of guitars and mandolins playing in lyrical Mexican folkmusic style. In this context it is marvellously tender and evocative; no consciously-composed 'emotive' or 'nostalgic' music would have worked half so well.

Steiner professed a particular liking for the romantic melodramas which stood Warners in such excellent financial stead during the 'forties, and certainly his music reached its greatest public through these pictures — *Intermezzo* (1939), *In this our Life* (1942), *Now Voyager* (1942), *Since you went away* (1944), *Saratoga Trunk* (1946), *Beyond the Forest* (1949), and the most popular of all, *Gone with the Wind* (1939). Yet eminently suited as Steiner's style undoubtedly was to this women's-magazine-type escapist entertainment, I question whether it ever really brought out the best in him. The characters in these films are mostly stock and two-dimensional, and the music generally moves on the same level of cliché and stereotype, emotionalism and sentimentality doing duty for genuine emotion, and rhetoric for eloquence. Of course we have those wonderful tunes — 'It can't be wrong' in *Now Voyager*, 'As long as I live' in *Saratoga Trunk* — and they *are* wonderful. Steiner was certainly one of Hollywood's finest melodists. His best-known tune (though not his best) is the Tara theme from *Gone with the Wind*, which has almost become a part of Americana. Other *Gone with the Wind* themes are superb — Gerald O'Hara's, Scarlett's, Mammy's Cakewalk, Bonnie's (a gloriously warm, rich melody), and the swaggering march for Clark Gable as Rhett Butler.[14] Sometimes Steiner developed such affection for a theme that he would reprise it in a later picture — this lovely tune, for instance, first written for *A Stolen Life* in 1946, subsequently re-surfaced not only in *This is Cinerama* in 1953 but also in *A Summer Place* in 1959 — for which latter picture the eighty-one-year-old composer gave Warners one of their biggest hit-tunes in years.

The Fountainhead (1949) evidently touched a different nerve in Steiner, and the music frequently approaches the level of vintage Herrmann. Gary Cooper plays Roark, an architect with innovatory ideas, who, unwilling to compromise his integrity, dynamites a half-constructed building when he discovers that his original design has been tampered with. Steiner's theme for the hero is fraught with a true emotion and a genuine idealism and aspiration. It surges upward in 'masculine' style, whilst Roark's mistress's theme wends downwards in curves of typically feminine shapeliness. The score brings dignity and grandeur to the picture: in the finale when the theme uniting Roark and Dominique (harmonically related to Roark's theme: the bittersweet yearning of the minor seventh chord impregnates the entire score) soars to impressive heights as he awaits her, straddled atop the tallest skyscraper in the world. He above, she travelling up in the workmen's elevator: the music seems to draw them together in mutual fulfilment. Music is also important in the early scene when Roark's one supporter, the ailing architect Cameron, is driven to hospital in an ambulance; an elegiac lyricism, proud yet compassionate, marks the sun pouring in through the window and lighting up the stricken man's face as he sees one of the buildings he built himself and warns Roark of what is in store for him.

Later, for Dominique's first encounter with Roark in her father's quarry, there is an anticipation in reverse of the finale. This time she is above, he below driving his drill into the side of the cliff; however, there is no question of consummation, and Steiner cleverly reflects this in the music. He takes the same theme but projects the melody on high violins, flute and vibraphone, with little harmonic or textural support other than the naturally reverberative properties of vibraphone, soft bass-drumroll and tam-tam. Their over-tones, mingling and lingering in the atmosphere, complement director King Vidor's insistence upon the heat-haze and white chalk dust which permeate the scene. The effect of this extreme starkness thrown into relief against a quasi-impressionistic glow is to communicate the full force of Roark's frustrated desire. It is the kind of underscoring which reveals depth and complexity under analysis but which nevertheless must have occurred naturally and spontaneously to Steiner, who was one of the least intellectual of composers.

All the cerebration would have been done by his innate feeling for drama.[15]

In general the best Steiner is to be heard in those films whose tenor is light-years removed from the synthetic glamour and hypersophistication of the *Now Voyager* genre. Steiner's warm and spontaneous melodic gift and the naturally unsophisticated character of his musical personality lent themselves without any sense of strain to films dealing with the lyric and the homespun, tales of simple people in rural American settings. The strength of Steiner's response to the beauties of the American landscape is attested not only by *This is Cinerama* and *Spencer's Mountain*, but also by many of his Westerns. *Dodge City* and *The Oklahoma Kid* (both 1939) are two of the most distinguished. Their sense of grandeur may be romantic-European rather than authentic-American, but it is genuine nonetheless.

Steiner brings to his brand of Americana a melodic grace and deftness of dramatic touch. *Johnny Belinda* (1948), *The Lion and the Horse* (1952), *So Big* (1953), *Come next Spring* (1955), *All Mine to Give* (1958) and *Cash McCall* (1959) are all notable examples, and his collaboration with Delmer Daves in *A Summer Place* (1959), *Parrish* (1961) and *Spencer's Mountain* (1963) reveal a freshness and fertility of invention astonishing in an ailing and near-blind septuagenarian, whose creative faculties we might reasonably have supposed exhausted after so many years of unrelenting pressure.

The Adventures of Mark Twain (1943) is typical. The greatest influence on Twain's life was the Mississippi river and the steamboats which sailed upon her, and in the main title music Steiner ingeniously refers to this in two ways. First, by building the principal theme of the picture out of the Mississippi riverman's cry whence Twain derived his name; second, in the heavily-accented horn-figure which repeats in the manner of an ostinato and seems to suggest the mighty river heaving and churning before the wheels of the paddle-steamer of which Twain becomes navigator.

The origin of the first is early explained when a bad accident brought about through young Clemens' inexperi-

ence is narrowly averted by his gruff old teacher's skill, and
the cry goes up from one of the boat-hands, 'Mark twain! Safe
water' (in the same key as the orchestra); throughout the
inexorable horn-figure surrounded by ebbing-and-flowing
figures on strings and woodwinds reminds us of the constant
river motion. So too in the memorable river-scene which
follows, as Twain attempts to negotiate a particularly
treacherous mid-river island in a thick fog. Here a further
subtlety is revealed: the rhythm of the horn-figure is
synchronized with the chugging rhythm of the steamboat's
funnels giving off their puffs of smoke at regular intervals. In
other words, the two ideas together amount to a composite
musical image of the Mississippi river and its steamboats. The
horn-figure is present all through this long sequence: it closely
follows the emotional tenor of the action, passing through all
manner of different harmonies and keys. Melodic details may
be modified but its general shape and contour is always
recognizable, always making us conscious of the waters
surging beneath us, keeping us adrift. Finally, the peril is past,
Twain is the hero of the hour and the Twain theme shares in
the general rejoicing, enhanced by a mosaic of 'safe water' and
related cries thrillingly delivered by solo black voices.

For the end title, as the boys and girls of Twain's fantasy
creations, Tom Thumb-size, lead the old man over the brow
of a hill into the sunrise of immortality, a chorus takes over the
Twain theme, singing — symbolically — of the 'safe water'.
The comet which coincides with Twain's death — and his
birth seventy-five years before — is reflected in a mystic
shimmer of string tremolos and tubular bells. The earlier
montage showing the mini-figures of Tom, Huck and his
friends slipping in to inspire an author stricken with grief after
the death of his son is the occasion for one of Steiner's most
enchanting flights of fantasy: the Twain theme turned into a
whistle; the quicksilver sonorities of piano, harp, celesta and
vibraphone; variations around a haunting bassoon theme that
had earlier accompanied Twain's own Tom Sawyer-like
boyish pranks. This and the double bassoon music for the
frog-jumping contest, with its sly Chaplinesque humour,

shows at its best the vein of genuine folk poetry which Steiner tapped in a manner peculiarly his own.

In many ways the apotheosis of Steiner's handling of this type of film came with the 1963 *Spencer's Mountain*. Inasmuch as it shows a response not only to character and situation but also to natural scenery (in this case the lake and mountain country of Wyoming), the score recalls another into which Steiner put much effort, the 1953 *This is Cinerama*. This was a massive portmanteau-type spectacular designed to show off the prowess of the tripartite screen to its best advantage, the second part of which was an aerial coast-to-coast tour of America — New York, Pittsburgh, Chicago, the wheatlands of the Middle West, the Rockies, San Francisco, the Grand Canyon, all displayed in a sequence of majestic landscapes. The latter strikes some powerful music from Steiner, and it seems a pity that his contribution is interrupted every few minutes to permit a large chorus singing 'America the Beautiful', 'Battle Hymn of the Republic', 'Columbia, the Gem of the Ocean' and other stalwarts, related to the visuals more sentimentally than musically. However, there is music of exhilarating splendour for the Sierra Nevada, turbid dissonance and sharp-tongued orchestral sonority for the sinister Mount Syon, the clangour of anvils as we pass the copper mines in Southern Utah, a steely lyricism for the heavy industrial area of Northern Indiana; and when one of the mightiest spectacles in the world — the Grand Canyon — bursts upon the Cinerama screen, Steiner's music helps burn the moment into the memory.

It is difficult to credit *Spencer's Mountain* as the work of a man of 75. The main theme is imbued with that sense of childlike wonder which is the trademark of a perennially youthful creative imagination. The film tells of a family in a remote Wyoming mountain valley struggling against the poverty-induced ignorance which has been crippling them for generations; the main titles and their music are wedded to some splendid panoramic shots of the valley. Prefaced by a quotation on horns from 'America the Beautiful', this theme in its main-title setting reflects both the tranquillity and beauty of lake, wood and mountain, and the peaceful temper of life in this uncorrupted area.

Finally, *The Glass Menagerie* (1950), which does not fit into this rural category but which engages unexpected sympathy for its subject — unexpected since most Tennessee Williams films have been so successfully scored by homegrown American composers (e.g. *A Streetcar named Desire* by Alex North in 1951), leading us to doubt that a more continental approach could be viable.

As far as overall strategy was concerned, Steiner had to determine whether to reinforce the claustrophobically sombre and desperate tone of explosive relationships in a slummy St Louis tenement district, or to view everything musically from the point of view of Laura, the heroine (Jane Wyman), and somehow capture in sound her escape from the tawdriness of reality into her make-believe world of glass figures. Steiner decided on the latter; for the former a jazz-orientated score like North's for *Streetcar* would certainly have been necessary.

In terms of orchestral sonority *The Glass Menagerie* is unique in Steiner. Brass are excluded until the end title, woodwind used only soloistically; the protagonists are the strings, and Steiner has the violins play in their topmost register, generally muted and in harmonics. The result is tone-colour of an appropriately glassy quality; and there tends to be a wide open space between this transparent sheen of sound and the bass line sustained by cellos and double basses. The effect is that of a huge sheet of glass bounded at either end by a frame. Finally, a free use of vibraphone, celesta, piano, glockenspiel and triangle enhances the fragility and beauty of the sound.

Thematically too the score is imaginative: as usual with Steiner, each motif distils the essence of the characters. The motif which represents the glass animals — and by extension Laura's dream world — is the simplest of tunes in the 'whitest' of white keys, C major. It simply runs five notes up the major scale, then down again. Its *alter ego* is strangely haunting — a sequence of chords rather than a theme. The two chords are built of superimposed fourths and have an aura of purity, largely because of their association with the five-note ('pentatonic') scale, a familiar musical image of purity and innocence.[16] The two chords forming this motif tend to repeat themselves, trance-like, and over the haze of pentatonic sound so produced, a string melody etches itself high in the stratosphere. Here is a symbol of Laura, the real person — not the Laura of a glass menagerie; and so the score is coloured principally by these twin themes, the glass world and Laura. The former is used for the montage showing Laura playing truant from business college and instead walking in the park, visiting the library and the glass-house full of tropical plants. When her mother comes home having discovered her deception, double basses and cellos bestride the theme menacingly as she tries to make her face reality. The sweet, aromatic chordal theme is rarely absent, reminding us of the tenderness and sympathy Laura's mother and brother both feel towards her.

Amanda's theme wittily reflects the Southern origins of which she is ever conscious. It is akin to Mammy's theme in *Gone with the Wind*, complete with cakewalk-style syncopation. Steiner ensures that every time we hear it we picture Amanda as a now humbled scion of a once proud and well-to-do house. Tom's theme has a big-city blues-type resonance. It is also rich and warm and so not only creates something of the atmosphere of the mid-western city with its dusty brick walls concealing furious and desperate living within shabby rooms, but also tells us something of Tom's good-hearted nature.

The most important thematic entity in this sensitive and soft-spoken score is a melody of great lyrical beauty, again tinctured with pentatonic purity, first heard in the main title and thereafter absent for three-quarters of the film. It is right to be thus given pride of place, however, for the character it represents: Jim O'Connor (Kirk Douglas), who turns out to be the long-awaited 'gentleman caller' who transforms Laura's existence. This clean-limbed melody reflects his likeableness and honesty, and several times occurs in conjunction with a wavering figure which, as Jim starts to talk to Laura and gradually wins her confidence, ceases to waver and resolves on to a radiant major chord. Elements of Jim's theme are built into the dance-band music at the 'Paradise' as he assures her of her essential beauty and begins successfully to counter her deep-seated inferiority complex. Upon their return home, the music darkens the scene in preparation for Jim's disclosure that he is already committed to another girl; but as he enjoins Laura not to forget the 'good advice' he has given her, we hear an echo of the music from the 'Paradise' — but now metamorphosed out of all recognition into a graceful waltz, just as Laura is now a new person. She gives Jim as a souvenir the unicorn he earlier broke, and a serene version of the chordal motif helps her to explain to her mother that, even if there was no possibility of a permanent relationship with Jim, he has at least forced her to overcome her shyness and to face the world with courage. Jim's theme closes the picture as it had opened it, with Laura now hailing Richard, her new 'gentleman caller'. *The Glass Menagerie*, rather than *Now Voyager*, should be one of the points of departure for anyone seeking to test the validity of Bette Davis's claim that 'Max understood more about drama than any of us.'

NOTES

1   Extract from *Notes to You* (Steiner's unpublished autobiography).

2 and 3   Extracts from Steiner's article 'Scoring the Film', in *We Make the Movies*, ed. Nancy Naumberg, London, 1936, pp. 218–20.

4   This changed somewhat in later years: men like Alfred Newman (20th Century Fox), Ray Heindorf (Warner Bros) and John Green (MGM) were all Heads of Department and distinguished musicians in their own right.

5   In a conversation with Elmer Bernstein, Friedhofer gives a fascinating glimpse of Steiner at work, and of the way his personality exteriorized itself in his work:

> Max always seemed to suffer a great deal, more than he actually did . . . everything became a big problem. It was largely histrionics because I think Max wrote rapidly and fairly easily, but strangely enough he always dramatized everything that he did. I know that when I was working with him, we would run the picture together and then I would go home and he would go home. Say we ran on a Thursday, he said, 'You should have something by Monday', and on Monday I would get this tearful, pathetic call from him saying 'Puppsy, I must have eaten something — I have food poisoning — I can't get anything off the ground', and I would say, 'OK Max, take it easy, whenever you're ready', so he would, two or three days later, come with a heap of sketches. The first picture I did for him, *Charge of the Light Brigade*, entailed close to 1,000 pages of orchestral score. I did 900 and something myself, and the rest was farmed out — the 'Charge' was the last thing of course, and it was murder — we really whipped it out fast. Outside of that, my total intercourse with

Max from the time we sat in the projection room together until the time we met on the recording stage consisted largely of notes on his sketches, 'Hugo, you remember what we did in such and such a place — I want something like that, only different.' The rest were mostly just telephone conversations, that's all — generally around 4 o'clock in the morning.'

(Elmer Bernstein's *Filmmusic Notebook*, Vol. I (1974), pp. 16–17)

6   This book deals only with the handful of best composers, and with the tiniest fraction of the total Hollywood product. In archives and studio music libraries I have seen unthinkable quantities of sketches, full scores and orchestral parts — the life-work of dozens of composers — all destined to irremediable oblivion, just like the ephemeral product they were designed to complement. But every age has produced its own form of mass-media entertainment music, which serves an immediate purpose and is just as immediately pulped and forgotten.

7   In one particular context, however, Steiner himself comes curiously close to an authentic Americanism. In Warners' 1941 'epic' interpretation of the life of General Custer, *They Died with their Boots On*, the 7th Cavalry is preparing to go into the Black Hills to stop the retaliation of the Sioux and Cheyenne. The bedrock of slow-moving harmonies bears only minimal relation to the melodic fragments superimposed upon it; the film's love theme, fanfares, and *Garry Owen*, the actual march of the 7th Cavalry and a particular favourite of Custer's. Here Steiner's use of popular and traditional tunes is akin to that of Charles Ives. So too in the music for Custer's Last Stand, scored for an army of musicians with many extra brass, woodwind and percussion players. Bugle calls run amok, six flutes and six clarinets shriek a hoarse and jagged Indian theme enthusiastically countered by *Garry Owen*, and again the resulting collage is reminiscent of Ives, although it is very doubtful that Steiner knew any of his music in the 'forties. The music for the burning of Atlanta in *Gone with the Wind* is another instance.

8   See André Previn's reminiscences of MGM in the mid-40s to mid-50s in *Music Face to Face* (Conversations with Antony Hopkins — London 1971) and elsewhere.

9   In conversation with Elmer Bernstein, John Green, Head of the MGM Music Dept from 1949–58, gives an instance of the kind of

pressure to which composers were subjected in order to meet deadlines:

> The architects of those ridiculous schedules put four or five guys on to finish a picture. I'll never forget the first time that I became involved in that. It was one of Miklós Rózsa's pictures and Miki couldn't possibly finish writing by the tax date when the film had to be shipped out of the state, not with five Eugene Zadors [Zador would write out the orchestral scores from Rózsa's detailed composition sketches]. I was in a meeting with executives Mannix and Cohen and I said, 'You cannot have this picture ready for the tax date. You just can't have it!' I thought Mannix was going to have a stroke — he grew purple. 'What do you mean "we can't?"' I said, 'You can't have it because you can't have it. You are not dealing with a sausage machine, you're dealing with a tremendously gifted artist, Miklós Rózsa.' 'Well, give him some help, put four or five guys on it.' I said, 'This isn't a hack, Eddie, it's Miklós Rózsa's score and he's going to write every last 32nd note or you get yourself another boy at my desk.'

(Elmer Bernstein's *Filmmusic Notebook*, Vol. III no. 1 (1977), p. 26)

10   *Flying Down to Rio, The Gay Divorcee, Top Hat* and *Follow the Fleet* were among Steiner's RKO credits as musical supervisor.

11   Another good example is *The Life of Emile Zola* (1939), where the main theme has a march-like tread and quietly heroic ring which tell us much about Zola's character: his integrity, unassertive authority and his tireless struggle for truth and freedom. Interspersed between phrases of the theme are distant bugle-calls to hint at the most important political issue to involve him: the Dreyfus affair.

12   In medieval times the 'tritone' (augmented fourth) was known as the '*diabolus in musica*', and it still remains the most sinister-sounding interval of all — hence its aptness for depicting devilry. Examples of its use are legion: for instance, Kastchei's Infernal Dance in Stravinsky's *Firebird* or the Demons' music in Elgar's *Dream of Gerontius*.

13   A slight break with convention. The usual Hollywood procedure for the finish of an end title was a long pause on a sustained chord, *fortissimo*.

14   *Jezebel* (1938) is an earlier Steiner picture also set in the Deep

South at the time of the Civil War, and a noteworthy achievement on two counts: first for the fine waltz first heard (outside the main title) in the crucial scene where Bette Davis outrages New Orleans society by appearing at the local ball clad from head to foot in red instead of white. This is what precipitates the tragic rupture between Davis and Henry Fonda, and so it is fitting that from then on — not before — the waltz should form the basis of the incidental music; it acts as a constant reminder of the cause of the trouble. Second, Steiner's treatment of Negro music is original. In the scene where Davis is preparing to welcome Fonda at a party on her plantation after not having seen him for a year, a Negro chorus is singing a spiritual somewhere outside the house, out of sight. Inside Davis is becoming increasingly nervous and excited as the hour of Fonda's arrival draws nigh, and, as if unconsciously reflecting her mood, the chorus gradually gains in tempo and fervour until a high pitch of intensity is reached. Only when a carriage is heard in the drive does the chorus break off and the orchestra take over. There is another imaginative touch a little later in the scene where Fonda and Davis are alone together and he reveals that he has brought a wife back with him to New Orleans, and that they are lost to each other for ever. Steiner here brings back the waltz — but gives it to the Negro chorus, who hum it very softly, slowly and expressively. The unusual sonority produces a strangely moving effect, not unlike that of the organ in the willow scene between Lucy and Eugene in Herrmann's *The Magnificent Ambersons*. Finally, after the evening has ended in catastrophe — all motivated by Davis' fury of jealousy and disappointment — she rushes outside in distraction and, gathering her Negros together, leads them in the old traditional 'Raise a ruckus tonight': she laughing through the tears streaming down her face, they, blissfully unaware of the irony, raising their voices in lusty abandon. We may surely see here and in the earlier spiritual episode the prototype of a technique which has come to the fore only comparatively recently in Bob Fosse's *Cabaret* (1972) and Lindsay Anderson's *O Lucky Man!* (1973): that of making quasi-realistic music serve as abstract commentary on the action.

15   An instance of Steiner's wit is his inbuilt commenting in *A Distant Trumpet* (1964), in a scene where the two leading ladies are scoring points off each other in a spirit of fierce feline aggressiveness. At one point a distinct 'mi-aow' can be heard on a solo violin in the accompanying music.

16   Many folkmusics employ this scale freely. If its constituent

notes are played together as a chord, the result is euphony. If the ordinary major or minor scales are played as chords, the results are cacophony. If we simplistically associate 'sin' with dissonance, there is no capacity for sin within the pentatonic scale.

ERICH WOLFGANG KORNGOLD

It was something of a coincidence that the two composers who materially influenced the development of Hollywood film music in its earliest stages were both Viennese. Erich Wolfgang Korngold was precisely nine years and nineteen days Max Steiner's junior. He was actually born in Brno (now in Czechoslovakia, then in Moravia, a province of the Hapsburg Empire) but his family moved to Vienna when he was two years old, so to all intents and purposes he may be accounted Viennese. Whether he and Steiner had any contact in Vienna is doubtful, since they grew up in such different musical *milieux*. Korngold was the son of one of the most feared music critics in Vienna, Dr Julius Korngold. Erich's talent developed precociously: he completed his first major work, the pantomime *Der Schneemann*, at the age of 11, and throughout his teens he continued to write music with the fervour and speed of a born composer. At 16 and 17 respectively he composed his operas *Der Ring des Polykrates* and *Violanta*, and was only 23 when he scored the greatest operatic success of his life, *Die tote Stadt*.

Korngold lived from 1897 to 1957, through one of the most fractured periods in music history. The general impression of his German late-Romantic idiom is one of familiarity; there is nothing much new or strikingly progressive. The strength of the music derives from the mode and quality of thought within the idiom. That is what tells in art. Idioms come and go and history finds little to choose between them. The enduring factor is the vitality of thought, which alone makes an idiom meaningful. The idiom of yesterday, however, is less likely to be the medium of commanding thought than the idiom of today or tomorrow, for its possibilities have already been explored and there is little room left for individual genius. It says much for Korngold's imaginative powers that although he grew up steeped in the traditions of an era already moribund at the time his own musical personality was developing, the conventions he inherited often seem in his hands not the empty mockery of a decaying impulse but the noble expression of one still living.

This combination of a certain spiritual *naïveté*[1] with the most fantastic flights of melodic, harmonic and orchestral imagination equipped Korngold superbly for the medium of the film score. In truth, Korngold was writing Warner Brothers music long before he set foot in Burbank. Korngold first came to Hollywood in 1934 when he accepted Max Reinhardt's invitation to adapt Mendelssohn for his film of *A Midsummer Night's Dream*. He returned in 1935 to write an operetta for Paramount with Oscar Hammerstein II, and was approached by Warners to compose an original score for an Errol Flynn swashbuckler just completed entitled *Captain Blood*. That was the first of the eighteen original film scores produced by Korngold between 1935 and 1947.

He arrived in Hollywood at precisely the right moment, since film music was still struggling to find its feet, and Korngold brought it a sorely needed dignity, stature and professionalism. He was excited by the medium and unstintingly gave his best. It is not difficult to understand both how Korngold adjusted so well to Hollywood — much more comfortably than most of his 'highbrow' colleagues — and how Hollywood adjusted so well to him. For Wagner and Strauss were the immediate progenitors of a self-indulgent style wrought with a Puccinian lusciousness and luxury of invention and occasionally tinctured with Impressionist atmospherics. Korngold's melody was sweepingly lyrical, his harmony heated and opulent. His orchestration was creamy and full-flavoured. He had a lavish and superabundant talent, one that, fortunately, had enough inbuilt vitality to stop short of the kind of maggotty over-ripeness into which the idiom degenerated in the hands of less accomplished practitioners — especially those on the film scene. The scores he wrote for pictures whose other component parts accorded perfectly with the inherent character of his music have survived the test of time to emerge as models of their kind, namely the handsome series of Warners costume dramas featuring Errol Flynn.

Korngold's stature was fully recognized in Hollywood at the time he was writing these scores. Aside from the fact that so internationally eminent a composer giving of his best in a medium held in almost universal contempt by his colleagues brought considerable prestige to the studio that employed him. Contemporary composers in Hollywood appreciated the quality and sense of occasion he brought to the idiom in which they themselves were working and little by little they began to emulate him. Alfred Newman's scores for *Son of Fury, Slave Ship, The Prisoner of Zenda* and *Captain from Castile*, Steiner's for *The Adventures of Don Juan* and *John Paul Jones*, Roy Webb's for *Sinbad the Sailor* and *At Sword's Point*, Franz Waxman's for *Prince Valiant*: they all bear the Korngold insignia. This influence however had both its positive and negative aspects — positive in that *The Adventures of Robin Hood* (1939) and *The Sea Hawk* (1940) showed just how effective the grand Wagnerian manner could be when applied to the two-dimensional swashbucklers then in vogue; negative, in that the very excellence of the scores encouraged and endorsed acceptance of the nineteenth century as the standard musical currency of Hollywood, regardless of the fact that Korngold was in a class by himself and that lesser luminaries would, through the inferiority of their talent, inevitably debase the currency.

For *The Adventures of Robin Hood* and *The Sea Hawk* Korngold paid in hard gold. Colour, pageantry, romance, immediacy of appeal, larger-than-lifeness — these are the mainstays of the Flynn spectaculars, and the mainstay of the Korngold style in its most extrovert guise. *Robin Hood* allowed him ample scope to realize his conception of film as opera without singing. The screen and screenplay are brought alive by music just as the stage and libretto are in an opera house. Pictures of this type are more closely related to fantasy and cartoon than to straight dramatic feature and, as we saw in the case of *King Kong*, the action is greatly dependent on the music to enhance credibility and to apply a gloss of reality. *Robin Hood* is, after all, kids' stuff, visually, intellectually and musically; hence its appeal to the child in all of us. As in much grand opera, *Robin Hood* is virtually a series of big set-pieces all of which call for musical support in the grand operatic manner. Of connective tissue, corresponding to recitative, there is comparatively little; therefore the composer is allowed very little respite. Korngold quailed at the *Robin Hood* assignment, and with good reason. In the event, however, the seven weeks in which he composed the score found him in prime creative condition.

At the very beginning he effects a neat transition from credits to first scene via a flourish of timpani that does duty both as commentary for the former and realistically for the latter:[2] but Korngold has been keeping a watchful eye on how much thematic material he exposes. We first hear a robust and jolly march, later to be associated with the Merry Men; also a full-hearted lyrical melody that proves initially something of a puzzle. For if this is played, as it is, under the card announcement that during King Richard's absence in the Holy Land his brother John has taken unscrupulous control of the country, why do we next hear it as a melting cello solo for the protracted *scène d'amour* between Robin and Maid Marian in Nottingham Castle? What have the two to do with one another? Is Korngold bandying the theme about indiscriminately? The riddle is not solved until the climax of the film when in Sherwood Forest the lately returned King Richard casts off his monkish apparel and reveals himself to

Robin and his men, who have all unwittingly borne testimony to their loyalty. Then the same theme peals forth nobly on a solo trumpet, telling us that Korngold has been equating Robin's love for Marian with love for his country.

Other themes bide their time. Robin of Locksley's is as perfect an embodiment of the character as Flynn himself; a virile, athletic trumpet motif that first rings out with crackling brilliance when Robin bursts upon the scene to save Much the Miller's son. Another fine theme is reserved for the famous Sherwood Forest ambush scene in which Robin's men swoop down from the trees to overwhelm and capture Sir Guy of Gisborne's retinue. At the climactic moment the Merry Men's March (on brass) is broken up into short sharp rhythmic segments interspersed with a flashing swirl and glitter of strings and woodwind, reinforcing not only the sight but also the sound of the action. Then with victory assured a brand-new marching tune is given its head by the full band. The manner is never far removed from opera: the music dashes recklessly to a full close as Robin leaps on to a high boulder and welcomes his 'guests' to his 'home'.

Other set pieces are no less histrionic. The banquet in Sherwood Forest after the ensnaring of Gisborne is done as a roistering Viennese waltz, and Robin's skirmish with Little John as a series of variations on the Merry Men's March. Muted trumpets crow in gleefully discordant anticipation of Robin's hanging. Here and in the final procession and coronation the composer comments on the proceedings from the point of view of the 'goodies'. Just as the supposedly 'religious' procession headed by the Bishop of the Black Cannon (thunderously smiling at knife-point) is in reality composed of Robin and his men heavily shrouded and distorted, so the accompanying music is a disguised version of the Merry Men's March. The coronation is heralded by a ghoulish jangle of bells (part-simulated by the orchestra) and some sourly dissonant ceremonial fanfares. In making these fanfares dissonant the composer is in effect taking a moral stand; he knows that the audience will be on Robin's side and he therefore interprets what is happening on the screen

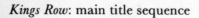

Kings Row: main title sequence

Erich and Luzi Korngold in the 1930s

through their reactions to it. When they want to laugh, he helps them; when they want to cry, he helps them too. This is a naive but lucid example of the way a composer must often act as liaison-man between screen and audience. And contrary to general belief, the scoring of a quasi-comedy picture needs essentially the same skill and sensitivity as the scoring of a dramatic feature. The score for *Robin Hood* is brilliant musical showmanship, but its dramatic premises are, and need to be, as sound and genuine as those on which are based the grandest of Korngold's grand operas.

The Sea Hawk, one of the great Warners sea-epics, has a score that combines the familiar panache with a number of detailed dramatic subtleties. The main Errol Flynn theme, like that of *Captain Blood* only more so, is nothing less than a fanfare-like figure extended into a fully-fledged melody and put to imaginative use in a variety of contexts. As Flynn's men make their way cautiously through the dank Panama jungle towards a Spanish ambush, muted echoes of the fanfare are superimposed on an instrumentation whose exotically oppressive sonorities contrast effectively with the strong primary colours elsewhere: saxophones, temple blocks and other similar percussion, all over a high sustained note to maintain the suspense. Later, when Flynn and his men, galley slaves on board a Spanish ship bearing secret news of the Armada, swiftly and silently contrive to work themselves free of their chains, we hear the fanfare, again muted but not this time foreboding — rather whispered, breathlessly excited. The scene immediately following in which they overpower the Spaniards, take over the galleon and set sail for Dover is handled in an overtly operatic manner. As the climax approaches the orchestra poises on a sustained note, great slashing chords punctuating each of the sailors' shouts as the ship makes ready to sail; then the fanfare and a triumphant *fortissimo* chorus for men's voices and orchestra, 'Sail for the shores of Dover' setting the definitive seal of victory on the scene. This is pure operetta — we almost expect to hear the characters singing their roles as the remaining scenes unfold.

Korngold seems to make a point in this score of letting his music tell what the camera physically (as opposed to emotionally) is unable to communicate. In the opening scenes on board the Spanish ship carrying Claude Rains and Brenda Marshall, and on Flynn's 'Albatross,' the music makes us feel the rushing winds driving the Spaniards into the pirates' arms long before these winds are actually mentioned, for music can give us the illusion of movement more effectively than a camera. Is it because music is authentically, naturally, a dynamic, temporal art, whereas the movie camera represents what is basically a static, spatial art (photography) turned synthetically, unnaturally, into a temporal one? We have perhaps here a clue to music's power of overlaying a basically unrealistic situation with the illusion of reality. The point is made even more emphatically in a later scene when Flynn's men, still chained to oars, resolve by hook or by crook to escape from servitude to warn Elizabeth I of the Armada. To create disorder on the vessel they agree on a given signal gradually to stop rowing. The camera does not at first show us the oars, since it needs to concentrate instead on the reactions of the Spaniards on the deck to the fact that the ship is slowing down. So the *music* picks up the rhythm of the oars — and gradually slows down. We see nothing, but we become aware through our ears that the ship is slowly coming to a standstill; and only then are we given a shot of the oars.

Korngold initially treats the love music for Flynn and Brenda Marshall in much the same way as the wind music described above: he puts it into circulation on the very first occasion the two meet, after Flynn has boarded the Spanish ship and taken her prisoner. Neither one responds to the other on this first meeting, but the music tells us (if we need telling) that they will eventually do so. And the love music fulfils all its expected promise in the scene where Donna Maria (Marshall) hastens to Dover to warn Captain Thorpe (Flynn) of the Panama treachery. She is too late; he has already sailed on the ebb tide and all she can do is watch through the mists as the vague outline of his ship disappears into the gloaming.

Her lone, sad figure standing on the harbour is intercut with that of Flynn on board ship, and the love music binds them together in mutual longing.

Robin Hood, The Sea Hawk and *The Private Lives of Elizabeth and Essex* (1939) make up an impressive trilogy of Korngold-Flynn spectaculars. In *Elizabeth and Essex* the set pieces are fewer and shorter, but they make for some moments of thrilling Walton-like pomp and panoply — particularly the triumphal entry of Essex into London at the very start of the film, accompanied by a proud marching trumpet tune aglow with all the romantic virility of medieval chivalry. However, the chief *dramatis persona* is always Elizabeth herself. Not only was the title of the Maxwell Anderson play on which the screenplay was based *Elizabeth the Queen*, but director Michael Curtiz, despairing of Flynn's unsuitability for the part of Essex, manifestly gave all his attention to Bette Davis as Elizabeth. This being the case Korngold clustered his chief galaxy of musical themes around the Queen herself. Everything is reflected musically from her point of view. The magisterial theme first given out early in the main title prelude establishes the regality of the monarch. It is the occasion for another of the brief set pieces scattered throughout the picture: the dramatic entry of the Queen into the crowded throne-room after the news that Essex and his army have arrived back from Ireland, winning the support of the people of London and demanding an audience. As in the setting sail for Dover in *The Sea Hawk* the moment is manoeuvred musically in quasi-operatic style: trumpets and horns in purple and gold; a huge tidal wave of orchestral sound marshalling itself and poising precipitantly; a flourish of trumpets; then, as Elizabeth appears in long shot in the doorway, the imperial sweep and passion of the main title music as she advances through her courtiers to her throne.

In sharp contrast to this 'exterior' theme of pomp and circumstance comes the 'interior' theme of the loneliness and constant suppression of personal feelings that Elizabeth's position thrusts upon her. This poignant melody (which later reappeared as the theme of the slow section in Korngold's

Deception Cello Concerto) is first heard in the first scene as the Queen declares to Bacon the necessity for publicly reprimanding and humiliating Essex, her great lover: 'Whatever he suffers I suffer a thousand times more intensely.' Essex enters and drops at her feet, but as he looks up expecting to see warmth and gladness in her face and encounters instead a cold stare of disapproval the music simply changes a major chord into a minor. The effect is one of a solar eclipse.

Later Elizabeth is playing chess with her ladies-in-waiting and overturns the board in a fit of pique: the 'loneliness' theme comments on the thoughts passing through her mind. Then Lady Penelope begs leave to sing 'Master Marlowe's' ballad, "The Passionate Shepherd to his Love", which includes interpolated verses by Sir Walter Raleigh containing a number of scarcely veiled references to the ageing queen *vis-à-vis* her youthful lover. As with Korngold's other realistic set pieces, the song is stylistically incongruous but better integrated inasmuch as it is prepared in the orchestra beforehand (as Penelope asks the Queen if she would like to hear the song) and later underscores the scene in which Elizabeth consoles Mistress Margaret Radcliffe who weeps for the absence of *her* love, just as Elizabeth is inwardly weeping for the absence of Essex. The song in this commentative context has the right innocent sweetness.

After the hysterical outburst in which the Queen orders every mirror in the palace to be smashed (intensified by Korngold in music of an almost expressionistic violence), the 'loneliness' theme seems to help her regain her composure and then movingly underlines her revelation to Margaret of the depths of her isolation and misery: 'To search men's hearts for tenderness and find only ambition . . . to cry out in the dark for one unselfish voice and hear only the dry rustle of papers of state . . . to be a Queen is to give up all that a woman holds most dear.' The music rises to an impassioned climax as Penelope goes to fetch Bacon and the Queen is left on her own; it alone speaks of the tumult raging within. Very differently scored — the last significant, and most unnerving appearance, of the 'loneliness' theme — is the moment when

Elizabeth, having committed Essex to the Tower and the executioner's block for treason, is left alone in the vast hall with the giant empty shadow of a giant empty throne. The 'loneliness' theme on high violins and vibraphone blows like a gust of chill wind through harp glissandi in a peculiarly cavernous sonority; one that helps fix in our minds an indelible musico-visual impress of Elizabeth in her stoic isolation.

The love theme is all the more effective for being excluded from the soundtrack until halfway through the first major love scene between the pair following Essex's return to court. Later, after the disastrous council chamber scene, it enters to moving effect as Elizabeth angrily claims that Essex, so bedazzled with his power to command an army, would 'follow the very devil in an assault on heaven' and he replies, 'That's one thing the devil doesn't know — heaven's always taken by storm. . .'. In the interview between them after his return from Ireland the love theme warmly underscores the first minutes while she is still overwhelmed by the fullness of her love for him; then a subtle change of mood in the music intimates his approaching revelation of the strength of his ambition. But as the gulf between them widens, the music drops out, and the cold and emptiness on the soundtrack of which we are suddenly aware is dramatically much more to the point than a continuation of the music, suitably chastened in nuance and inflection, could ever have been. The music is — intentionally and literally — conspicuous by its absence.

King's Row (1941) is perhaps the acid test of whether or not we can accept the Korngold approach in the context of a quasi-contemporary drama. On the face of things it seems probable that a Viennese-born composer would be hopelessly out of his depth in the ambience of a small turn-of-the-century Mid-western American town. How could he interpret sympathetically the characters of its inhabitants? When I first saw *King's Row* the main title music caused me to fear the worst. On its own, the music is marvellous: the heraldic main theme, melodically fine and upstanding and with bold and trenchant harmonic progressions, is as arresting as anything in Korngold. But what, I wondered, could it possibly have to do with what I imagined to be a homely, winsome little piece of Americana in the manner of *Our Town* (by the same director, Sam Wood) to which Aaron Copland's score, sparing of gesture and economical in texture, seemed perfectly tailored? In fact *King's Row* proved to be a big pulsing melodrama, and Korngold's big pulsing melodramatic score helped give it its stature and depth of reality. The Copland approach, I came to realize, would have been as inadequate here as it was appropriate to *Our Town*.

The effect of the music is in fact to delimit the characters, to create the impression that the screen is reaching out to envelop us, to make us participate directly in what it is portraying. The outstanding example of this is the love scene where Parris and Cassy first 'find' each other and are suddenly, without any warning, thrown into an inferno of passion. Magnificently stage-managed — the climax is set amidst a terrific thunderstorm, with James Wong Howe's photography a kaleidoscope of flashing darkness, movement and light. The music, massively Wagnerian, brings to the scene a dimension of macrocosmic intensity. It is *Tristan und Isolde* all over again; and the lovers' love proves no less destructive. No question here of inflation or gratuitous grandiloquence on the music's part: the theatricality is inherent in the direction and camerawork and the music supplements it.

Elsewhere there are well-judged strokes. The main theme is scaled down to a thistledown set of mini-variations for Parris and Cassy as children frolicking through the trees and diving into the pond — which is particularly effective coming as it does hard on the heels of the rhetorically imposing main title version. The latter is also a major factor in the beauty of the transition between Parris as a boy and as a young man. We see him as a boy vanishing across the stile in the direction of the Von Elm estate, and soft strings are playing the theme. The camera remains focused on the stile, and presently a pair of long-trousered legs come into view from the direction whence the boy had disappeared; and as the main theme is transformed into a triumphant ringing *fortissimo*, Parris Mitchell (Robert Cummings) is revealed as a young man.

Korngold matches in his score the twin themes of innocence and horror. The children's tripping dance-like variations in the main theme lie at one end of the expressive spectrum; at the other is the music hinting at Cassy's incipient madness even before the audience (and Parris) is made consciously aware of it. Korngold here uses the whole-tone scale, a scale which has no tonal centre and therefore generates a feeling of vagueness and instability. It is a favourite cinémusical cliché for dream-dissolves and the like, generally with sweeping waves of harp. In these scenes Korngold contrives to make it sound extraordinarily cold and sinister. He avoids giving Parris and Cassy a theme of their own, as if to emphasize the fact that their love has no future; instead he reserves the big romantic love theme for Randy and Drake (Ann Sheridan and Ronald Reagan). Theirs is a love that grows into something deep and enduring through suffering; this is reflected in the warmth and expressiveness of Korngold's theme, which is not so much glamourously lyrical as human and poignant. Another theme is Parris's grandmother's, charmingly portrayed by the diminutive Maria Ouspenskaya; it seems to enshrine her qualities of gentleness, honour and dignity. The melody first springs to life at the start of the picture as Parris arrives home from school and greets his grandmother through each window of her drawing room in a different language. The music seems to light up her face with serenity and courtliness.

The Constant Nymph (1943) and *Deception* (1946) were 'musical' films about composers and yielded additional fruit in the form of two pieces that later became concert compositions in their own right.[3] From the finale of *The Constant Nymph* came the miniature tone poem *Tomorrow* for contralto, chorus and orchestra. *Deception* wove what later became the Cello Concerto, Op. 37, into its fabric in a way strongly reminiscent of Herrmann's *Hangover Square*: small excerpts played on the piano (by Korngold himself), the central *Adagio* section at a dress rehearsal, and a complete performance that (in the picture) jumps from the opening *Allegro* to the fugato finale. George Korngold claimed that the Concerto (*Concertino* would be a better term) 'contains enough thematic and developmental material for a piece twice its length', but brevity and concentration are its virtues.

Another Dawn (1937), *Of Human Bondage* (1946), the Brontë 'biopic' *Devotion* (1943) and *Escape me Never* (1947) were all mediocre pictures that owe whatever staying power they possess to Korngold's music. *Anthony Adverse* (1936), *Juarez* (1939) and *Between Two Worlds* (1944) were superior, and the first half-hour or so of *Anthony Adverse* — continuously scored — represents the high water mark of Korngold's attempts to turn his pictures into songless operas. The odd man out is *The Sea Wolf* (1941), which contains music of a greater harmonic asperity than usual. Much of it borders almost on Rózsa 'forties' territory, and the strangely simple music for the love scene between the two convicts John Garfield and Ida Lupino — played on a harmonica[4] — is unlike anything else in Korngold.

After 1947 Korngold returned to films on only one occasion — to supervise the Wagner 'biopic' *Magic Fire* (1955) in which he also impersonated conductor Hans Richter during a performance of a four-minute *Ring* montage. He died of heart failure in Hollywood on 29 November 1957, at the age of 60.

He died, it seems, feeling he had outlived his usefulness, in films, the theatre and the concert-hall. Yet it was Charles Gerhardt's RCA Korngold anthology entitled *The Sea Hawk*, first issued in 1974, which gave to symphonic film scores a new lease of life. And not just on records. It has often been remarked how the high-quality sci-fi spectaculars on which modern audiences feed so avidly — the *Star Wars* series, the *Superman* series, *Close Encounters of the Third Kind*, *E.T.* — are the contemporary equivalent of the great westerns and Errol Flynn adventure-epics of the 30s and 40s. What more natural than that John Williams, who grew up in a Hollywood musical context at a time when the master-composers of that legendary era were either still active or exerting a pervasive influence, should take their work — above all Korngold's —

as a model for his own? A professional craftsman like Williams, a musician of taste and style, an artist, transforms and recreates what he borrows, repays his debts with interest: and so it is that *Star Wars, The Empire Strikes Back* and *Superman* (the first, the prototype — the sequels employ his material but are not his original work) have already attained the status of pop-symphonic classics. In Korngold's time the release of *King's Row* led to a spate of letters to Warner Brothers asking if recordings of the music were obtainable. But this was during the war, when soundtrack albums of dramatic scores had barely been thought of: even *Gone with the Wind*, astoundingly, was unprocurable. (Rózsa's *Jungle Book* was the first). How spoiled we are today, when almost every film released brings with it a video, LP, cassette and CD. So it is relatively easy for a score like *Star Wars*, receiving maximum exposure, to become a permanent fixture. Korngold has had to wait much longer, but it would surely please him, not only that his own music is being revived and re-appraised, and that the re-emergence of his screen music has led record companies to investigate also his operas, symphonic and chamber music, but also that he is playing a prominent part in the cyclic processes of history and popular taste. *The King is dead: long live the King.* Popular music of whatever genre has always had its place in films; of course it has, for film is entertainment and has to be popular. But unless it ever reaches, and remains and sticks to, a complete nadir of non-quality and eccentricity, there will, equally, always be a place for music of a more serious intent, and for music, moreover, made live by human beings, not manufactured in a laboratory (although the latter too has its contribution to make). That is one of the most marvellous things about film — its all-embracingness and diversity. It can feed on all things and, therefore, give something back to all people in return to establish its own traditions and criteria and continually refashion them. Only what is bad gets totally discarded: what is good may go out of fashion in its more superficial aspects, but the principle, the essence, the core of quality — star quality — remains as a vital regenerative force. Of nothing is this more true than of music.

NOTES

1   Korngold's was basically a genial disposition, warm, impulsive, childlike. The unselfconscious good humour of his music is one of its most attractive qualities.

2   Roy Webb's score for *The Leopard Man* rings an interesting change on this idea; see p. 172.

3   Exceptionally, Korngold was given permission by Warners to make whatever use he pleased of his film compositions in other fields. Hence *Juarez, Anthony Adverse, Another Dawn* and *The Prince and the Pauper* were quarried for melodic material for the Violin Concerto, Op. 35.

4   In theory — but in theory only — it is realistic music, the unseen source (referred to by Garfield) being a lonely cabin boy.

ALFRED NEWMAN

In 1959 Stravinsky, in conversation with Robert Craft, told him that he still liked the music of his *Oedipus Rex*, 'all of it — even the Messenger's fanfares which remind me of the now badly tarnished trumpets of 20th Century Fox.' Tarnished or untarnished, those trumpets sound what is perhaps the most familiar and prototypical of all Hollywood trademarks. It was the work of a man whose name is practically synonymous with 20th Century Fox music: Alfred Newman.

Newman was born in New Haven, Connecticut, March 17 1901. His family was of Russian-Jewish origin and he was the oldest of ten children. In spite of the family's straitened financial situation, a little money was found to enable the six-year-old boy to begin piano studies, and by the time he was ten he was showing such promise that a businessman named Everard Thompson not only arranged an audition with the Polish pianist Sigismond Stojowski in New York but, when Stojowski offered the boy a scholarship, persuaded a ticket inspector with whom he was on friendly terms to allow the budding pianist to use the same train ticket more than once on his trips to and from lessons! At the Von Ende School of Music Newman studied not only piano with Stojowski but

harmony, counterpoint and composition with Rubin Gold-
mark and George Wedge. At the age of thirteen he was obliged
to start supporting his entire family; the Newmans had always
been desperately poor, and upon their removal to New York
the father could not find work. Alfred was engaged for twelve
weeks as piano soloist at the Strand Theatre, an establishment
which maintained a full orchestra that gave a short concert
before the film was shown. Here he performed portions of
well-known concertos and other concert numbers. Paderewski
heard him at this time and asked him to play at a concert given
in support of the Polish Relief Fund. After his twelve weeks at
the Strand were up, young Alfred got a job as pianist at
Reisenweber's Restaurant, and it was there that Grace La
Rue heard him and signed him as her accompanist for a
vaudeville tour. When she appeared in 1916 in the Broadway
revue *Hitchy-Koo* she arranged for Newman to play piano in
the pit. The conductor was William Daly, the same William
Daly who was later to play an important part in Gershwin's
career. In fact Newman first knew Gershwin when
he was still a song-plugger at Remick's. Daly befriended
Newman, gave him instruction in the rudiments of conducting, and allowed him to conduct at matinees when the show
went on tour. This was the beginning of Newman's career as a
conductor. At 17 he became the youngest musical director on
Broadway. He conducted (among other shows) the *George
White Scandals* of 1920 and 1921 (music by Gershwin), the
Greenwich Village Follies of 1922 and '23, Jerome Kern's *Criss
Cross* in 1926, and Gershwin's *Funny Face* in 1927. In 1926 Fritz
Reiner was so impressed by Newman's conducting that he
invited him to appear as a guest conductor with the
Cincinnati Symphony Orchestra.

During the run of Rodgers and Hart's *Heads Up* in 1930,
Irving Berlin recommended Newman as musical director for
his film musical *Reaching for the Moon*, to be produced in
Hollywood by Joseph M. Schenck. He left New York for
Hollywood in 1930 intending to stay no longer than the
stipulated three months. He remained for the rest of his life.
He wrote his first original film score in 1931 and also worked

with Chaplin on *City Lights*. In 1933 he was appointed General
Musical Director of Zanuck's new production company, 20th
Century, and in 1935 composed and recorded the 20th
Century Fanfare. When 20th Century merged with Fox,
Newman remained with Goldwyn (with whom Zanuck had
been sharing the United Artists studios) but in 1939 rejoined
Zanuck as Musical Director of 20th Century Fox. He resigned
from this post in January 1960 and died February 17 1970,
having written the scores for 187 dramatic and comedy
features and supervised the music of 63 musicals and shorts —
a total of 250 films. He won nine Academy Awards and was
nominated 45 times.

Newman had the ability — more frequently found in
America than in England — to move easily and with authority
from one sphere of music to another, and differentiated solely
between good music and bad. As a conductor he was greatly
esteemed. John Williams, who played piano under him in the
20th Century orchestra, remembers that 'he had a wonder-
fully expressive technique, a great feeling for nuance and
shading. To watch him in action was often to be reminded of
Sir John Barbirolli. He could easily have made a career as a
concert conductor if he'd wanted to, but on the other hand his
brand of musicianship was much needed in Hollywood. He
was specially adept at shaping music to the rhythm of a
picture, moulding and mixing it in with the grain and texture
of a sequence.'[1] Newman occasionally made guest appear-
ances with symphony orchestras, but preferred the seclusion
of the recording studio. He made a number of albums, chiefly
for Capitol with the Hollywood Bowl Symphony Orchestra;
among them was an important recording of two of Gershwin's
lesser known works for piano and orchestra (the Second
Rhapsody and the Variations on *I Got Rhythm*) and two
lavishly produced and lushly exotic albums, *The Magic Islands*
and *Ports of Paradise* — the culmination of a long love affair
with the exotic which began in the late 1930s and had
embraced the scores for *The Hurricane* (1937), *Trade Winds*
(1939), *Gunga Din* (1939), *The Black Swan* (1942) and the
screen adaptation of Richard Rodgers' *South Pacific* (1958),

for which Newman composed some music of his own based on Rodgers' material.

It is reported that composing never came easily to Newman — a fact not readily apparent from his music's fluency. According to Bernard Herrmann, Newman's great achievement was that he was the first composer (and in many ways perhaps the last) to match in his music the highest technical finish of film performance. This perfectly proportioned and scrupulously varnished element is one which commands admiration. Yet whereas in the hands of lesser artists, particularly commercial arrangers, these qualities can easily become synonymous with slickness and sentimentality, the best of Newman is personally motivated. He did not write every note of the scores assigned and credited to him: as head of department he could not be expected to. He surrounded himself with an expert staff and was not afraid to delegate;[2] nor was he afraid to employ composers regarded by other studios as untrustworthy on account of their supposedly progressive inclinations: David Raksin, Hugo Friedhofer and Bernard Herrmann. Just as in all the major studios there were many instances in which a number of directors, resident or non-resident, worked in part on films credited solely to one, so Newman would on occasion prepare themes, compose important sequences and pass the remainder over to one of his colleagues — Cyril Mockridge, David Buttolph, Edward Powell, Herbert Spencer — all of whom were long steeped in the Newman manner. Frequently, however, a film would engage Newman's sympathies so deeply that he made himself responsible for every note. This was certainly true of *Wuthering Heights*, *The Song of Bernadette* and other major scores discussed in this chapter.

Newman, like most of his colleagues, wrote in a traditional, late nineteenth-century romantic rhetorical style, painting with broad, colourful strokes on a large canvas. His individuality lay chiefly in his treatment of the strings, with which he had a particularly felicitous way, oddly for a man who was primarily a pianist. The Newman string 'sound' has an identifiable ring and is capable of a high degree of

The Twentieth Century-Fox Fanfare

Alfred Newman

expressive intensity: a burnished quality of melodic continuity, a firm but always lyrical consistency. Newman's
sonorous, sometimes almost Brucknerian use of the brass, and
his balance and shading of the woodwind choir are other
personality traits. Always a concern for blend and integration
is predominant. In general, Newman is little interested in
polyphonic interaction between instrumental groupings. He
prefers to think in terms of blocks of sound, either individually
or as a unit. Of course, like all made-to-measure styles his took
some time to perfect. Fred Steiner, whose study of Newman is
one of the most valuable pieces of American film-music
criticism ever written,[3] has examined Newman's evolutionary
growth in some detail. Like Max Steiner, Newman first left
Broadway for Hollywood to work on a screen musical, and
later that year superseded Hugo Riesenfeld as Head of the
Music Department at United Artists — where he soon came
into contact with Samuel Goldwyn, whose favourite composer
he became. Like Steiner, Tiomkin, Webb, Waxman and the
others, Newman the composer evolved with film music. Early
pictures like *Street Scene* (1931)[4] used little music and small
orchestras, although Fairbanks' *Mr Robinson Crusoe* (1932),
being essentially a 'silent' movie with sound dubbed on later
(Fairbanks shot it on a yacht trip to the Southern seas), is
virtually through-composed, for the most part in a quasi-
cartoon style. The 1933 Eddie Cantor musical *Roman Scandals*
has a virtuoso chase sequence running for more than seven
minutes; the score for *Clive of India* (1935), though substantial,
adheres fairly closely to military-historical convention, with
much use of familiar songs and pseudo-oriental colour. Fred
Steiner also cites the sewer sequence in *Les Misérables* (1935) as
a definite pointer to the Newman of the future. He claims that
in Goldwyn's *Dark Angel* (1935) Newman is more consistently
himself — has 'found' himself more surely — dramatically,
linguistically and orchestrally, than in any previous score.
Beloved Enemy (1936) and *Dead End* (1937) were other
landmarks, likewise *The Prisoner of Zenda* in the same year (the
1952 re-make is also a note-for-note adaptation of Newman's
score). In fact, much of the best of Newman is to be found in

the adventure stories and romances, historical pageants and swashbuckling epics which proclaimed him a legitimate musical offspring of Korngold.

Newman absorbed the Korngold manner in a way that generally contrived to elude Steiner who, as a native Austrian, was the more obvious successor. *The Prisoner of Zenda* is a typical example of one of Newman's many Richard Straussian scores, even though the Strauss may be derived at second hand through Korngold. But if the music is basically pastiche (the overriding influence is Strauss' *Don Juan*) it is pastiche of a high order, which draws tolerably close to the distinction of its prototypes. The main theme is an impetuous summons for unison horns, picturing Rassendyll's Flynn-like bravado, and is answered by a singing melody for strings: the hero in love. Both themes are put to impressive use. The love-theme poignantly envelops the scene where Flavia, deeply in love with Rassendyll/Rudolf, voluntarily renounces him for the sake of her country and her house; and there are even pre-echoes of Korngold's *Robin Hood* (1938) in the manner in which Newman diverts his main theme to underscore Rassendyll's Flynn (or Tarzan)-like escape over the treetops as he swings from bough to bough in equal defiance of danger and credibility; and later as he duels with Rupert of Hentzau to the death. Elsewhere, Newman's economy throws these extravagances into exciting relief: a dissolve neatly bridged by a few sinister trombone chords, Hentzau's first appearance marked by a few equally sinister single notes on the stopped horn. The only other 'purple patch' is the ceremonial music for organ, brass and percussion to precede and punctuate Rudolf's coronation (the procession moves up the cathedral aisle in step with Handel's *See the Conquering Hero Comes*).

For *Captain from Castile* (1947) Newman provided not only the famous 'Conquest', a robust march for the Spanish conquistadors in the New World, but also some impassioned love music in the conventional Spanish idiom for Tyrone Power and Jean Peters. A better film, and one which provoked an interesting score, was William Wellman's 1939 version of *Beau Geste*. Newman showers the picture with music, but rarely superfluously, except perhaps the scenes with the Geste boys in their garden at home. The main theme represents Gary Cooper in the title role, and has an appropriately heroic ring; it is sturdily oriented around the major scale of C. This theme is the musical backbone of the scenes of the Arabs' repeated attacks on the fort which Geste and a small body of men under the sadistic Sergeant Markoff (Brian Donlevy) are attempting to hold. Newman scores these scenes with great panache, and the musical argument between his main theme and a stylized exoticism is cogently articulated; for once the dubbing allows us to experience the excitement which music has the power to generate in battle. The identical opening and closing scenes in the deserted fort with dead men propped up between the parapets are poetically conceived. Here Newman creates an eerie atmosphere: a small women's wordless chorus sings in high register, but softly enough to produce a pinched, strangulated tone (we shall meet this evocative use of choral sound again in Newman). Far below them, low brass maintain a sombre commentary interspersed with ghostly bugle-calls which seem to persist like a question-mark. What has become of the bugler sent into the fort to reconnoitre? By the time the action has turned full circle and the scene come round again, we are in a position to give the answer.

One scene aptly demonstrates the effect of the cessation of music. When the commander of the fort, stricken with fever, expires in the presence of Markoff, we would expect music to indicate the moment of death. Here, however, it simply stops as Markoff listens for the commander's heartbeat and finds it missing. When the man dies the music dies.

Newman's last tribute to Korngold was contained in the screen version of the musical *Camelot* (1967). Musicals do not come within the scope of this survey, since the dramatic responsibility of their music is very different from that of the music in a feature film. The man who brings a filmed musical to life is an arranger rather than a composer, and his creativity is channelled into presenting the songs in their most attractive and appropriate guise. In the case of a stage musical transferred to the screen this often involves elaborate restructuring in cinematic terms, the extending of dance routines and the providing of connective material and other incidentals, all related directly to the songs. However, the fact that the musical is a screen spectacle demands commentative or dramaturgical music as in the dramatic feature, music subject to the same rules and requirements. This music has to be *composed* by somebody. The dividing line between composing and arranging in this context is slender. A full-length screen ballet built around one or more songs is virtually an original 'composition'. Stravinsky once said that in Hollywood Haydn would be known as the composer of the *St Anthony Variations* and Brahms as their 'arranger'.

There was more scope than usual for commentative music in *Camelot* since it was director Joshua Logan's intention to treat it not as a musical but as a straight dramatic feature in which certain scenes assumed musical form. An original component of these 'musical' scenes is the use of vocal arranger Ken Darby's chorus in Merlin's magic forest. When Arthur (Richard Harris) in the prologue invokes Merlin outside the castle of Joyous Gard, distant voices — 'forest murmurs' — with a fairy tinkle of celesta and glockenspiel, are heard singing 'Follow me' to create an atmosphere of sylvan enchantment. It is a song reminiscent of an opal slowly revolving, revealing new colours and hidden traceries, and this mystic quality is recaptured in the flashback when Arthur goes into the forest with his bow and quiver in an attempt to find solace among the animals after the strife at court. It was a good idea on the part of Newman and Darby to have here a children's chorus singing 'Follow me', as if opening a magic window onto Innocence. The effect is enhanced through the final cadence which repeats the words 'Follow me' to the same notes over and over again until lost in the distance. The children's chorus gradually merges into the adult chorus, just as youth yields to age.

In those scenes which call for ordinary commentative music, Newman work wonders with his material. He could scarcely have gone wrong with 'If Ever I Would Leave You', the love song of Lancelot (Franco Nero) and Guinevere

(Vanessa Redgrave). Newman first introduces it on a solo cor anglais as the pair first look into each other's eyes — after Lancelot has resuscitated Sir Sagramore — and know that they are in love. Later, after they realize that they can never part of their own free will, there follows a montage in which they recall memories of their love-life together. Newman, having scored the song itself in alternating blocks of strings and woodwind, now releases the full orchestra to scale the heights and plumb the depths.

It is not hard to recognize the scenes where Newman takes a last look backwards at his 'epic' achievements of the 1940s and their progenitor Korngold. For when Lancelot escapes from Mordred's henchmen after being discovered with Guinevere *in flagrante delicto*, and then rescues his lady from the stake — all performed with a dashing derring-do against impossible odds — we can see that this is the very stuff of English legend, the same stuff of which the heroic tales of Robin of Locksley are woven. And to any Hollywoodian like Newman this scene and others like it would automatically have brought Flynn and Korngold to mind: hence the nature of the musical treatment. For Lancelot's rescue of Guinevere Newman adroitly combines Lancelot's '*C'est moi*' with the choral song 'Guinevere', and as in comparable scenes in *Robin Hood* and *The Sea Hawk*, the music brings the action flashingly to life and helps bridge the credibility gap.

More original composition than arrangement too is the finale of Act I, which shows the Round Table at the pinnacle of its glory. Here the title song 'Camelot' is decked out in ceremonial style, each phrase encrusted with horn and trumpet fanfares. The later 'Guinevere' chorus starts as a romp, inappropriately perhaps, since it accompanies the preparations for the Queen's execution. But as we pass to the interior of the castle and close in on the King sitting alone in the huge darkened throne-room, a note of hysteria begins to creep in. A harrowing climax is reached which breaks off at the booming of the bell summoning the King to witness the execution — the logical outcome of the earlier scene in which Arthur and Guinevere, dismayed both at the news of

Mordred's subversive activities, and at the terrible secret of Guinevere's adultery not spoken of by either, make a token attempt to clear the air by singing the innocuous 'What do the Simple Folk Do?' One of the answers is, 'they dance', and the King and Queen begin to dance. So far from dispelling their gloom, this prompts them to give vent to their agony of desperation; the music turns into a dissonant *danse macabre*, and leads straight into the scenes of Mordred's men invading the Great Hall, plundering, brawling, killing, and riding their horses on the Round Table. The music is a powerful element here, for it not only intensifies the turbulent mood of both scenes, but draws the one into the other and unifies them.

Films like *The Snake Pit* (1948) brought out a streak of iron in a creative temperament which generally preferred the glorious past to the sordid present. *The Snake Pit* was the first picture set in a lunatic asylum and to portray the horrors of institutions. Newman's music — which may reflect some of Herrmann's influence in its use of low tubas in octaves and high piccolo shrieks reminiscent of *Hangover Square* — is carefully placed and unsentimental. It intensifies the terror and inspires sympathy, especially in two of the most traumatic scenes. The first is when Dr Kik (Leo Genn) decides to try electric therapy in order to cure Virginia Stuart Cunningham (Olivia de Havilland) of her mental disorientation. Here the music accentuates each of the electric shocks administered to her in such a way as to cause the audience literal physical discomfort; we experience the pain vicariously. The second scene is the moment of Virginia's recovery — 'it was strange! Here I was among all those people . . . and at the same time I felt as though I were looking at them from some place far away. The whole place seemed to me like a deep hole, and the people down in it like strange animals, like snakes . . . and I'd been thrown into it . . . yes . . . as though I were in a snake pit.' The camera pulls up and back as if out of a huge shaft, leaving the inmates of the asylum grovelling like reptiles at the bottom; and the full orchestra complete with cymbal clashes peels off layer after layer of dissonance, as if cleansing Virginia of the accumulated filth of centuries.

Pictures with a religious undercurrent were a speciality of Newman's, even though those who knew him say that he was never an overtly religious man. The strength of these scores suggests that Newman may have sought an outlet in his music for a spirituality he suppressed in everyday life.[5] In the four films which stand out — *The Hunchback of Notre Dame* (1939), *The Song of Bernadette* (1943), *The Robe* (1953) and *The Greatest Story Ever Told* (1964) — there is a process of cross-reference unique in Newman. Themes and even whole sequences are repeated or re-worked in contexts of like emotional nature. In this respect *The Hunchback* is the 'father of them all' in that the 'Hallelujah Chorus' which bursts out *subito fortissimo* to spotlight Quasimodo's rescue of Esmeralda and later returns to close the picture, recurs in the finale of *The Song of Bernadette* (Bernadette's Death and Transfiguration) and in that of *The Robe* (as Marcellus and Diana are led to be martyred by order of Caligula). The energetic music which accompanies Captain Phoebus as he prevents Quasimodo absconding with Esmeralda returns in a similar context in *The Robe* as Demetrius the gladiator is rescued from his torture dungeon. Two memorable musical sequences in *The Hunchback* are not, however, duplicated in any subsequent score. The first is the march of the mob on its way to hang Esmeralda, which voices a savage splendour, a kind of blood-drunk exultation. The second is the development of Esmeralda's motif as she offers water to Quasimodo, as he languishes at the whipping-post in the full glare of the sun. Esmeralda's theme has previously sounded merely sweet and clinging. Here it attains a new dimension of compassion and feeling. Beauty is drawn to the Beast, and the Beast to Beauty. The music articulates emotions which can be felt but neither spoken nor acted.

The Song of Bernadette contains some of Newman's loveliest music. The main title presents three motifs, each of which colours a main issue of the story. First, a brass chorale to represent Mother Church. This is a clever move, since the Church is mostly shown as a hostile, reactionary and unenlightened force; and when played heavily on the lower reaches of the brass, sometimes with mutes, this motif (though neutral in substance) can wear an appropriately stern, even sinister aspect. Bernadette's theme, for strings, has that blend of richness, warmth and tenderness characteristic of Newman. Finally, the theme of Bernadette's vision, a romantic Wagnerian melody with (at least to *my* ears) a true spiritual fervour.

Sensitively handled are the scenes of Bernardette's visions at the Grotto of Marsabielle. Newman began by taking the Grail Music in *Parsifal* as his model, but soon realized he was on the wrong track. It came to him that Bernadette had never claimed to see a vision of the Virgin, only of a beautiful lady, and he decided (no doubt influenced also by the naturalness of Jennifer Jones' portrayal) to interpret it in a manner less divine than human. Tiny natural disturbances provide the mainspring of the music: little gusts of wind (flutes and clarinets), the rustling of the rosebush (strings), leaves trembling in the breeze (fluttering flutes), the twitter of birds (oboe and cor anglais), all interwoven with fragments of Bernadette's theme. Wordless voices are superimposed, so distantly to begin with that the ear has cause to wonder whether it is not imagining them; as the Lady appears to Bernadette the music works towards a climax until with a fanfare of trumpets the screen is ablaze with light and the full sound of the chorus. Only at this point does the 'vision' theme emerge on ethereally high strings over rippling harps and celesta.

This impressionistic nature-poem in miniature recurs for every one of Bernadette's visions and their associated happenings: the miracles of the underground spring and the healing of the crippled baby. When Bernadette goes to the grotto at the Dean of Lourdes' request we do not actually see the vision — the camera fixes on her face and we are dependent on the music's climax to indicate the moment when the apparition materializes.

The music not only depicts the character of Bernadette and her vision, but also relates their effect on those around her. For instance it helps to indicate the gradual softening of the Dean of Lourdes' heart towards Bernadette, and his final conviction (after he has tempted her to deny having heard the phrase 'Immaculate Conception' from the Lady's lips) that she is without guile. And when the doctor presents his medical report to the municipal council of Lourdes, there is no music until he is asked whether the crowd at the Grotto, having failed to see what Bernadette claimed she saw, laughed at her and denounced her as a fraud. 'No', replies the doctor (the music begins), 'there was something in her demeanour which precluded laughter. Her expression was so genuine that the observer almost had' the impression he saw what the child saw.' Music here adds an aura of mystic feeling which enhances the import of the doctor's words and suggests that he too has become a believer; the secret lies in the precise moment of its entry. The music 'sees what the child sees' and enables us to see it too.

Two other scenes made powerful by music are the father's search for work at the beginning, and Bernadette's farewell to her would-be husband Antoine at the end. Mr Soubirous is desperate for work, and all he can find is a cartload of infected hospital waste which he is ordered to take outside the town and burn. The music emphasizes the heaviness and weariness of his actions but also expresses the hopelessness and sordidness of the task. The young Antoine falls in love with Bernadette and she with him, and when she decides to enter the convent at Nevers he stops the carriage and vows to her, on the pretext of having a widowed mother to look after, that he will remain single all his days. Their outward relations remain formal — they are scarcely even on Christian-name terms — and only the music tells of their undisclosed passion and the sacrifice they are making.[6] In his essay on Prokofiev and film music, Eisenstein quotes from a letter written in 1547 by Benvenuto Cellini on the merits of sculpture as against painting: 'Sculpture is eight times greater an art than any other of the fine arts, for a statue has eight angles from which it should be viewed and from each of which it should be equally perfect. A painting is a kind of statue presented from only one of these eight angles.' Eisenstein comments: 'a scene photographed from one angle is plastically flat and lacking in depth, whereas if it is photographed from eight individual angles which are then juxtaposed in a montage, a sense of its three-dimensional nature and volume is obtained. In the same way "illustrative" music is trivial and expressionless if presented "from one angle", that is, if it illustrates one aspect, one element only of the material to be illustrated.' This metaphor demonstrates one of the cardinal responsibilities of film music. Newman does not merely 'paint' the two scenes just described in his music; had he done so the result would have been 'flat', 'lacking in depth'. Instead he sculpts them, views them from that multiplicity of angles which alone can give them their fully realistic, 'three-dimensional' character.

Franz Werfel, the author of *The Song of Bernadette*, attended the recording session with his wife Alma Mahler-Werfel, widow of the composer (both of them had settled in Beverly Hills) and was profoundly moved by the music for the vision scenes. Yet Newman's score has come under heavy fire on a number of occasions, never more so than when it was described in public by the English composer Benjamin Frankel as the nadir of vulgarity. To which a good reply is contained in a letter by Thomas Mann to an American friend who in a lecture had subjected Dieterle's moving *The Best Years of Our Lives* to scathing attack. Mann wrote: 'My dear friend, how many corrupt and corrupting pieces of hackwork there were to pillory instead of this film! It belongs to the finest things of its kind to have come my way. . .'

Newman's 'Hallelujah Chorus' makes its third and last screen appearance in *The Robe*, the first film in CinemaScope — for which process (though not for this inaugural film) Newman composed an extension of his 1937 Fox Fanfare. The film is not very highly regarded today, yet it inspired Newman. Perhaps he was affected by its ethos rather than its quality. He was anxious that aurally as well as visually the new process should offer a further-ranging experience, and his music for *The Robe* has a spaciousness, grandeur and simplicity of conception rarely to be found in scores for epic 'blockbusters'. *The Robe* was also the first picture in stereophonic sound and Newman experimented with nondirectional microphones covering only the centrally placed strings and woodwind and so admitting brass and percussion in natural perspective only. It is possible that this had some bearing on the uncluttered quality of the textures. Another factor was the character of the melodic and harmonic language. *The Robe* was a New Testament epic, and here, as with all period dramas, the problem was to reconcile the claims of commentative music with the archaic element necessary to give the soundtrack location in place and time. Newman solved the problem in a manner similar to Rózsa in *Quo Vadis* (see page 214). He observed in the cast of his thematic material the spirit rather than the letter of Hebrew monody and Oriental chromaticism, which meant that motifs and themes were free to follow their natural bent without playing havoc with stylistic consistency. I use the terms 'theme' and 'motif' advisedly since the film's 'main theme' is not really a melody. In order to stress the fundamental idea of faith and belief, the triumph of Christianity over its antagonists, Newman devised a harmonic sequence consisting of juxtaposed major and minor chords unrelated by key. This was a device patented by Debussy (for example in *La Cathédrale Engloutie* and *Le Martyre de Saint Sébastien*) and taken up by many later composers to suggest the remote, the mystical, the transcendental; it is a Rózsa fingerprint (the Christ theme in *Ben-Hur*) and Herrmann employs it frequently (in *Journey to the Centre of the Earth*). Its roots lie in the medieval church modes of plainsong or Gregorian chant in which there seem to be no true closes. The effect is one of archetypal solidity and strength, a type of utterance to which Western man has been responding for centuries; and in that it represents the film's underlying concept. In essence it remains unchanged throughout, adapting itself to new situations through variations in orchestral colour and dynamic. We hear it on divided high strings with wordless voices in the background when Marcellus is finally convinced of the healing power of the Robe and is converted to Christianity by his slave Demetrius. Later, when Simon Peter brings Demetrius, on the point of death after being tortured by the

Praetorian Guard, back to life, Peter emerges from the room where the slave has been lying and the 'chords' sound serenely in the brass, telling us more eloquently than words of the miracle which has been wrought.

In the Procession to Calvary (a sequence the emotional tenor of which calls to mind Newman's Jewish origins) the chords assume the character of a funeral dirge, punctuated by dragging drum-figurations and gong-strokes: against which high strings project a passionate, quasi-improvisatory melody of Hebraic cast. On Golgotha the wordless chorus takes up this melody imitationally (one voice following another with the same motif or permutation thereof) in a hypnotic manner suggestive of ritual keening. The orchestra gradually joins in to intensify the climax, and then the music fades into the natural sounds of a thunderstorm.

The most dramatic scene is one which in every respect save its music (and its music saves it!) is a failure — the rescue of Demetrius from the torture chamber by Marcellus and a band of Christians. In the chamber before the rescue a rugged march-like tread with heavy percussion both impresses with the apparent invincibility of the Praetorian Guard and charges the atmosphere with electricity. Then, as the Christians suddenly drop down out of the skies, an energetic burst of music provides all the missing excitement and exhilaration. Herrmann once remarked 'music is designed to supplement both what the actors and technicians have been able to do and (mostly) what they've been unable to do.'

The Robe is a musical masterpiece. One of its greatest admirers was Franz Waxman, who re-worked some of its thematic material in a sequel, *Demetrius and the Gladiators* (1954). He favoured particularly a major-minor motif which later assumed a prominent position in *The Greatest Story Ever Told*. For Newman, however, what he envisaged as perhaps the project of a lifetime eventually turned into the Saddest Story Ever Told. The full tale of woe has been related by Ken Darby (*Films in Review*, June/July 1969, pp. 348–9) but only the aesthetic aspects of the débâcle need concern us here.

The most contentious is director George Stevens' insistence on the use of the 'Hallelujah Chorus' from the *Messiah* for the scenes of the raising of Lazarus and the Resurrection. There are two basic objections to this. First, the very familiarity of the Handel draws attention to it in a way that must always be shunned by film music: because it is a cliché it fails to provoke the necessary strength of emotional response. Second, there is no thematic connection. Originally Newman had written his own 'Hallelujah Chorus' (his second) for these two scenes, which with its purposefully striding *moto perpetuo* bass line invoked a quasi-Handelian spirit, but whose substance was thematically derived from other material in the score, ensuring a musical continuity. Stevens decided to replace it in both scenes by the *Messiah*. He also jettisoned Newman's original 'Via Dolorosa' in favour of the opening of Verdi's *Requiem*. Stylistically this is more in keeping with Newman's score than *Messiah*, and in fact the emotion it projects is in keeping with the character of the visual representation; but again the music bears the burden of over-familiarity and is liable to distract. Instead of drawing us into the screen it momentarily sets up an irrelevant train of thought: 'Don't I know that music? Yes, it's the Verdi *Requiem*.'

That said, we must admit that the scene of the raising of Lazarus — a superb piece of cinema — is tolerably well-handled musically as it now stands, *pace* Handel. The musical transitions are nicely managed. As Jesus (Max von Sydow) disappears in the doorway of the tomb, thunder rolls and re-echoes around the hills and instigates a long quotation from the Crucifixion sequence in *The Robe* (another of Stevens' unwelcomed ideas — but at least there is a natural congruence between the Newman of *The Robe* and of *The Greatest Story*). We see nothing distinctly: but then all at once the screen is a dynamo of excited activity. Men are seen running in all directions, passing on the joyful tidings: and at this point the music breaks into the opening of Newman's original 'Hallelujah Chorus' with its stalking bass. The Handelian quality of the latter facilitates the transition into the *Messiah*. It is so cut that the pause just before the final cadence may coincide with the response of Old Aram (Ed Wynn): now cured of his blindness, he answers the question posed by the men at the gates of the town: 'Who has done this thing?', with the line: 'His name is Jesus'. This marks the end of Act I, and is good musical dramaturgy; but it might have proved much better had Newman's original music been retained.

For quiet beauty and sincerity Newman never surpassed the concentrated lyricism of his main theme, 'Jesus of Nazareth'. In this he sought to portray a flesh-and-blood Jesus, destroying the waxen doll image of Sunday School and Scripture Class. Further than this it is unsafe to submit the score to detailed analysis since we cannot be sure to what extent it corresponds in its released state to the composer's intentions. The film's original running time, over four hours, was gradually whittled down to two. Moreover, Stevens was constantly re-editing, shortening and shifting scenes; in some cases music designed for one scene was placed in another, and when further cuts were insisted on by the distributors, Hugo Friedhofer and Fred Steiner were assigned the task of boiling down Newman's music to suit. Small wonder that in the face of this Newman should have declared 'it's my name but it isn't my score. I'd be happy if my name were removed from the credits.'

The Diary of Anne Frank (1959) touched a similar nerve in Newman. He chose to concentrate not on the tragedy of the Frank family and the horror and degredation of their ordeal, but on the character of Anne herself as played by Millie Perkins. Viewed in this light the magnitude of the tragedy is perceptibly diminished, for Anne is too young and unsophisticated to be seared by pessimism. She regards her attic life in hiding as a great adventure, and confides to her diary that, in spite of everything, she still believes people to be good at heart. It is Anne's girlishness and guilelessness which sets the tone of Newman's music. He makes in his main title for a sweetness and sunniness, even a nostalgic *alt-wienerisch* quality, a remembrance of happy things past, as when Anne tries on Peter's mother's coat just before her first date with

Peter to a lilting Straussian waltz. Arguably this softens the impact of the drama. But this is, after all, the story of Anne Frank and the film is designed to express everything from her point of view. Moreover, the general policy of understatement means that those moments when Newman *does* depict fear and oppressiveness — the families' first day in their makeshift garret home (in which the music seems to well out of the sepulchral sound of deep tolling bells) and the scene of the night-burglar — make their points tellingly. Nor can the musical treatment of the scenes between Anne and Peter Van Daan be faulted. As they look through the trapdoor to the open sky, with the snow on the rooftop glistening in the spring air and the birds flying, the music blends these impressions with the first glimmerings of adolescent love. The revelation comes only seconds before the Gestapo arrive to arrest them, and the music evokes the wonder and tenderness of their feelings — rising, in one of Newman's most moving passages, to an agonized, ecstatic climax as the dreaded knocking on the door prompts them to a first and last passionate kiss. The music may be 'old-fashioned', 'conservative', 'derivative'; yet it is not pastiche. Like the best of Newman it has style, elegance, integrity, and is 'felt'.

The last four major scores of Newman's life comprised two ensconced in 'tradition' (in more than one sense) and two which point in the direction of new paths of development. *The Greatest Story Ever Told*, in the first category, has already been discussed; there remains *How the West was Won* (1963) and, in the second, *The Counterfeit Traitor* (1962) and *Airport* (1969). Although Newman's musical language was European, like many of his Hollywood colleagues he acquired a certain dexterity in integrating the legacy of Americana — indigenous American folk and traditional music — within the European symphonic tradition. A *tour de force* in this respect was *Wilson* (1944), Zanuck's mammoth tribute to the 28th U.S. President, for which Newman spent some time on research. It was necessary to establish what songs the Wilson family sang around the piano, what music Wilson and his daughter used for their soft-shoe dance, what bands played at political rallies in the 1900s, what kind of music Wilson and his wife would have heard in vaudeville acts they witnessed on their visits to the New York of 1912, what the theme-songs of the different candidates at the 1912 convention were, what music was played at White House functions by what types of bands and orchestras. *Wilson* finally contained some forty realistic numbers, all authentically American, ranging from college songs and sentimental ballads to patriotic anthems.

This and the similar (if smaller-scale) experience gained in films as diverse as *Barbary Coast* (1935), *Drums along the Mohawk* and *Young Mr Lincoln* (both 1939), *The Grapes of Wrath* (1940), *Belle Starr* (1940), *The Westerner* (1940, credited to Dimitri Tiomkin), *Yellow Star* (1948), *The Gunfighter* (1950) and other more or less conventional Westerns, all served to prepare Newman for the vast undertaking of *How the West was Won*. This was a massive historical Cinerama spectacular, each panel assigned to a different director, which chronicled the history of the American West from the pioneer settlers of the 1830s through the Civil War to the era of railroad expansion and the final establishment of law and order in the 1880s. A fair portion of the score is of Newman's original composing, but folk and traditional materials play a large part in determining its overall melodic complexion. The overture is a miscellany of such material (including 'Shenandoah' and the evocative 'Endless Prairie') freely arranged and adapted by Newman and Ken Darby; likewise the *entr'acte* which features among other well-known tunes 'When Johnny Comes Marching Home' and 'I'm bound for the Promised Land' linked together in counterpoint. The latter serves as a kind of motto-theme for the whole picture, and incidentally serves to illustrate Newman's adeptness at absorbing borrowed material into his musical bloodstream. For his own original main theme — a melody of pioneer sturdiness announced at the onset of the main title by the six horns, and later surrounded by driving *Big Country*-like high violin figurations — becomes in the finale something resembling a folk-hymn.

Here it acquires a Darby lyric and pulses to the rhythm of massed guitars over a series of travelogue views of America as it is today.

On other occasions Newman gives his own themes the outline and imprint of American folksong, memorably in the scene showing the aftermath of the buffaloes' stampede over the railway workers' encampments. Even apart from the action whose shape it helps articulate, the music forms a logical emotional sequence in its own right — the numbness of the initial shock as the dust clears and the desolation becomes apparent, then the outburst of grief (violins climbing to a pitch of elegiac intensity); finally a period of calm and solace leading to a resurgence of optimism. Here Newman's quasi-folktune (the theme associated with George Peppard as Les Rawlins) comes into its own and gives expression to Rawlins's determination to rebuild his life in the face of apparently insuperable odds. There is no better example of the power of Newman's rich, translucent string writing.

Of the authentic folk melodies, the most poetically employed is 'When Johnny Comes Marching Home' in one of the John Ford scenes which shows the young Les Rawlins saying goodbye to his mother (Carroll Baker), leaving his farmhouse home and wandering away to the horizon and war. We hear the well-known song sung by a soft, spectral men's chorus overhung by strings, and punctuated by distant bugle calls, so distant as to seem to be coming from beyond the horizon. This image-in-sound recalls another of Newman's celebrated sequences – the beginning of *Twelve O'Clock High* (1949), when the ghostly men's voices in the deserted aerodrome recall to Dean Jagger the comrades he has lost in the war. Earlier, in *Wuthering Heights* (1939) a wordless female chorus suggested Lockwood's vision of the ghost of Cathy, just as in the grotto scenes in *Song of Bernadette* it evokes the 'beautiful Lady'. Few composers in Hollywood conceived of the *pianissimo* chorus as a potent musico-dramatic entity in this way.

Newman incorporated a number of expressive cameos in *How the West was Won*; one of the best is the picture of gambler

Van Valen (Gregory Peck) astride his donkey. In a
scherzo-like vignette Newman captures his mixture of
wiliness and lovableness. The music is reminiscent of the
quaint old stowaway Ada Quonsett's (Helen Hayes) theme in
Airport, Newman's last score. But before *Airport* came the
Seaton-Hunter *Counterfeit Traitor*, (1962) their common
denominator being Newman's transmutation of noise into
music. *The Counterfeit Traitor* was an espionage thriller set in
occupied Europe and shot in Stockholm, Copenhagen and
elsewhere; and Newman decided to make the racket of the
modern city a musical symbol of the tension and terror
experienced by those who lived through the Nazi nightmare.
Accordingly he visited Copenhagen and steeped himself in its
everyday din — pneumatic drills, footsteps, the cacophony of
tyres, exhausts and brakes and the myriad other noises which
cast their mite into the symphony of a great city. Years before,
in *A Tree Grows in Brooklyn* (1944), he combined a hurdy-gurdy
with the 'symphony' of street noises and other naturalistic
sounds, all 'orchestrated'. Here, however, in the title music,
he turns these metals into gold: a declamatory opening,
then a sense of implacable flux with obsessively repeated short
rhythmic figures, dissonant harmony, pungent scoring — of
which a passage for percussion alone is the inevitable upshot.
This is the brutal big-city ambience; while a long cantilena
for strings against throbbing harmonies, and a sombre
chordal sequence for brass, presage the personal tragedy
which is the secondary theme of the picture.

Newman enlarged upon this new line of development in
Airport, another Seaton-Hunter picture. Here, as in the theme
for Lilli Palmer and William Holden in *The Counterfeit Traitor*,
Newman proves in his themes for Dean Martin/Jacqueline
Bisset and Burt Lancaster/Jean Seberg that his old feeling for
rhapsodic romance is as active as ever; and in the scene where
Van Heflin (he plays a psychopathic failure, planning to blow
up an aircraft with himself on board so that his wife can claim
the insurance) bids his wife a last goodbye, the music seems
to probe into his half-crazed mind with understanding and
sympathy.

But the main glory of the *Airport* score is its modern airport music, i.e. the main and end titles: bustle, excitement and nervous tension is contained in the mamba-like rhythm heavily marked by Latin-American percussion, but there is romance too — for taking off in an aeroplane is still, will always be (we hope) a romantic adventure — in the swelling lyrical theme which 'takes off' just like the plane. The music projects that same crazy dance-like sensation of man at war with the cosmos as Herrmann's *North By Northwest* main title, and in not dissimilar musical terms. Was Newman, in this score, experiencing that rejuvenation of creative energy in old age which other composers have enjoyed, among them Steiner and Waxman? The snazzy up-beat feel of this music, with its rhythmic snap and colourful percussion, suggests that Newman may have been listening to the work of younger colleagues. It has perhaps a flavour of Elmer Bernstein, though nothing so specific as to suggest the latter's direct influence. The love theme on the other hand is unmistakably Newmanesque in its voluptuous, long-lined curvaceousness; Newman always had a special feeling for beauty of melodic contour. Much as we may regret Newman's premature death (already a mortally ill man when he embarked on *Airport*, he died a matter of months after its completion), at least he was spared the tragic fate of Steiner, whose last few scores were described by Tony Thomas as 'a weak coda to a mighty career'. Newman's 'mighty career' ended not with a whimper but with the resolute bang of *Airport*.

NOTES

1 In conversation with the author.

2 Some interesting parallels could be drawn between the professional activity of a man like Newman at 20th Century Fox and Bach at Weimar and Leipzig. For instance, they both worked under constant pressure. They had to combine a hectic schedule of practical music-making with an ongoing commitment to composing, to fulfil which assistants were employed in various degrees of creative capacity, and much transcribing, re-arranging, re-editing and borrowing (of their own and others' material) went on.

3 *The Making of an American Film Composer: A Study of Alfred Newman's Music in the First Decade of the Sound Era.* Unpublished dissertation, University of Southern California, 1981.

4 Dassin's *The Naked City* (1948) launched a crop of gangster films and thrillers with big-city locations bearing the word 'city' in their titles; several were Fox productions, and the use of *Street Scene* as main title music became almost mandatory in these cases, whether or not Newman himself composed the remainder of the score — for instance *Where the Sidewalk Ends* (1950, composer Cyril Mockridge). Robert Siodmak's *Cry of the City* (1948), which Newman *did* score himself, reveals this to have been a rather foolish convention, in that the cool, Gershwinesque sophistication of the music is at variance with the sombre poetry of the city as captured in this film and others like it.

5 Or was it rather a question of atavistic racial impulses taking control? See below my remarks on the Procession to Calvary sequence in *The Robe*.

6 Antoine's chant-like theme recurs in a minor key some twenty years later as one of the motifs in *The Greatest Story Ever Told*.

FRANZ WAXMAN

It was the composer of Dietrich's 'Falling in love again' who made a film musician out of Franz Waxman. Friedrich Holländer (who later became 'Frederick' and dropped the Umlaut in Hollywood) engaged Waxman at the age of 24 to orchestrate and conduct his score for the celebrated *Blue Angel* in 1930 (though Waxman received no screen credit). Three years later Waxman composed his first original score for Fritz Lang's screen adaptation of Molnár's *Liliom* (1933). As in the case of *The Blue Angel* his producer was Erich Pommer of UFA, and when the latter eventually joined Fox in Hollywood as a producer, he decided to import Waxman from Paris to supervise the music of his film version of the Kern-Hammerstein operetta *Music in the Air* (1935). Waxman had left Germany the previous year after being attacked by Nazi hoodlums on a Berlin street. His arrangements of Kern's music were much appreciated in the United States; and after his original score for James Whale's *Bride of Frankenstein* (1935) met with a similar success, Waxman was appointed head of the music department at Universal. Here he supervised the music of some fifty pictures as well as scoring a number himself; but wishing to devote all his time to composition he signed a contract with MGM as a staff composer, moving to Warner Brothers in 1942.

In 1948 he became a free-lance and it was at this juncture that his musical horizons began to broaden. For Waxman was a musician of wide — and ever-widening — sympathies, and the range of his musical intellect and musical activities increased as he grew older. He approached his art in a spirit of Teutonic conscientiousness. In later years he became more interested both in concert music and conducting. The latter was what the French term a *passion* with Waxman, and the highly remunerative nature of his film work provided him with the wherewithal to indulge it on a lavish and benificent scale. In 1947 he founded the Los Angeles Music Festival and for twenty years was its principal conductor. He introduced many important works to the West Coast — Honegger's *Joan of Arc at the Stake* (in the Hollywood Bowl), Britten's *War Requiem*, Debussy's *Le Martyre de Saint Sébastien*, symphonies by Shostakovich, Prokofiev and Walton, Stravinsky's *Soldier's Tale* and his opera *The Nightingale*. Stravinsky conducted the American premiere of his *Canticum Sacrum* during the 1957 Festival, and at the same concert the world premiere of his ballet *Agon*. Waxman from time to time brought out a new 'serious' composition of his own, and in 1956 directed the West Coast premiere of Miklós Rózsa's Violin Concerto. Otherwise the Festival's links with the film world were negligible. It is worth pointing out, however, that Waxman's true stature as a composer first came to be recognized as a result of his work in the film medium.

Waxman often extracted material from his film-scores for concert use. From Lewis Milestone's saga of anti-Nazi activities in Norway *Edge of Darkness* (1943) came the symphonic fantasy on the Luther chorale 'Ein' feste Burg'; and *Old Acquaintance* in the following year yielded an attractive *Elegy* for string orchestra and harp. Neatly-made single-movement concert suites exist from *Rebecca* (1940), *Sunset Boulevard* (1950), *A Place in the Sun* (1951) and others; and the *'Carmen' Fantasy* for violin and orchestra (written for Jascha Heifetz) was a by-product of *Humoresque* (1947). Writing the score for the Spencer Tracy version of *Dr Jekyll and Mr Hyde* (1941) led to a special fascination with Stevenson's weird allegory, and Waxman worked intermittently at an opera on the subject which he never lived to complete.

The last decade of Waxman's life, however, saw the production of three major concert works: the Sinfonietta for Strings and Timpani (1955); the dramatic oratorio *Joshua* (1959); and, most important of all, *The Song of Terezin* (1965), a song-cycle for mixed chorus, children's chorus, mezzo-soprano soloist and orchestra, based on a collection of poems entitled 'I never saw another butterfly', written by children imprisoned in the Theresienstadt concentration camp in Czechoslovakia in World War II. Minor concert pieces include a Theme, Variations and Fugato (1955), a Trumpet Overture (1946), and *Goyana*, four sketches for piano and string orchestra (1960). None of these works is in any way associated with Waxman's film scores, except that in *Joshua* the main theme of Billy Wilder's *Spirit of St Louis* (1957) becomes a *cantus firmus* as part of the contrapuntal scaffolding of the chorus 'Shout, for the Lord has given you the city'.

These works, and the film scores composed contemporaneously with them, reveal a clear progression away from the stylized suavity and euphony of the music Waxman was producing for the cinema in the late thirties and forties. The more faded aspects of Hollywood romanticism are superseded by contrapuntal textures and dissonant harmonies. Much in Waxman certainly stemmed from the elder statesmen of Germanic romanticism — Wagner, Strauss, Korngold: the score for *Prince Valiant* (1954) is an enjoyably outrageous compendium of elements drawn from *The Ring, Don Juan, Heldenleben* and *Robin Hood*. Elsewhere he seems to be looking more to the post-romantic generation of Russian composers — to Prokofiev and particularly Shostakovich, with whom he had an undoubted affinity. This trend was typical of Waxman's enquiring and receptive mind, ever searching for ways to expand his own stylistic universe, though never at the expense of facile or fashionable mimicry. Herrmann said, 'He was dissatisfied with what he was doing and wanted to do it

better — which is a hallmark of the true artist'. His versatility
expressed itself in jazz (*Crime in the Streets*, 1956), the oddly
painless intermingling of occidental and oriental idioms in
Sayonara (1957), the Hebraic severity of *Joshua*, the powerful
tenderness of *The Song of Terezin*, the barbaric beauty and
flint-and-steel-struck splendour of *Taras Bulba*. When he lost
his battle with cancer in February 1967, two months after his
sixtieth birthday, Waxman was at the zenith of his powers.

We can easily follow the logicality of Waxman's stylistic
development if we remember that there were always two
complementary, not conflicting, elements in his musical
make-up. One was melodic invention. Although he was never
much interested in song-writing *per se* he created many
popular and distinguished melodies: the Katsumi love theme
in *Sayonara*, Rosanna's theme in Hemingway's *Adventures of a
Young Man*, the lovely title song of *Beloved Infidel* composed in
1959 to lyrics by Paul Francis Webster, 'The Wonderful
Season of Love' in *Peyton Place* (1957), the song 'Lisa'
incorporated in Hitchcock's *Rear Window* (1954) as an integral
realistic part of the scenario, the title song for Lang's *This is my
Love* (1954), and 'Ariane' for Wilder's *Love in the Afternoon*
(1957). But if the musical impulse was primarily melodic,
contrapuntal disciplines later came to take precedence.
Waxman enjoyed working within an extraneously imposed
structural framework (although he allowed himself maximum
freedom within the broad outlines of the structure) and
produced some of his best music in this form. Fugatos and
fugal textures especially attracted him, and there is a famous
example in *Objective Burma* (1945), in which a hill-climbing
episode is fugally dramatized, strand added to strand
methodically and insistently, until at the climax, with Flynn
and his co-climbers having reached the summit, the music is
abruptly dispersed and all that remains is the howling of a
desolate dry wind. Another spectacular moment in *Objective
Burma* is the first mass parachute jump, accompanied by an
onslaught of fighting high violins, a single line, *allegro furioso e
fortissimo* (a variant of the celebrated opening sequence of *God
is my Co-Pilot*, where Waxman interestingly claimed to 'hear'

The Spirit of St Louis: the 'Building of the Ryan'

Franz Waxman receiving his Oscar for
Place in the Sun from Gene Kelly

massed violins on his first viewing of the footage without initially being sure of the precise music they were to play — the specific sonority being in this case the all-important factor). Montgomery Clift's flight through the woods in *A Place in the Sun* is predominantly fugal[1] (a sequence much admired at the recording session by, among others, Bernard Herrmann and Alma Mahler), likewise the street fight in *Sayonara*. *Taras Bulba* (1962) contains two fine fugal episodes: the chase at night through the streets of Kiev with its nerve-shattering snare-drums and Andrei's frantic search for Natalia among the plague-ridden Poles of Dubno. A vivid passage in the oratorio *Joshua* is the chorus 'Shout, for the Lord has given you the city', already mentioned, which approaches the stricter canons of fugal procedure and is one of Waxman's most sinewy and muscular inspirations.

The sequence depicting the building of the plane in *The Spirit of St Louis* would have been ideally suited to fugal treatment, but Walton had already achieved fame with his *Prelude and Fugue: The Spitfire* written for a similar montage in the British film *The First of the Few* (1942). Waxman (who conducted the West Coast premiere of this piece in 1947) was no doubt loath to imitate Walton and drafted instead a long paragraph whose knotty, fibrous textures whirred, hummed, spun and bustled with all manner of contrapuntal — but studiedly unfugal — activity. In the Walton the completion of the 'Spitfire' is marked by the return of the broad, confident Elgar-like marching tune from the main title. Waxman's overall design is different. First, the main theme is not a march, but a sharp, angular, upward-striking motif imbued with the kind of star-reaching spirit often found in Austro-Germanic music. Second, this motif is not reserved for the climax but appears relatively early in the sequence as a leading thread in the contrapuntal complex. At the climax, however (as the finished plane is wheeled out), the theme is allowed to stand clear, naked and unashamed, and this very starkness and bareness has an exhilarating ring and flash of triumph. So does the great moment when James Stewart finally lands the plane at Le Bourget, the music having sympathetically accompanied and supported him throughout the various stages of his ordeal.

Waxman was also drawn to the passacaglia, a musical form in which a short phrase (primarily bass-ic) is subject to constantly varied repetition. The passacaglia's pace being generally slow and deliberate, it can easily give the impression of massive reserves of power concentrated into one single organism, and released slowly but with relentlessly cumulative effect. The form has therefore a dramatic potential which Waxman was quick to take advantage of. A classic instance is the entire last scene of *Sorry, Wrong Number* (1948) with the crippled Barbara Stanwyck alone, terrified, helpless and awaiting the murderer; here the passacaglia conveys both a mounting tension and sense of approaching horror with a directness and insistence that no other musical form could have rivalled. The final climax, as the passacaglia theme riding the full orchestra coincides with the footsteps approaching the door, and everything, including Stanwyck's demented scream, is lost in the roar of the overhead railway, is one of the most frightening in film music. Waxman made the orchestral sinfonia 'The Siege of Jericho' in *Joshua* a passacaglia, again demonstrating the usefulness of the form in sustaining an unbroken arch of tension over a long time span: also the first movement in *The Song of Terezin*, 'On a Sunny Evening', where the dramatic intention is quite different, namely to drive home the world-shaking anguish and despair belied by the innocent lyricism of the text.

When constructing a passacaglia a composer at least has a phrase of definite meaning and shape to work with, however neutral emotionally. But in one of his earliest scores, *The Bride of Frankenstein*, Waxman achieved an even greater *tour de force*, for the long sequence portraying the creation of the female monster is in effect a fantasia on one note. The one note is the repeated E hammered out by the timpani to represent the beating of the monster's heart. Waxman was stimulated by any imposition or restriction, and, although he makes no direct reference to it, he must have remembered this high watermark of his early career when he came to write the second movement of his Sinfonietta for String Orchestra and Timpani, which is entitled 'Dirge' and is built around a repeated timpani A.

After *Bride of Frankenstein* Waxman was frequently called on to score films of horror and suspense. Hitchcock's *Rebecca* (1940) was the first to bring him fame and is conspicuously successful in its underlining both of the fairy-tale atmosphere Hitchcock tried to create in his Manderley and of the *Laura*-like omnipresence of Rebecca. She is never seen, for she is dead: only her malign influence can be felt, and the music helps us to feel it. We are enveloped from the moment the main title opens — an ominous tread in the bass over a repeated note, string and woodwind figurations writhing in quasi-impressionistic mists, an imperious horn summons. Then, as the credits come up over a series of dissolves from one dream-like distorted view of the Manderley estate to another, the 'Rebecca' theme is heard for the first time. Joan Fontaine's opening narration begins, 'Last night I dreamt I went to Manderley again'. Romantic-impressionist music creates a dream-like aura as the camera tracks forward up the deserted, overgrown drive on which 'Nature had encroached in her stealthy, insidious way with long tenacious fingers.' This passage is based not on the 'Rebecca' theme but on another shorter but pregnant motif associated with Manderley alone and not with Rebecca.

For the 'Rebecca' problem does not really arise until a third of the picture is over, and Joan Fontaine is installed in Manderley as second wife to Max de Winter (Laurence Olivier). How to suggest the potency of the past, of the evil and ghostly presence of the dead Rebecca? Waxman's solution is the use of the novachord, an electronic keyboard instrument with a sound not unlike that of a Hammond organ. Now in disuse, it enjoyed huge popularity in the Golden Age. Employed in a certain way its sound had supernatural overtones. Every time Rebecca's name is mentioned, or her presence is invoked — almost invariably by the frightening Mrs Danvers (Judith Anderson) — the 'Rebecca' theme sounds on the novachord, its peculiarly spooky sonority pointing us ever in the direction of the world beyond the veil.

When Joan Fontaine first stumbles across the deserted beachhouse, the 'Rebecca' theme — as it were a musical monogram — overwhelms, telling us straightaway that everthing here is a relic of the dead woman, all preserved as it was at the time of her death. And because the malevolent spirit of the drowned Rebecca lives on in Mrs Danvers, the novachord comes to stand as a musical symbol for the latter also; its sinister purr seems to deepen the undercurrent of lesbianism and necrophilia through which the past contrives to poison the present.[2] It is a wonderful moment when the new Mrs de Winter first penetrates the (implicitly forbidden) west wing of the mansion. This is Rebecca's wing where, again, everything has been left as she left it. There the second Mrs de Winter encounters Mrs Danvers, who tells her of Rebecca's bedroom, 'the most beautiful room in the house' with its windows looking down across the lawns to the sea. We focus on the large double doors leading into Rebecca's quarters, and lying there in front of them is Jasper, her pet spaniel. Over a soft timpani pedal soft unmuted trombones (in the manner almost of a low growl) and novachord sound the 'Rebecca' theme, and the effect is one of *sotto voce* triumph: gloating, sadistic, sweet as honey.

Quite different is the transformation this same theme undergoes in the finale. As de Winter and Crawley are driving home after establishing the real cause of Rebecca's death, they see a glow in the sky that they quickly surmise must be Manderley ablaze. We close in on the burning building. The de Winters' love theme pulses through the orchestra as Max searches for his wife, reaching a climactically triumphant A major (one of the brightest of keys) as he finds her with Jasper on a lead. Then we see Mrs Danvers still inside the blazing west wing, darting wildly from one room to another; as she does so the orchestra picks up the 'Rebecca' theme and races ahead with it in the manner of a mad waltz. But there is no escape for Mrs Danvers; and as she resigns herself, like Brünnhilde, to follow her mistress in death, the low brass in octaves proclaim the 'Rebecca' theme *tutta forza* in broad augmentation. The camera closes in for a final shot of the pillow slip with the embroidered 'R', and a massive chordal treatment of the musical 'R' has the last word.

In 1950 and 1951 Waxman won the Academy Award for two years in succession. The Oscar itself is no guarantee of a score's quality, but it does occasionally happen that good films inspire good scores that are recognized and honoured accordingly, as in the case of *Sunset Boulevard* (1950) and *A Place in the Sun* (1951).

Sunset Boulevard, the most famous of all the 'Hollywood on Hollywood' movies, inspired what is arguably Waxman's masterpiece.[3] It must have been a difficult task since the music has to move on the same constantly shifting levels of unreality as the scenario, and take due account of the many areas of pastiche through which it passes. The first is encountered in the opening scene. The titles open with Sunset Boulevard speeding away behind us, and as Gillis, the dead man (William Holden) begins his narration, we realize that we have been travelling in a police car to the scene of his murder. The genre for the present is that of the gangster movie of the thirties and forties, and the accompanying music perhaps casts one sidelong glance in the direction of Rózsa's 'gangster' scores of the latter period, another towards Gershwin's form of 'big city bustle' music. Nevertheless it is relevant to what is to come: for not only is the insistence on one note — trilled, jabbed and pecked out, heavily accented, syncopated, or merely repeated in fast notes — prophetic of Norma Desmond's (Gloria Swanson) obsession, her mental imbalance, but her own theme is also introduced, as if incidentally, beneath the racket of roaring, screeching brass and motoric rhythms. The theme is set in the Phrygian mode, the mode most commonly employed in Hispanic musics; for which three reasons. First, the use of this darkly exotic-sounding mode invests the theme with an appropriately bizarre, even sinister quality; second, the tango, a dance of South American origin, is an important motif on two occasions in the film, and a melody with Hispanic overtones is obviously appropriate. Third, Norma Desmond's film script is the story of Salome and, again, the exotic flavour is apposite.

As we move into the swimming pool in Norma Desmond's mansion — still over Gillis's narration — and see his body floating in the water, a softly ominous trill begins in clarinets (a clearer symbol of Desmond's madness) and Gillis's own theme tentatively asserts itself, more firmly as the flashback begins. It is an aimless, nonchalantly syncopated melody, deliberately flat in tone, grey in colour (it is usually given to the piano) and so reflects something of Gillis's ingrained hopelessness. The 'gangster' movement and music is resumed when Gillis, after failing to borrow money from everyone he can think of, is spotted and chased by the two agents out to seize his car for non-payment of the dues. He takes refuge in the driveway of what proves to be Norma Desmond's residence: 'a great white elephant of a place, the kind crazy movie people built in the crazy twenties . . . a neglected house gets an unhappy look . . . it was like that old woman in *Great Expectations*, that Miss Havisham. . .' Already the trills and repeated notes are sounding again, this time softly on mid-area strings, but the music cuts out just before Norma hails Gillis; only to cut back in almost immediately on alto flute with Norma's theme. Subtly, almost imperceptibly, the music exhales its exotic aroma, spinning its web of weirdness and fantasy. It does not play continuously, only a few bars here, a few bars there: the wind allegedly blowing through the pipes of a chamber organ thereby emitting a mysteriously evocative sound, especially when it chimes in with the key of the orchestra: 'It sure was a cosy set-up — that bundle of raw nerves, that dead monkey upstairs, and the wind wheezing through that organ once in a while. . .' By this time the genre has changed. We are back in the past-haunted world of *Rebecca* as Gillis takes stock of his surroundings. The music helps to settle us there.

Late that night Gillis observes the funeral of the monkey, commented on with a nice touch of irony by a grotesque quasi-Mahlerian funeral march in miniature. On going to bed he has a dream of an organ-grinder whose face he cannot see but whose instrument is draped in black; on it a chimp is dancing for pennies. As Gillis gradually stirs to life and opens his eyes he realizes that the organ music is still audible. It is Max, Norma's manservant (Erich von Stroheim) playing Bach's D minor Toccata and Fugue on the chamber organ. Waxman handles this transition with great skill: a bassoon (earlier associated with the dead monkey) dominates the first few seconds, while Gillis is still dreaming. Then, as he slowly becomes aware of the organ music, the whirring triplets of the Bach Toccata are introduced *but still within the orchestra* (first piccolo then clarinet) i.e. still within Gillis's dream. Gradually, as he comes to, the woodwinds' tone is merged with that of the 'real' organ, the orchestra is mixed out, and as Gillis leaps to his feet fully awake, the organ dominates the soundtrack.

Gillis starts to work on Norma Desmond's *Salome* script, which is, we are given to understand, conceived in terms of silent-film technique — the technique of Gloria Swanson's own glittering past. The music hints at as much when, as Norma starts out of her seat and challenges Gillis on seeing him throw a sheaf of script into the trash can, it reverts to one of the favourite devices of silent-film music (as in *The Informer*): anticipating a sharp reproof or retort — verbal violence rather than physical — by a *sforzando* diminished seventh[4] chord. Shortly afterwards Norma has Max show a clip from one of her early (Swanson) movies, *Queen Kelly*. In the middle, wildly agitated and almost hysterical, she explodes 'Those imbeciles! Have they forgotten what a star looks like? I'll show them! I'll be up there again, so help me!' She stands there defiantly, her profile quivering in the interrupted light from the projector, and the orchestra suddenly blazes with trills — the first time that these trills are overtly associated with Norma's mania, and, in fact, the first time that the audience is made aware of it. The trills complement the crazed expression to produce an unforgettable visual-aural image.

Slowly Gillis becomes part of the petrified Desmond household. The first 'crunch' comes when Norma persuades him to let her buy him some proper clothes. They go to the best tailor in town. When offered two ranges of material Gillis automatically chooses the less expensive. But the assistant whispers in his ear, 'But if Madame is paying for it . . .' and Gillis realizes with a shock that he is nothing more nor less than a kept man. The shrill piccolo points his horror-struck reaction. Soon, however, he accepts the situation, is moved to the main house and his own theme, formerly listless, now becomes sleek and well-fed. Suddenly it is surrounded by lush harmonies and smooth velvety strings, just as Gillis's outward appearance changes from scruffiness to elegance, and he leaves his spartan accommodation in the garage for the wild extravagance of the former husbands' bedroom.

Only at her New Year's ball does Gillis become aware that Norma has fallen in love with him and wants exclusive possession. He flees the house and joins another party at the house of a friend, Artie Green (Jack Webb), who is engaged to a reader in the Paramount script department, Betty Schaefer (Nancy Olson). In the midst of all the clamour of the party, Gillis hears over the phone from Max that Norma has slashed her wrists. The commentative orchestra enters during the cut to Max in which he informs Gillis of what has happened. It persists as we cut back to Gillis at the party; a many-tiered succession of rising fourths that seems to stretch his nerves to breaking point and that, incidentally, is rooted in the same key as the realistic party piano, so effecting a neat musical transition between the shots. Equally neat is the realistic/commentative interchange at the point where Gillis's attention to Norma's Mack Sennett/Charlie Chaplin imitations is distracted by thoughts of Betty. An unseen orchestra plays as Norma does her Bathing Girl impression, but as she disappears to change, Gillis's thoughts turn to Betty, and the orchestra 'changes' as well. We hear Betty's theme on viola, seconds before Gillis's voice-over, 'I was thinking about that girl . . .'

Norma is called into Paramount to see Cecil B. de Mille about her *Salome* script (or so she believes); he bids her sit in his director's chair while he investigates the real reason for her summons. The moment she seats herself she is overcome by the same complex feelings — nostalgia, exultation, *hauteur*, a growing longing to be back on the screen, the centre of attraction — as we have already seen assail her at her private screening at one of her silent films. Now, as then, trills in the orchestra match the fanatical light that invades her features, everything craning forward to the ultimate catastrophe. As de Mille learns that all Paramount wants of Norma is to borrow her car, a solo viola with a pathetic variant of Norma's theme underlines the pity he feels for her as he slowly walks back to rejoin her. He cannot, however, bring himself to reveal the truth to her; and she leaves the studio confidently expecting that the first day of shooting on *Salome* is merely a matter of weeks away. The beauty treatment montage that follows immediately is scored by a solo violin executing a virtuoso *moto perpetuo* obbligato above Norma's theme, suggesting the merciless frenzy both of her ambition and the means she is employing to fulfil it.

Clandestinely, Gillis and Betty begin to work on their script together late at night in the deserted studio. They grow closer together, and their two themes are intertwined contrapuntally; Gillis's theme is heard in an attractive celesta/harp variant as they walk together down one of the studio's sham streets. Betty's theme, incidentally, is a musical 'in'-joke, since it is none other than the theme of the Paramount newsreel, 'The Eyes and Ears of the World', here transformed (almost unrecognizably) from a blustering march into a melodious and lyrical love theme. As a muted trumpet solo it accompanies the studio stroll and is also responsible for one of the great musical climaxes. Norma discovers the reason for Gillis's nocturnal absences — she finds the script with its heading, 'An Untitled Love Story by Joe Gillis and Betty Schaefer'. A spiralling crescendo of strings, gathering momentum like a tornado, erupts *con somma passione* into a *fortissimo* statement of Betty's theme as Norma reads the title and realizes its import. The climax is the more overwhelming in that this love theme has never before been heard in this uninhibited guise: and now it is so heard, it is invoked not by the two lovers themselves, on their own account, but by the Other Woman.[5]

Betty comes to the house at Gillis's request, and he puts a stop to their romance because he realizes he would make her a defective husband. Dying embers of their love theme glowing on cellos, a quickening of the pulse as he bids her farewell for the last time, and then a forlorn solo violin as she disappears into the driveway — *literally* solo in that no other instrument is playing. Back upstairs, Norma goes to Gillis's room, but as she stops outside his door she catches a glimpse of herself in the mirror. It is as if she sees herself on the screen. Her theme, set *pianissimo* to a tango rhythm, tells us that her 'apotheosis' is at hand (a tango, presumably, because it was this dance, so she told us as she moved to its rhythm with Gillis at her New Year's party, that Valentino claimed could be danced much better on a tiled floor). In the scene between Norma and Gillis that follows there is again the threat of personal danger to Gillis and the music alludes to the earlier 'gangster' music. He makes the disclosure to Norma that the studio wanted her only for her car, and that her 'fan letters' are all written by Max. Max tries to reassure her: 'Madame was the greatest star of them all'. Norma, now showing unmistakable signs of insanity, snatches at the word 'star': trills in the orchestra help her. She is again a star, and no one ever walks out on a star; when Gillis tries to, she shoots him (her theme overlaid by the crazy tango rhythm on strings in two keys at once). As he falls headlong into the pool, his theme is given out for the last time on heavy brass — a final stark comment.

By the time the police and reporters have invaded Norma's house she is in a state of complete mental shock. Oblivious to the barrage of questions fired at her, she comes to life only when she hears one of the policemen say, 'The newsmen are here with the cameras.' The magic word 'cameras' registers immediately, aided again by the trills. 'Lights!' calls Max, and a bevy of unseen trumpeters, as if in the far distance, sound a muted fanfare, always over the sustained trills. The cameras turn, and the savage tango built out of Norma's theme sweeps her in an ecstasy of madness down the stairs and into the camera for her close-up. One last, lugubrious reminiscence of Gillis's theme on saxophone; then, as the end title looms, Waxman pulls one of the most dramatic punches of all. For just as the ear is preparing to accept D flat or G flat as the home key, at the very last moment the music nose-dives quite without warning, into a sardonically triumphant — and totally unexpected — C major. It — and we — exult in the fact that Norma has in the final analysis outwitted the world. All that remains is for the end cast to take 'The Eyes and Ears of the World' as their outgoing bow.

The fifties, recent enough to tap into many people's experience, sufficiently remote also to admit of nostalgia, is a period which seems, in movie terms, particularly familiar and appealing to today's audiences. The decade began with Swanson's pronouncement, in *Sunset Boulevard*, that the movies had 'gotten small' — a challenge to which the producer-director George Stevens threw down the gauntlet in the form of his so-called 'American' trilogy: *A Place in the Sun* (1951), based on Theodore Dreiser's novel *An American Tragedy, Shane* (1953), and *Giant* (1956), all 'big' pictures, 'epic' in terms not only of space and time but also of the myths and moral complexities they embrace.

I mentioned *Sunset Boulevard* advisedly in this context, for it was Waxman's work on this Billy Wilder masterpiece which may, I think, have led directly or indirectly to some of the problems he encountered in *A Place in the Sun*. *Sunset Boulevard*, being a comment by Hollywood on Hollywood, needed the music's connivance in underlining its ironic tone and making its critical points. Waxman clearly felt this to be a suitable departure point for *A Place in the Sun* which was, if reduced to its most basic terms, a love-story gone madly, badly wrong. So Waxman created one of his most glorious love-themes but subjected it to some inglorious treatment. The music is often cynical and jazz-inflected and is of a piece not only with the temper of the film — and of the times — but also with Waxman's own continuing development, influenced as it surely was by contemporary trends in Hollywood music. Jazz and jazz-oriented idioms were definitely flavour of the month, of the year, of the decade: *A Streetcar Named Desire*, with Alex North's music, appeared in the same year as *A Place in the Sun* and the next few years saw Leith Stevens composing *The Wild One* (1954), Elmer Bernstein's *The Man with the Golden Arm* (1955) and Leonard Rosenman's *Rebel Without a Cause* (1955). These are all composers of a newer generation than Waxman's; in fact Waxman responded to jazz more positively than any of his Hollywood contemporaries, as one can hear in *A Place in the Sun* (albeit *en passant*) and, more consistently and confidently, in his scores for Alfred Hitchcock's *Rear Window* (1954) and for *Crime in the Streets* (1956), a pre-*West Side Story* drama of rival gangs. In other words, starting with *A Place in the Sun*, Waxman may be said to have made his own contribution to the evolving 'teenage' idiom of fifties film music, anti-romantic and neo-expressionistic.

A 'teenage' idiom, however, was not precisely what George Stevens had in mind for *A Place in the Sun*, and he was far from happy with much of Waxman's music as he originally composed it, so much so that he called in two other Paramount composers, Victor Young and Daniele Amfitheatrof, and asked them to re-write certain scenes. This they did (they would have had no choice in the matter, being under contract to the studio), using Waxman's thematic material with the result that the score in the film as we know it, the one for which Waxman won his second Academy Award, is only about sixty per cent authentic Waxman. Clearly Stevens wanted something considerably more conventional, something that would soften the pictures' edges rather than harden them; something that would sweeten the medication. He loved the saxophone theme for Elizabeth Taylor, but expected it to indulge and luxuriate in the old-Hollywood style to which he was accustomed. Waxman's approach was often too stark, too dissonant and comfortless to engage audience-sympathy for the anti-hero, played by Montgomery Clift. (I have completed a 'Scenario' for Orchestra based on Waxman's original cues — a chance to sample Waxman's original prescription in all its tartness and dramatic sharp focus).

The score as we actually hear it in the picture, rather than as Waxman intended, is inspired, though arguably flawed. The flaw is the saxophone theme for Taylor. She plays Angela Vickers, the wealthy and attractive girl with whom George Eastman (Montgomery Clift) falls hopelessly in love after fleeing from the repressive poverty and piety of the mission run by his mother. The trouble is that the saxophone has such a long history of 'low life' associations (it is typical, for instance, that Waxman himself in *Joshua* uses the tenor saxophone in connection with the pious harlot) that it cannot but create an immediate impression of Angela as a floozie or *femme fatale*. The latter she may be in effect, though not in the sense the saxophone would have us believe; the former she certainly is not, and in this connection the music creates a misleading impression. Even the eminently *un*decadent quality of the melody cannot dispel the aura of decadence: a conclusive demonstration, in fact, of the overriding power of sonority. For *A Place in the Sun* Waxman auditioned many saxophone players until he found Ted Nash who, he thought, played in a manner suited to the character of Elizabeth Taylor. Evidently he had it fixed in his mind that the saxophone's tone colour was the only one suited to express the intoxicating attraction Angela exerts over George. Theirs is a genuine love affair; Angela is never presented otherwise than in a sympathetic light, and the love theme is the focal point of the entire score in that George's love for Angela is the dominant factor in his life. This precipitates the tragedy of Alice (Shelley Winters). This love theme is therefore the *main* theme and assumes many guises. During the early scenes between George and Angela at her parents' home it is even heard realistically as party music; saxophone chorus setting the party scene, strings as they meet and talk in the billiard room, strings and saxes as they dance together. Echoes punctuate the progress of the unhappy liaison between George and Alice, reminding us that George is ever conscious of his first view of Angela.

The theme's most passionate full-orchestra rendering is prompted by the lovers' final embrace, just before George's arrest for the murder of Alice. They do not know it is to be the last. At least, George may have a notion that he will be apprehended sooner or later, but Angela has not the slightest inkling that anything is amiss. Only the music advises us that this is the last time they will be free together. The next time they meet is in the execution block, where George is waiting to be taken to the electric chair. Here the saxophone announces Angela's approach; and here the fact that it plays entirely on its own creates a sense of pathos and loneliness. A solo cello with soft orchestral support takes up the theme as the lovers say their last goodbyes. Phrases from it are woven into the march-like apotheosis as George is escorted through the prison on his last journey, accompanied by the muttered prayers of the priest and the farewells of the other prisoners.

On several occasions music is called upon to clarify psychological issues. The first is when Alice, having discovered she is pregnant, begins to put pressure on George to marry her. George realizes that to do so would be to shatter all his dreams of promotion and of a future with Angela. He is driven to turn his thoughts to murder as the only way out and, when he comes home, turns on the radio and hears a newscaster talking about fatalities in lake resorts and warning non-swimmers of unpatrolled beaches, the colour and character of the music leave us in no doubt as to what is in his mind.

Then, when Alice and George are alone together in the boat on Loon Lake, the very calmness of the music aggravates the suspense; for although the music *is* calm, it is not peaceful. As evening settles on the lake, darker colours obtrude, and the shattered state of George's nerves is suggested in a worryingly insistent rhythmic figure in which is contained the germ of the much-admired fugato accompanying George's flight through the evening woods immediately prior to his arrest.[6] The rhythm gradually gathers momentum, culminating in a *fortissimo* outburst as Alice at last notices the distracted expression on George's face. Unthinkingly, she continues to prattle about her expected child. It is at this point that the strings refer plainly, if distortedly, to the George/Angela love theme, telling us what George is thinking; that Angela and her world are lost to him forever. Then comes the climax, the boat keels over accidentally, and the next shot is of George stumbling ashore alone. The music is thus involved in the moral dilemma: whether George's failure to save Alice was due to mere incompetence, or whether it was determined by the nature of the thoughts passing through his mind seconds before the accident happened. When George is awaiting execution in prison, he has a long conversation with a priest, during the course of which the latter asks him, 'Who were you thinking of when the boat capsized? Were you thinking of Alice — or of the other girl?' George does not answer. He has no need to; the music answers for him. The music proves the case for the prosecution.

By the mid-1950s Waxman was at the height of his powers, producing one distinguished score after another, often for mediocre pictures: *Elephant Walk* (1954) for instance contains one of his loveliest romantic themes and, in the climactic elephant stampede sequence, a spectacular compositional tour-de-force that has few parallels in the work even of this extraordinarily resourceful composer. Other major scores include, *The Silver Chalice* (1955), *The Nun's Story* (1959), *Beloved Infidel* (1959), *The Story of Ruth* (1960), *Sunrise at Campobello* (1960), *My Geisha* (1961) and *Hemingway's Adventures of a Young Man* (1962). In many ways, however, his most significant contribution to the 1950s — in fact to film music in general — was *Sayonara* (1957). This magnificent film is set in Japan at the time of the Korean War, and probes a sensitive area — the attitude of the American military authorities to the idea of Americans in the armed forces 'fraternising' with Japanese girls. Waxman sets the American Scenes to American (i.e. European) music, the Japanese to Japanese, with Irving Berlin's title-song 'Sayonara' poised somewhat uncertainly in between. Whereas such a procedure would be commonplace today, the idea of using ethnic music, not merely scenically but also *dramatically*, to underscore important action and dialogue scenes, was almost unheard of in the Hollywood of the 1950s. Ten years before it would have been completely out of the question. But just as in the aftermath of World War II many parts of the world began increasingly to open up to knowledge and understanding — films like *Sayonara* itself were valuable in this regard — so a new liberality, and a new curiosity, came to prevail in many artistic and cultural walks-of-life, even in the notoriously self-regarding sphere of Hollywood film-music. Waxman was a pioneer in the use of jazz and in *Sayonara* he respects the integrity and independence of non-Western music while meeting the needs of film-music as *drama*, not merely as decoration. With admirable skill and sensitivity, he effortlessly weaves the Berlin song into the tissue (that it is both simple and pentatonic, like the basic profile of the ethnic music, helps). In other words this most remarkable man, Waxman, emerges as something of a pioneer of interests and assumptions that are now widely shared.

Waxman's last important score, *Taras Bulba* (1962), shows no sign of age and mortal sickness taking their toll. Rather it is a young man's music in its exuberance, dashing colours and whiplash energy. It so happened that just before his work on *Taras Bulba* Waxman was invited by the Soviet Government to conduct a series of concerts in various parts of Russia. In Kiev — in part of the setting of Gogol's story — he was able to hear and buy copies of Ukrainian folk music; and the *Taras Bulba* score is based both on authentic Russian folksongs and Waxman's own simulation. The result does not, of course, possess the authentic Slav ring of Janáček's symphonic poem of the same name, since the context in which the melodies are employed is romantic-Germanic and not Slavonic; but the music is strong enough to be listened to in its own right, without the support of the film, as an extended symphonic poem in the late-romantic tradition. The ride to Dubno is mightily impressive — Ravel might have likened it to his *Bolero*, 'orchestral tissue without music'. The only 'music' is contained in the Cossack brotherhood theme, although there is a fleeting glimpse at one point of Taras' sons' theme on a high trumpet; the rest is 'tissue'. The huge army of Cossacks on horseback that gradually takes shape at Taras' behest is matched by a huge sustained orchestral *crescendo*. It is a virtuoso showpiece, a great finale — not only to *Taras Bulba* but to one of Hollywood's finest musical careers.

NOTES

1 The term 'fugue' is derived in part from the Latin *fuga* meaning 'flight', and the very consistency of fugal textures renders them especially suitable for depicting the same (c.f. Rózsa, *The Naked City*, p. 204).

2 There are echoes of the 'Rebecca' theme in Waxman's main theme in his score for Hitchcock's *The Paradine Case* (1948), which again portrays an honest man (Gregory Peck) falling under the baleful spell of a superhumanly beautiful woman (Valli). These echoes are particularly noticeable in the scene of their first meeting alone together when he first begins to yield to her quasi-hypnotic power.

3 Waxman and Wilder had known each other since their refugee days in mid-30s Paris. At one time the same cheap boarding-house, the Hotel Ansonia, was the home of Waxman, Hollander, Wilder and Peter Lorre.

4 Up to the end of the nineteenth century the diminished seventh was virtually the only dissonance (in the modern sense of the term) in common use, and in later music it generally has an archaic ring. On the other hand all 'consonances' are, for some reason, quite timeless.

5 Another film in which the score enables the audience to share a character's perceptions is *Possessed* (1947). In an interview with Lawrence Morton, Waxman described his work on this film as follows:

> In *Possessed* there was a direct cue given by the picture itself. Let me describe the situation in the film: Joan Crawford plays the part of a young woman emotionally unbalanced, a real psychiatric case. Her condition has, of course, a complicated history, but for our purposes it is sufficient to say that it is

based on an unreciprocated love for an engineer, played by Van Heflin.

A number of times Van Heflin plays on the piano a passage from Schumann's *Carnaval*. Frequently, in the underscoring, I used this piece as an expression of Miss Crawford's attachment to Heflin. Now at the point in the film where she realizes that he doesn't really love her, which is the point at which her mind and emotions begin to crack up, Heflin plays the Schumann again. Heflin is apparently playing the piece correctly, but what the audience hears this time is a distorted version, omitting all the sharps and flats, which suggests what Miss Crawford is hearing. That is, the distortion of the music corresponds to the distortion of normal emotions. What formerly had been a beautiful piano piece now sounds ugly to Miss Crawford because the man who is playing it does not return her love.

This is what I mean by *getting inside* a character.

(reprinted in *Pro Musica Sana*, Vol. VIII no. 1, Winter 1979–80)

6   The resemblance of this sequence — thematically and formally — to the fugal *Allegro* in the second movement ('The 9th of January') of Shostakovich's epic Eleventh Symphony ('The Year 1905') is astonishing in that the symphony *post*dates *A Place in the Sun* by about seven years. The likeness between the fragmented *pizzicato* passacaglia theme in the third movement of the same symphony ('Eternal Memory') and that of the *Sorry, Wrong Number* passacaglia — composed some ten years before — is also worth remarking.

DIMITRI TIOMKIN

In 1955 the Academy of Motion Picture Arts and Sciences presented Dimitri Tiomkin with an Oscar for his music score for *The High and The Mighty*. The speech he made in reply is one of the most famous in the annals of Hollywood:

> Ladies and gentleman, because I am working in this town for twenty-five years, I like to make some kind of appreciation to very important factor which makes me successful and adds to quality of this town. I like to thank Johannes Brahms, Johann Strauss, Richard Strauss, Richard Wagner ... (*laughter*) Beethoven, Rimsky-Korsakov. . .'
>
> *More laughter and speech ends in uproar. A voice [Bob Hope's] rising above the din:* 'You'll never get on *this* show again. . .'[1]

Time proved Hope wrong: Dimitri Tiomkin *did* get on the show again, when he collected a fourth Oscar for *The Old Man and the Sea* in 1959. But that wasn't at all the kind of speech that recipients of awards were expected to make, and Tiomkin gained considerable notoriety as a result. He undoubtedly knew he would. It was a typical gesture on the part of a man whose extroverted public image constantly diverted attention from the serious side of his art and from his originality as a film composer. He had charisma: he brought a sense of gala to film music. He was a great melodist: 'Do not forsake me' (*High Noon*), 'Thee I love' (*Friendly Persuasion*), and 'The green leaves of summer' (*The Alamo*) have all passed into Americana. He was a Slav, and therefore ebullient rather than restrained. He did things *his* way, he made people sit up and take notice. Sometimes they liked it (and his music), sometimes they didn't. No other composer in Hollywood has inflamed such contradictory passions, inspired such controversy as to the real nature of this stature and talent. Is he genius or showman? Something of both, most likely. But one thing is for sure: he had a great sense of theatre, both off screen and on. He knew what worked. It was, perhaps, a hyperactive sense: it is never easy to distinguish theatricality and legitimate showmanship from vulgarity — and let us not forget that an element of vulgarity is, in fact has to be, endemic in the nature of everybody involved with the practice of theatre, cinema, entertainment in general. Look at Wagner. Tiomkin was a great entertainer. He sailed perilously close to the wind on many occasions, particularly when he was adapting others' music as opposed to composing his own;[2] which is not to deride the many great — and theatrically effective moments (an epithet one returns to again and again *chez* Tiomkin): for example in *The Great Waltz* after Strauss at the beginning of Tiomkin's career, and *Tchaikovsky* after Tchaikovsky at its end. It was typical of his expansive nature that a time came — late in life — when he felt that he had outgrown what film music had to offer in terms of prestige and public acclaim and made a number of in many ways misguided forays into producing films, i.e. purchasing properties and involving himself in realizing them. *Tchaikovsky* was probably the most cherished of all such projects, and that he concerned himself painstakingly with every aspect of its production accounts both for its defects and its qualities.

The Tiomkin artist/showman paradox is the very paradox of Hollywood itself. Tiomkin was of the essence of Hollywood. He did everything on the grandest scale. He had a vision. He

was one of those expatriates of immense energy, determination and resilience who actually helped create the Hollywood
myth. Deprived of their own traditions and cultural
institutions they made for themselves an environment in
which they could fulfil themselves both materially and
spiritually. Tiomkin's larger-than-lifeness was prototypical,
as were the contradictions within his musical personality.
There was crudeness and bombast; there was sensitivity and
sweetness. Over the past few years I have had the chance —
through sorting and cataloguing his music, and working from
his holograph sketches in re-orchestrating and reconstructing
his music for record albums and concert performance — to
become familiar with most of Tiomkin's vast output. As a
result I am probably more aware of his strengths and
weaknesses than any other film music critic. This familiarity
has bred greater admiration, not contempt. Many disparage
his work; but how well do they actually know it? Have they
bothered to explore behind the facade? I have, and am
endlessly fascinated. Earlier, Tiomkin did himself no great
service by almost always refusing to discuss his work
seriously in public. The mechanics, the technique, the real
raisons d'être: that was his private business. The public — and
the critics — got the jokes. Sadly, this belied a sincerity,
devotion and conscientiousness no less sincere for having at
times followed some bizarre directions.

It is no accident that Tiomkin's most enduring claim to
fame lies perhaps in his treatment of great 'Western' epics: *Red
River, Duel in the Sun, Giant*; in fables of the American West like
High Noon and *Gunfight at the OK Corral*. These scores are
'rhetorical' in the non-pejorative sense: they persuade and
impress. In a sense, of course, the American West, as evoked
in his music and as portrayed in the films for which the music
was written, never really existed. It was all part of the
Hollywood myth, and in this respect we can draw an
interesting parallel between Tiomkin's work and that of the
late-nineteenth century painters Frederic Remington and
Charles B. Russell. They, like him, viewed the West from an
expansively romantic, essentially nineteenth-century view-

point, and their pictures decisively influenced the ideology and iconography of the Hollywood Western. This is not to suggest, however, that Tiomkin merely perpetuated a received tradition or cliché of commercial Americana. He received this tradition certainly, worked within its bounds, and in his earlier Westerns (*Red River* and *Duel in the Sun*) employed its conventions; but he quickly stamped it with his own distinguishing mark, and later works like *Gunfight at the OK Corral* and *Last Train from Gun Hill* are almost completely lacking in its stereotyped vernacular. After all, he had reason to feel an empathy for the American West. He came from a Big Country too, and in America's vastness, particularly its vast all-embracingness of sky and plain, he must have seen a reflection of the steppes of his native Ukraine. So the cowboy becomes a mirror-image of the Cossack: both are primitives and innocents, etched on and dwarfed by a landscape of soul-stirring immensity and rugged masculine beauty. And as an exile himself, Tiomkin would have identified with the cowboys, pioneers and early settlers who people the world of the Western. They, like him, were itinerants, wanderers in search of a home and in search of money, because money brought security in a foreign and, as yet untried, land where the only law was the survival of the fittest. Those like Tiomkin who blazed a trail in Hollywood were actually winning the West all over again. This is surely why his Western music has such dynamism and commitment, for in it he is actually reliving a part of his own experience. Prince Sergei Obolensky could easily have been writing of his friend Tiomkin when he described himself as 'one man in his time, simply an ex-Russian of a particular background and family, the foundations of whose existence were destroyed'. Yet Obolensky, Tiomkin and their like were survivors, even in the permanence of exile.

Being young enough when they *were* uprooted, they perceived and embraced the potentiality of America, the resources and relative openness of a young culture and dynamic society very different, no doubt, from the 'old' culture they had left behind in Imperial Russia. And

Lost Horizon: entering Shangri-La

Dimitri Tiomkin in Moscow, circa 1969

throughout his film-career Tiomkin reacted to films which enabled him to celebrate this or that feature of his adopted land, most regularly its landscape. Ironically the one film which — towards the end of his career — he wanted to score so badly that he actually bought the property and set it up with himself and Carl Foreman as co-producers, ultimately slipped through his grasp. This was *Mackenna's Gold*, the tale of a quest for a legendary Apache treasure-trove buried somewhere in the canyons of the American south-west (stunningly photographed on location principally in Arizona). Tiomkin must instinctively have recognized this as a picture made, god-sent, for him to score. It would have been an apotheosis. He would have turned it, musically at any rate, into one of the great screen epics in the tradition of his *Lost Horizon* and *Search for Paradise*. Alas, politico-practical considerations intervened and Quincy Jones composed the score. Jones's utterly un-Tiomkin approach — cool, cynical, pragmatic, even anti-romantic — robbed the film of the special aura Tiomkin would have undoubtedly supplied. For Jones it was just another western.

Tiomkin came from St Petersburg via Berlin, Paris and New York.[3] When he arrived in Hollywood he had practical experience of vaudeville but hardly any of composing (if we discount the numerous songs and piano pieces written in the American popular style of the day, none of which bears any trace of individuality). He had been trained as a pianist, not as a composer, and it remains something of a phenomenon that at the age of forty and more he taught himself what was virtually a new trade. The achievement is the more remarkable when one recalls that composing is scarcely an ability that lends itself to being 'picked up' in middle life. If one has a talent in that direction one naturally practises it from an early age, and it is rare for a composer to be as old as forty before he reaches stylistic maturity. But Tiomkin was around forty before he even started, and some sixty years of age before, in the 1950s, he reached the zenith of his powers.

He began to conduct his own scores even later: in his fifties. The very fact that, at an age when most men have ceased to be malleable, he was prepared to face and overcome enormous technical challenges bears witness to that indomitable will-to-succeed characteristic of Hollywood men who, like Tiomkin, came from a background of deprivation and instability. No one starting to compose so late can hope to acquire real technical fluency. Yet in Tiomkin's case, in a way, this was all to the good. It meant that his dramatic sense developed out of instinct rather than intellect: he had to rely more on inspiration than on technique. Hence an element of the unconventional and unpredictable: if an idea seemed right for a scene he would use it, regardless of whether it was the conventional or unconventional thing to do. Highly unconventional is his handling of *Gunfight at the OK Corral*, in which the ballad singer sings throughout the film, summarizing, commenting upon and even anticipating the action in the manner of the chorus in Greek tragedy. Conversely, Tiomkin could take a disreputable musical cliché and reinstate it as meaningful expression; which is what all clichés were before they became stock formulae. The wonderful unaccompanied choral music behind the scene of the travellers' first sight of the celestial Shangri-La in *Lost Horizon* is not in any way a Hollywoodian 'Heavenly Chorus', simply because it represents Tiomkin's natural spontaneous response to the poetry of the scene. The affinity is more with a work like Delius's *Song of the High Hills*, where the wordless choir is also used to convey the related emotions of awe, rapture and ecstasy. To point to the lack of surface polish and elegance in Tiomkin's work is simultaneously to draw attention to one of its greatest sources of strength, its rough-hewn quality, its quasi-primitive vitality, its earthy peasant-like directness. It can pierce to the core of a dramatic situation with an instinctive, instinctual soundness.

With the one starry exception of *Lost Horizon*, little Tiomkin prior to the mid-1940s is at all distinguished. We might also except the discarded 'John Doe Requiem' in *Meet John Doe*, the romantic title-music to *Only Angels Have Wings*, and the quasi-fugal action music in *Battle of San Pietro*, which foreshadows *The Guns of Navarone*. He was still developing and learning; the war years, which he spent scoring war documentaries (though he managed to fit in a few 'unofficial' features), had to a degree impeded his stylistic progress.[4]

On the basis of these patchwork wartime scores, and of much later war films such as *Cease Fire*, *Take the High Ground*, *The Command* and *Bugles in the Afternoon*, one is tempted to aver that Tiomkin's sympathies were little engaged in this genre. Then we remember *The Guns of Navarone*. This was a much better film than those others; and orchestrator Leo Shuken's description of his friend and colleague of many years, Victor Young, comes to mind: 'When the film was great, Victor wrote great. When it wasn't, he just sloughed it off'. *Lost Horizon* also undoubtedly was 'great', and for it Tiomkin 'wrote great'. The Shangri-La scenes disclose a type of musical response which lay outside the Hollywood mainstream and which may be ascribed to the composer's Russian origins. Most of Tiomkin's work from this time on bears signs of a Russian romantic derivation, and much of its interest consists in the fact that these Russian elements — dormant throughout his early professional years — are precisely what lent his style its distinction. Tiomkin's music is profoundly Russian, not so much in the sense of actual reminiscence as in the ways of thinking, feeling and reacting musically that it reveals.

The distinguishing marks of the Russian creative musical mind were first comprehensively tabulated by the English musicologist Gerald Abraham, whose studies of Russian composers, published in the 1930s, have attained the status of classics. If we turn to his chapters entitled 'The essence of Russian music' in *Studies in Russian Music* and 'Some psychological peculiarities of Russian creative artists' in *On Russian Music*, we find on almost every page meaningful observations as applicable to Tiomkin as to any of the composers Abraham cites. First — and basically — he finds that most Russian composers prefer to start with a *trouvaille* or *donnée*, a 'given fact', rather than create in a vacuum. This partially explains the outstanding success of such composers as Tchaikovsky and Stravinsky in ballet, or Prokofiev and

Shostakovich in film. The fact is that the basis of modern musical construction in Western Europe, the system of logical development of germinal ideas, is entirely foreign to the spirit of Russian music. Progressive thinking is not the Russian's way; his mental process is more akin to brooding; a continual turning over of ideas in his mind, viewing them from different angles, throwing them against strange and fantastic backgrounds, but never actually evolving anything from them. Even the greatest of Russian operas — Mussorgsky's *Boris Godunov*, Borodin's *Prince Igor*, Prokofiev's *War and Peace* — consist more of a series of tableaux than of dramatically unfolding action. It is as natural for a Russian to think episodically as for a Frenchman to think logically. Now episodic thinking is an essential qualification for any film composer. The 'system of logical development of germinal ideas' is as foreign to the nature of film music as it is to Russian music, there being neither the time nor the opportunity . So that the process of film composing is well suited to the Russian creative temperament. And as for Russian composers not developing but continually modifying their material, viewing their ideas from different angles, we can instance a number of the finest moments in Tiomkin's work: the *Lost Horizon* funeral cortège, 'Pharaoh's Procession' in *Land of the Pharaohs*, the magnificent 'Pax Romana' sequence in *The Fall of the Roman Empire*. All these processional movements are cumulative in effect, but colouristically and two-dimensionally so, not symphonically. The monothematic structure of *High Noon* and *Gunfight at the OK Corral* also falls into this category. The idea of basing an entire score on a single theme could scarcely be put successfully into practice were a typically Russian resourcefulness in repetition with modification not to replace symphonic evolution, for which the filmscore framework offers minimal scope.

In the light of this it becomes easy to understand the attraction folksong has always exerted over Russian composers from Glinka on. For folksong, being already a fully developed whole, contains no growing power: it can therefore be varied and modified *ad infinitum*, but not symphonically treated in any positive way. Russian folksong inflections, cadences and turns of melodic phrase turn up quite often in Tiomkin's scores, even whole melodies of a Russian profile, such as the theme of the barbarians' devastations in *The Fall of the Roman Empire*. Most explicit of all is the second strain of the *Guns of Navarone* main theme, with its Volga Boatmen-like interval of the falling fourth.

One wonders, too, whether the wordless choral music which marks the first sight of the Celestial City in *Lost Horizon* would possess the magic it does without some recollection of the chant of the Russian Orthodox Church. However, we may feel that Tiomkin's partial folksong orientation proved most greatly of value in that it enabled him to acquire elements of other folk cultures as and when they proved dramatically necessary. Think of his handling of the American folk idiom in *Giant*, *The Big Sky*, *Mr Smith goes to Washington*, *Canadian Pacific*, *Friendly Persuasion* and others. Two classic non-American examples are the Iberian fishermen's scenes of early-morning departure and return off the coast of Cuba in *The Old Man and the Sea* (male choir *a cappella*) and the extraordinary measureless theme in *Lost Horizon* which has something of the 'continuous continuation' of true oriental music. It is perhaps significant too that *Lost Horizon*, which represents the first real milestone in Tiomkin's career as a composer, should have an oriental setting. Exoticism has always bulked larger in the work of Russian composers than in that of their Western contemporaries, and in fact the kind of glamorous fairy-tale musical orientalism which served Hollywood so well was basically the creation of Rimsky-Korsakov, following in the wake of Glinka and Balakirev. Later Tiomkin scores in which an important exotic element is present include *Land of the Pharoahs*, *Return to Paradise*, *The Adventures of Hajji Baba*, *Tarzan and the Mermaids*, *Search for Paradise* and *55 Days at Peking*; and 'exotic' can easily embrace the strong Latin-American elements in *Blowin' Wild* and *Strange Lady in Town*.[5]

The same taste for sugar and spice is reflected in the Russians' love of bright primary orchestral colours, and a recurring feature of Tiomkin's orchestrations is their spectacular colourfulness. His is almost a childlike delight in sound for its own sake. This is characteristic of the impressionistic tendencies in Tiomkin's work which are particularly noticeable in *Search for Paradise, Tarzan and the Mermaids* and *The Old Man and the Sea*; and there is some fabulous water music in *Canadian Pacific*.

Gerald Abraham has also pointed out that in more purely musical matters, such as counterpoint, the working of the Russian mind differs essentially from that of the Western:

> Genuine contrapuntal feeling, the natural flowing together of parallel, simultaneous streams of thought, is practically unknown in Russian music. On the other hand, some of the Russians have been very fond of using contrapuntal means in constructing their music, a fundamentally different matter. Borodin, in particular, frequently shows great ingenuity in juggling with combinations of themes, but the themes (as in the well-known *In the Steppes of Central Asia*) are only fitted together: they have not grown together. There is nothing forced or unnatural about the fitting.

For 'Borodin' in this quotation substitute 'Tiomkin', for this contrapuntal dovetailing of themes is one of his fingerprints. Sometimes whole themes are worked together, as in the *Lost Horizon* finale; or the *Search for Paradise* epilogue where, at one point, 'Happy Land of Hunza' in the brass combines with the baritone soloist's 'Somewhere in the Distance' (the main theme). Elsewhere the two complementary strains of a single theme are fitted together, as in the *Land of the Pharaohs* finale, the epilogue to *The Guns of Navarone*, and at the climax of 'Pax Romana' in *The Fall of the Roman Empire*. Yet again, in some cases themes which have essentially nothing whatever to do with each other are brought together for special dramatic effect. As for instance when 'Happy Land of Hunza' is superimposed on the wild native dance in the 'Bucephalus ritual' in *Search for Paradise*; or the moment in *The Fall of the Roman Empire* when the Neapolitan tarantella becomes gradually overwhelmed by the 'Fall of Rome' theme in heavy brass and organ. Most effective of all, perhaps, is the merging of the 'Western' and 'Eastern' themes during the Lama's funeral cortège in *Lost Horizon* at the moment when Conway is forced to flee the valley.

On a more general level Abraham observes that 'perhaps the most valuable of all the qualities of Russian music is its compressed force and directness of expression . . . the Russians have always been remarkable for their pointed, forceful brevity'. The ability to write with 'compressed force and directness of expression' is a valuable asset for a film composer, the nature of whose medium is of necessity opposed to prolixity. Tiomkin may be no miniaturist and prefer to fill a large canvas, but actual size has nothing to do with it; the point is the nature and quality of the thought expressed. Tiomkin frequently comes up with short, pithy musical sayings the impact of which is like a blow straight from the shoulder and, as a result, effective dramatically — as for instance the parachutists' motif in the *Search for Paradise* prologue.

Closely akin to this is the famous Russian realism. To quote Abraham again:

> The most superficial student of Russian literature knows that its predominant note is realism: the tendency, that is, to start from a basis of given facts and, broadly speaking, to portray them closely and accurately. The music of Dargomizhsky and Mussorgsky, which had next to nothing in common with Wagner's, was a sort of literal translation of words and even gestures into tones, a type of music very close to its verbal or pantomimic *donnée*.

Now is this realism not the nub of Tiomkin's thought again and again — the 'basis of given facts' being the motion picture scenario, the task he sets himself the 'literal translation' of its action into tones? Two examples immediately spring to mind, both from *Land of the Pharaohs*. 'The building of the tomb' is conceived with a quasi-operatic realism, the mainspring of the musical action being the singing of the myriad workers engaged in constructing the pyramid where the rhythmic sound of hammering and chiselling is also incorporated in the orchestral texture. And in 'The sealing of the tomb' Tiomkin's main business is to reinforce the physical sound of the pouring sand which inexorably forces the stones into immovable position. The cartoon documentary *Rhapsody of Steel* demands and receives a consistent realism of musical treatment, and this little-known score must be accounted one of Tiomkin's finest achievements.

Abraham also remarks that 'the excitement which Russian music manifests . . . is almost always physical, a direct glorification of the animal joy of living'. Do we not owe to this the particular kind of bustling energy and hectic exuberance — hysteria even — that must rank as one of Tiomkin's most readily recognizable characteristics? In this connection we should bear in mind his early experiences as pianist for his wife's ballet troupe. The peculiar nervous electricity demonstrated by (to quote four examples among hundreds) the safe-robbing scene in *The Steel Trap*, the car-chase music in *Dead on Arrival*, the tennis game in *Strangers on a Train* and the ambulance-call at the beginning of *Angel Face* suggest a balletic origin, as does the virtually choreographic approach adopted to the showdown scenes in *Red River*, *High Noon* and *Gunfight at the OK Corral*.

Abraham concedes, however, that there are certain areas of expression in which the Russian composer is notably deficient: 'Hardly any of the best Russian music is inspired by erotic emotion . . . and when Russian composers are unable to scamp the love-interest altogether, they generally provide it perfunctorily'. Abraham goes on to point out that, on the credit side, 'a quick reaction to any suggestion of the grotesque is noticeable' (*Cyrano de Bergerac*) and that all Russian composers show a penchant for the romantic (in the widest sense) and the heroic: *Lost Horizon*, *The Alamo*, *The Old Man and the Sea*, *Search for Paradise*, *Land of the Pharoahs*, *Red River*, *55 Days at Peking* and *The Fall of the Roman Empire* obviously qualify for inclusion here.

Tiomkin's colourful grandiloquence well suited epics: the 'public' persona. Yet we must remember that he was also capable of effects of delicacy and subtlety. The Hollywood convention was that every film should open and close in a blare and blaze of sound, regardless of dramatic appropriateness. Yet *55 Days at Peking*, Bronston's multi-million dollar reconstruction of the Boxer Rebellion, opens with the serenity of muted strings playing one of Tiomkin's tenderest melodies. A Western epic, *The Big Sky*, begins and ends *pianissimo* with music reflecting the majesty and beauty of the Missouri riverscape, an omnipresent feature of the film. *The Guns of Navarone* end-title has probably never been literally *heard* in the cinema: it is so quiet — muted strings, solo winds, bazooki — as to be helplessly drowned out in the noise and disturbance of the audience leaving. Yet should we hear it we would appreciate its making a poignant comment of its own: sorrowing that so much human skill, courage and dedication must be squandered in the criminal futility of war. This is the 'private' Tiomkin.

In fact Tiomkin's scores embrace a wide emotional range. It is a far cry from the tender melodiousness of *Friendly Persuasion* to the racy effervescence of *The Happy Time*, *Champagne for Caesar* or *The Fourposter*, with its interpolated cartoons; from the *alfresco* magnificence of prairie and river as evoked in *The Big Sky* or *Canadian Pacific* to the claustrophobic big-city nightmare of *Dead On Arrival*; from the rampant, extravagant exoticism of *55 Days at Peking* to the spare, clipped, piano-dominated sonorities of *36 Hours*; from the tense interior drama of *I Confess* to the witty stylistic time-travelling of *Cyrano de Bergerac*; from the sustained symphonic hysteria of *The Steel Trap* or *The Well* to the jazz-inflected emotion of *Town Without Pity*; from the intimidating atmospherics of the theremin-fraught *The Thing* to the sunny, folksy innocence of *The Sundowners*; from the gaudy swashbuckling of *Hajji Baba* or *Lady in the Iron Mask* to the Disney-like picturequenese of *Tarzan and the Mermaids*, from the blustering jingoism of *Take the High Ground* to the compassionate commitment of *The Men*; from the ardent romanticism of *Wild is the Wind* to the sharp-featured, neon-lit cynicism of *Champion*; yet everything bears the stamp of a unique personality. *Tension at Table Rock* and *Last Train from Gun Hill* would be different kinds of Westerns without Tiomkin's music. This may sound like a truism; but it is too little appreciated that the colour of the music can affect our apprehension of a film just as profoundly as — perhaps even more than — the character of the photography or the quality of art direction. Tiomkin was grateful to the cinema for allowing him to write in as fine a style as he was capable of; and in return he left his mark on other aspects of the films with which he was associated. The day would have obviously come when he would take charge of a film of his own; and his chance came in the 1960s when the post-Stalinist 'thaw' enabled him to realize his lifelong ambition to shoot, produce and score a film biography of Tchaikovsky in Russian, in Russia. For a composer who, as man and artist, never (as I have tried to show) relinquished or gainsaid his specifically Russian identity, it was a fitting swansong. (Tiomkin finished his work on *Tchaikovsky* in 1970. He died in London nine years later — November 1979 — at the age of 85).

As we know, the first landmark of his career came in 1937 with *Lost Horizon*. The James Hilton novel tells of a plane hijacked while flying from revolution-torn China and taken with its passengers over uncharted areas of the Himalayas to the paradisial valley of Shangri-La where the inhabitants have discovered the secret of an almost perpetual youth. West meets East and is ennobled and transfigured by the encounter. With the exception of Robert Conway's brother George, all the occupants of the hijacked plane find peace in the Tibetan community. This dichotomy is mirrored in the two main musical themes. The first represents the harassed world-weary West and is a stylized Hollywood love theme. The second theme is an inspiration. The written score has bar lines, but they mean nothing: strong and weak beats, metric definition, conventional Western phrase structure that involves one phrase ending and another beginning — all are absent. Should we try to phrase the melody, the phrase mark would never come to an end. Instead there is an affinity with oriental or medieval monody in which tune is never-ending; it just flows on and on, perpetually regenerating itself — the 'continuous continuation' of the Orient as opposed to the Western concept of 'moment in time'.

There is no 'stress' here — in the technical, musical sense — much as there is no 'stress' — in the wider, general sense — in the Valley of the Blue Moon. Here is the ageless beauty and serenity of Shangri-La in a musical nutshell: immortality, *lux perpetua*. Anything further removed from the tradition of trumpery *Chu-Chin-Chow*-like confection that so often in Hollywood does duty for the Orient would be hard to imagine. The pull-and-thrust between these two disparate thematic entities complements the conflict on the screen, most skilfully in the scene of the funeral procession of the High Lama. Here the 'Eastern' theme is given to the mixed chorus keening wordlessly over the persistent funereal thudding of the timpani. The orchestral texture incorporates a variety of exotic percussion, metallophones, gongs, xylophones and bells redolent of the Javanese gamelan or percussion orchestra. The procession files up the hill to the lamasery. Torches flicker round the courts and pavilions, the musicians blow and beat, the keening voices fade on a veer of the wind, returning to fade again. But at this very moment of the Lama's obsequies, Conway is persuaded by his brother to flee the valley, and is pursued by Sondra. This posed a problem, since the 'on-stage' music of the cortège had in some way to be reconciled with the dramatic music required by the new turn of events. An easy solution would have been artificially to fade the one down and the other up, but Tiomkin's solution is to build the love theme contrapuntally into the cortège and write the overlap directly into the music. As the sound of the cortège — the 'Eastern' theme — is lost in the distance, the 'Western' love theme gains in ascendancy and comes into full focus, raging desperately as Sondra reaches the entrance and looks out helplessly after the disappearing party. Ultimately Conway finds his way back to his lost paradise, and the finale, resplendent with bells and chimes, is a *grandioso* restatement of the 'Eastern' Shangri-La theme.

Yet surely the 'Eastern' theme should first emerge *in toto* at the climactic moment when the travellers first stumble upon the entrance to the Valley? Here, as often, Tiomkin fails to do the expected thing; and incidentally, it is worth noting the careful timing of the chorus's entry during the main-title statement of the theme: the voices join in not at the beginning but half-way through, to fine effect. In the immediately preceding scenes, music has reflected the melancholy and inertia of the kidnapped passengers marooned somewhere on the vast Tibetan plateau, the loftiest and least hospitable part of the earth's surface. Then dour, nasal woodwinds — imitating their primitive prototypes — announce the arrival of Chang (H.B. Warner) and the caravan that escorts the party on the long trek across the stormswept mountain country to the secret crevice that alone gives admittance to the Valley of the Blue Moon. A march movement builds itself up with a scale reminiscent of Mussorgsky in its massive size, the many 'wrong' notes serving to emphasize the strangeness of the journey. A climax is reached, but suddenly evaporates; only the chiming of monastery bells is heard in the distance, for the travellers have come in sight of the Celestial City. And here, as Conway looks on the sunlit valley, a myriad voices sound from afar. The sound of massed voices singing or murmuring wordlessly in the distance has a mystical quality that almost defies analysis. (The much-later *Friendly Persuasion* is another score that is original in this respect). Here it seems to stand as a symbol of Conway's feelings of rapture, wonder, mystery, a withdrawal from common life and common consciousness. Near the end of this scene voices and bells are raised in a chant based on the Chinese penta-tonic or five-note scale which has already been heard once *fortissimo* at the climax of the caravan sequence. Like the main Shangri-La theme, it conforms to no Western standards of metrical regularity: it has rather the cold and tranquil beauty of ancient Chinese lacquers. It is heard again as a nocturne during which Conway tries to explain to his brother the strange feeling of fulfilment he experienced upon first encountering the valley; and a particularly felicitous touch is its appearance on the celesta to mark the end of Conway's first interview with the High Lama. The music in this scene, incidentally, creates a real aura, though since it is all under dialogue it can easily pass un-noticed. Tiomkin handles it almost as melodrama in the strict sense: the music being sensitive to, and unobtrusively supportive of, every nuance of emotion and import in the conversation. In general Tiomkin is little interested in scenes involving intimate human relations; but what the two men are discussing here is a *concept*, the idea and ideals of Shangri-La; and the music invokes forms and even moves us into the poetic, mystic, timeless dimension they are envisaging.

The Tiomkin saga of the American West began in 1947 with *Duel in the Sun*, an attempt on the part of David O. Selznick to make a Texan *Gone with the Wind*. However, it was Selznick's policy to involve himself extensively and often intrusively in all aspects of his productions, not least the musical. Tiomkin liked to tell the story of his efforts to find a love theme (for Jennifer Jones and Gregory Peck) passionate enough to satisfy the producer, but in fact the musical issue was more complicated. Very few areas remain in the score that were not at some point subjected to major revisions, either because Selznick did not like them as they sounded originally (for instance, it is easy to sense Selznick's hand at work in the interminable repetitions of Stephen Foster's 'Beautiful Dreamer' in the scenes at Paradise Flats), or because the picture was re-cut after the music had been composed. Nonetheless, inasmuch as it was the first of his great Western epics, the score was a landmark. The prelude is a blasting and blistering evocation of the Texan cowboy country with all its heat, noise, dust and intimidating magnificence. It is launched by a broad, lyrical theme associated in the picture with Jennifer Jones and Joseph Cotten (borrowed, incidentally, from Tiomkin's 1941 score for Capra's *Meet John Doe*). This leads into a fiery fanfare-studded *Allegro Maestoso* in which the main theme is presented (which interestingly, was conceived many years before in a much slower tempo for a quite different dramatic purpose in another Capra film — the caravan scene in *Lost*

Horizon). There follows music which is melodramatic in the strict sense: designed as accompaniment to the spoken word, in this case the voice of Orson Welles:

> Deep among the sun-baked hills of Texas the great weatherbeaten stone still stands. The Comanches call it Squaw's Head Rock. Time cannot change its impassive face, nor dim the legend of the wild young lovers who found heaven and hell in the shadows of the rock. And this is what the legend says: 'A flower known nowhere else grows from out of the desperate crags where Pearl vanished. Pearl. . .! who was herself a wildflower, sprung from the hard clay: quick to blossom, and early to die.'

The music, making subtle and evocative use of the wordless chorus, turns the words into poetry. As it does so it sets forth themes of the desert and of Pearl Chavez (Jennifer Jones) which are to play the dominant roles in the picture's *dénouement*, Pearl's and Lewt McCanles's (Gregory Peck) rendezvous at Squaw's Head Rock where they shoot each other, then die in each other's arms. This final sequence opens with the sight and sense of the desert conjured up on stark harmonies, hoarse woodwind figures, a heavy *basso ostinato*: wordless men's voices add a strange primitive element of the inhuman. The emotional stance changes abruptly after the shooting: the music surges in a perfervid development of the love-theme reminiscent of Skryabin in its impassioned character already established in earlier love scenes. (It comes as something of a surprise to discover this selfsame theme lending itself so naturally to a piquant, scherzo-like transformation for a springtime scene of frolicking colts; and it is also heard, in an arrangement for four solo guitars, as a serenade, i.e. as quasi-realistic music.) Skryabin's music is impregnated with a mystico-erotic emotionalism deriving from Wagner's *Tristan and Isolde*, reminding us of Charles Higham's description of *Duel in the Sun* as a 'Wagnerian horse-opera, a *Liebestod* among the cactus'. Pearl, herself mortally wounded and bleeding, drags herself slowly and painfully under the scorching Texas sun in an attempt to reach the dying Lewt. Tiomkin's music sets out to squeeze every last drop of emotion: the full orchestra develops the love theme to a pitch of almost unbearable intensity, and the climax, when it comes, represents the supreme ecstasy, the love-in-death. This scene described in the abstract seems to represent the romantic cinema at its hammiest and most cliché-ridden. In the theatre it can move a modern audience, and it would be a rash critic who would seek to disallow Tiomkin's share of the credit. The neo-Wagnerian extravaganza of the finale demanded a corresponding degree of stylization in the music. Different forms of stylization are encountered also in the 'western' music (the buggy-ride) and in the Mexican scenes (the children's 'El Bailero' and Pearl's Casino Dance).[6] *Duel in the Sun* marked Tiomkin out above all as a composer who was not afraid to take the centre of the stage and make a strong, direct and meaningful statement. He refused point-blank to stand in the wings fumbling with his hat; in this he is notably unlike many of his present-day colleagues in film. He was prepared to take the risk of overstepping the bounds of conventional 'good taste' and like most artists of his generation and outlook, he would prefer to be indicted for sins of commission rather than omission.

If *Duel in the Sun* was a Texan *Gone with the Wind*, the Edna Ferber–George Stevens *Giant* was a kind of Texan *Forsyte Saga*, or even *War and Peace*. The main theme, a march, is a musical microcosm of that empire to the West vaster than the minds of urban men can conceive, 'where the infinite plains and restless cities still beat with the pulse of frontier adventure as did the Chisholm Trail when the first herds of longhorns thundered eastward to market'. It is one of Tiomkin's grandest inspirations. After the massive, sprawling main title statement it finds its most natural outlet in the scene where Leslie Lynnton (Elizabeth Taylor) is first brought to Reata as a bride by her husband, Bick Benedict (Rock Hudson). They are set down in the midst of a vast, arid plain; the sun 'burning like a stab wound', the hot wind giving no relief and blowing wind-rock in all directions. It is from this all-present Texan wind that the music takes its cue. Rags and tatters of the

'Giant' theme, barely recognizable at first, are scattered and borne aloft on a tireless pitter-patter of strings, playing softly, lightly and very quickly. Gradually these dabs and dashes of tune assume coherent shape, broaden, lengthen, and grow louder, until at the climax, as the Reata Ranch heaves into view — a huge edifice of towers and domes and balconies and porticoes and iron fretwork — the complete 'Giant' theme is blared forth *fortissimo* in bold and brassy splendour.

The love theme (which later became a popular song under Paul Francis Webster's title 'There'll never be anyone else but you') is a melody which, in one of the early scenes of Bick's courtship of Leslie, underlines in a sudden burst of eloquent lyricism their tacit decision to marry — the starting point of the whole saga. More subtle is its two-edged application in the barbecue scene where Leslie faints dead away after watching men eating ox's brains straight out of the skulls. Despite her love for Bick, Leslie feels lonely and insecure, cast adrift as she is among foreign people in a strange overbearing landscape. As she wanders around undecidedly, unable to integrate, the love theme, heard as a single-line melody with no accompanying harmony or support reflects her forlorness. But she is not the only unhappy one present. Lounging in the background is the moody, disconsolate figure of the no-good job boy, Jett Rink (James Dean in his last role). We have earlier heard his own theme, given to an accordion; we have also seen that he is strongly attracted to Leslie Benedict. So in this barbecue scene Tiomkin cleverly links Leslie's loneliness with Jett's by playing the love theme solo, as described above, but on an accordion. In other words, the theme itself stands for Leslie, but the instrument on which it is played involves Jett; and, of course, the theme's overtones as a love theme automatically invoke something of Jett's inarticulate feelings for Leslie.

Jett himself is given a deliberately trivial cowboy theme. Innocuous enough in the early stages on accordion with banjo and guitar accompaniment (when Jett is still the problem child of the ranch), it is inflated to proportions of vulgar monstrousness on heavy brass as the oil derricks start springing up all over the Reata ranchland, bringing him unheard-of wealth and fame. The contrast between the vastness of his riches and the smallness of his mind is tellingly brought out.

Tiomkin with his innate sense of grandeur was better suited to films like *Giant*, *Red River*, and *The Alamo* than any other Hollywood composer. The two last-named form part of a 'John Wayne Trilogy', three films, two directed by Howard Hawks, all musically cross-referenced. First had come *Red River* (1947), an epic that told of the men who made the first cattle drive up the Chisholm Trail from Texas to Kansas under the leadership of Tom Dunson (Wayne). The title music immediately sets the 'epic' tone. The unison horn-call is an invocation: the gates of history are flung open, and the main theme, high and wide as the vault of the sky, rides forth in full choral-orchestral splendour. The first big moment is the crossing of Red River itself, made to music of a crude, pioneer vitality. Based on a ponderous rhythmic transformation of the 'cattle' theme (which like so much 'primitive' and 'innocent' music is contained within the five-note or pentatonic scale), it suggests grit, energy, determination and the sheer weight of physical effort involved in negotiating a mighty river with a herd of cattle. Tiomkin even builds the sound of the animals, their long-note lowing, into his scoring for brass. The great feat is exultantly accomplished as the main 'Red River' theme (strings) is superimposed contrapuntally on the 'cattle theme' (brass). The climax is reached in the long-awaited confrontation between Dunson and Matt (Montgomery Clift). The theme of revenge is sounded ominously in the horns and gathers momentum through persistently accelerating repetitions as the music assumes a march-like character. The scene is conceived musically in quasi-choreographic terms and is one of those which may well refer back to the composer's pre-Hollywood involvement in the ballet world.

In the 1958 *Rio Bravo* (part 2 of the 'Trilogy') the *Red River* main theme is fitted to a new lyric ('My rifle, my pony, and me') and sung in the film during a natural break in the action by Ricky Nelson and Dean Martin. The trumpet solo called

'De Guella', associated with the Mexicans who in 1836 wrested the fortress known as the Alamo from the Texans, was actually written not for the film *The Alamo* (although of course it reappears in it) but for *Rio Bravo*, in which that particular episode in Texan history is made symbolic of Dude's (Dean Martin) struggle against alcoholism. As later in *The Alamo*, 'De Guella' forms the thematic basis of much of the score.

Critic John Belton contrasted the 'epic expansiveness' of *Red River* with the 'lyric density' of *Rio Bravo*, a contrast reflected in the character of the music. As in *High Noon* Tiomkin relinquishes the *tutti* of the conventional symphony orchestra, but this time in favour of the more exotic, specifically Mexican sonorities of marimbas and guitars (reinforced by domras and harpsichord), harmonicas, and plucked rather than bowed lower strings which include the 'guitaron', the Mexican bass guitar. The result is a score of almost chamber-like music in character, much of it nocturnal and atmospheric. The film drifts in and out *pianissimo* (like *High Noon*) to the strains of the simple folksong-like main theme; which in the end-title sequence Dean Martin marries to Paul Francis Webster's lyric with its hauntingly repeated last line ('While the rollin' Rio Bravo flows along').[7]

The Alamo (musically) is the best of the great Tiomkin Westerns, and an apotheosis. Here we find the composer responding once again to a crucial event in the history not of his own country but of the land where he had rebuilt his life after its foundations had been destroyed. By chronicling this landmark in Texan history in music of great vitality and fervour, Tiomkin repays his debt to his adopted country with interest. The score's thematic protagonists are the outstandingly popular 'Green Leaves of Summer' (the score's biggest hit-tune); another original Tiomkin composition in folk-ballad style, the 'Ballad of the Alamo'; and the 'De Guella' already mentioned, heard at the outset (Mexican trumpet over a rustling continuum of guitars) in one of Tiomkin's typically understated main-titles. The end-title too is unconventional: 'The Green Leaves of Summer', 'Tennessee Babe' and 'Ballad of the Alamo' set for unaccompanied chorus. 'The Green

Leaves of Summer' is employed with laudable discretion in the context of the score itself, while both 'De Guella' and 'Ballad of the Alamo' find their apotheosis in the great battle-sequence which forms the climax of both film and score. Tiomkin does not merely reinforce the noise and tumult of the visual image but adds a dimension. He gives voice to the heroic spirit in such a way that we are drawn into the conflict. Particularly effective are the triumphant proclamations in the major of the refrain of the 'Ballad of the Alamo' which contrast with the predominantly minor tonality of the rest of the music, to the roughly rhythmic thrust of General Santa Ana's theme, and assert the frontiersmen's dogged will to overcome. At the end of the scene the 'De Guella' trumpet expresses the anguish and despair of defeat and disintegrates amid the debris of bugle-calls and drum-rolls.

Tiomkin's trail-blazing Western *High Noon* was markedly *un*-epic in character, and it was this that gave him the opportunity to take a relatively novel stance. Doubtless the fact that *High Noon* was not produced by a major studio but independently by Stanley Kramer and Carl Foreman gave him an unprecedentedly free hand and enabled him to break with Hollywood convention in three main respects. First: *High Noon* begins and ends *pianissimo* with a ballad-singer accompanied only by a guitar, accordion and drums.[8] Second: the idea of threading through a single tune, words and all, as an integral part of the dramatic underscore was unorthodox. Tiomkin is here anticipating his strategy in the masterly *Gunfight at the OK Corral*. *High Noon*, like *Gunfight*, is virtually monothematic; the tune is the source of practically every bar of the orchestral incidental music, thus a unique musico-dramatic unity.[9] Tiomkin intuitively realized that the film's thematic *idée fixe* — the deadly approach of 'High Noon' — should be complemented and reinforced in the music. Third: Hollywood stipulated the use of the standard symphony orchestra in which the main expressive burden fell upon the strings. In *High Noon* Tiomkin dispenses with violins altogether, and the lower strings that remain — violas, cellos and double-basses — are totally subordinated to a wind, brass and piano-dominated sonority. The result is a darker, starker, de-glamorized quality of tone-colour.

The most elaborate orchestral treatment of the tune occurs at the film's climax, primarily in the montage of suspense which culminates in the arrival of 'High Noon' and with it the 'deadly killer' bent on gunning down Gary Cooper. The clock's ticking is heard first as a throbbing pulse in harp and *pizzicato* strings but grows gradually into a relentless hammering; the sequence is a kind of 'fantasia on one note'. Over this *ostinato* the full orchestra throws out a nerve-shattering development of the melodic phrase set in the ballad to the words 'Oh to be torn 'twixt love and duty', the climax being reached with an ear-splitting blast from the whistle of the arriving train. The showdown sequence takes the theme to pieces in an eight-minute *tour de force* of variation-cum-symphonic development, and puts it together again, momentously, only in the closing bars as the conflict is resolved.[10]

Rumour has long had it that the *High Noon* tune originates in a Russian (Ukrainian?) folk-tune, but this seems to me to miss the point, or rather points. First, the originality of treating a Western *dramatic feature* — not a musical with a Western setting — musically in this way. Second, the fact that, whatever its roots when surgically anatomized, the music in its final transmogrification sounds authentically and instinctively American. It is foolish to seek to deny the extraordinary quickness, accuracy and receptivity of Tiomkin's ear. He could assimilate and then replicate the characteristics of a music — and a culture — other than his own with phenomenal skill (cf Kurt Weill in the popular-theatre works of his American years, and Benjamin Britten in the 'American' folk-opera *Paul Bunyan* he wrote with W.H. Auden). In these two scores Tiomkin authentically — and brilliantly — exploits the hillbilly idiom more familiar in later years in the context of (e.g.) Blue Grass and Country and Western.

As for *Gunfight at the OK Corral*, I submit that the Greek chorus-like ballad-singer is a stroke of Tiomkinian genius. I know that *High Noon* came first, but the technique is better practised in *Gunfight*: the tune itself is much better — it has a fine feel and shape and flow to it — lends itself more creatively to dramatic variation and elaboration, and the solo singer is most effectively 'shadowed' by a chorus of male voices (their whispered rhythmic repetitions of key-words in the 'Boot Hill' verse is particularly chilling). The minor-key colour is also to the point. Such treatment imperceptibly adds cubits to the film's stature: it is not a mere Western but a myth of the West and touched with the objective inevitability of classical tragedy. The restraint of *Gunfight*, in the face of Tiomkin's familiarly extravagant temperament, is startling.

Of Tiomkin's other epics, two stand out as cinema and as music; *The Guns of Navarone* (1961) and *The Fall of the Roman Empire* (1964). The setting of the former — Greece and the Islands of the Aegean at a crucial stage in the Second World War — proved especially congenial to Tiomkin. It is well known that at the time of the break-up of the Roman Empire, Russia inherited not the Latin civilization of the West but the Greek or Byzantine civilization of the East. When in the tenth century priests from the Eastern Empire were brought in to teach Christianity, Byzantine culture began to permeate the land — the Greek alphabet, literature and liturgical music. Beneath the complex network of Slavonic languages and cultural traditions there thus lies an ancient classical foundation to which it is only natural for a Russian artist to be particularly drawn. Tiomkin steeped himself in the contemporary folk idioms of the Greek Islands and reproduced them with a sureness of touch, for example, in the music for some native wedding celebrations which form a colourful backdrop to scenes of arrest and capture; and in fashioning a Greek-sounding melody, 'Yassu' ('Farewell'), which is used at intervals throughout. The main theme's two contrasting segments prove capable of all the necessary dramatic development. For instance, it rears up threateningly in the nether regions of the orchestra in the cliff-climbing scene, suggesting both the frightening sheerness of the cliff face itself and the everpresent danger of discovery by the German patrol. The theme's second strain assumes a beleaguered aspect at the moment when young Pappadinos is shot. Most important is the climactic sequence in which the blowing-up of the German guns within the fortress before the arrival of the British Navy becomes a desperate race against time. The music's function here is not only to underline the mounting suspense but to thread together the changing scenes of focus (the Germans outside the fortress, the saboteurs inside, and the navy ploughing through the Aegean) into a dramatic whole. The music takes the form of a free fantasia on the main theme and on 'Rule Britannia'. At the climactic point the full orchestra falls suddenly away to leave muted strings and a few solo winds musing quietly on the main theme and on 'Yassu' elegiacally harmonized; the two parts of the theme are even blended in counterpoint. Finally, Paul Francis Webster's lyrics are sung *pianissimo* by the chorus, and as the fishing-boat bearing the survivors sails quietly out of the twilit harbour, 'Yassu' and the splashing of the celesta wind one of the most poetic of Tiomkin's codas to stillness.

The Fall of the Roman Empire was Tiomkin's last major undertaking and perhaps his masterpiece. Russian composers have always been drawn to tales of heroism and pageantry enacted against a panoramic landscape: Borodin's *Prince Igor*, Mussorgsky's *Boris Godunov* and Prokofiev's music for Eisenstein's *Alexander Nevsky* and *Ivan the Terrible* are cases in point. This is connected partly with an intense national and historical awareness, partly with an almost child-like preoccupation with colour and with directness and trenchancy of utterance. So Tiomkin's enthusiastic response to Bronston's Roman Empire project was predictable. How to interpret his role? He took his cue from the scriptwriters, who had decided to isolate and develop two only of the many factors leading to Rome's downfall: the pressure of barbarians on the frontiers and the tragic reign of the half-insane Commodus. In this way the story-line avoided all trace of diffuseness and allowed scope for the development of plot and character on the purely dramatic plane; and it was this that determined the nature of Tiomkin's approach. He began to feel a degree of personal involvement with the *dramatis personae*, as he explained in the sleeve-notes for the recent album of the score:

> . . . I decided I must dismiss all idea of giving this picture quasi-documentary-style music. My plan was to react spontaneously to the dramatic element which I gradually began to appreciate in *Roman Empire*. I excitedly started to block important dramatic and lyrical passages and found myself, to my great surprise, involved not with characters from eighteen centuries ago but with characters whose problems were remarkably like our own and practically co-incidental with all human drama. They were amazingly alive, close to me . . . and then the melodies started to come.

The musical symbolism in *The Fall of the Roman Empire* is intricately worked, the sense of grandeur oddly unbombastic: in the title music Tiomkin massively, but simply and meaningfully, deploys three disparate instrumental groups — organ, symphony orchestra and separate brass group — in what is basically a lyrical theme with Slavic overtones of melancholy. He foregoes conventional fanfares in favour of playing this theme, with its singing lines and rolling periods, for all its worth. In addition to symbolizing the downfall of Rome this theme is also used, in a poignant chromatic harmonization for strings, for the sundering of relations between Lucilla (Sophia Loren), daughter of Marcus Aurelius, and Livius (Stephen Boyd), thus neatly dovetailing the element of personal tragedy with the broader issue of nationwide catastrophe. A later use of this theme shows how music may invest a scene with an added dimension of meaning, conditioning the audience's reactions in such a way that they become subconsciously aware of the shift in emphasis. Towards the end, the entire population of Rome seems to be dancing a primitive version of the twist, accompanied musically by a tarantella, a fast Italian dance with alternating major- and minor-key sections. However, as the orgiastic climax approaches, the tragic main theme suddenly stalks in, spectre-like, first on the organ pedals and then throughout the main body of the orchestra, but retaining the garrulous tarantella rhythm as counterpoint. Two orchestras, two musics — as in the funeral cortège of *Lost Horizon*. The irruption thrills with the sense of approaching doom and charges the sequence with irony; it lends the frenzied revelry the character of a *danse macabre*, which is exactly what it is — but the music makes the point. This main theme returns in the finale but the farewell appearance of certain other motifs in these final moments gives a clue to the nature of their symbolic import. First a reminiscence of the scene in which Marcus Aurelius (Alec Guinness) had received tribute in turn from all the provinces enjoying the Pax Romana — the Roman Peace of orderly government. The music for this scene is modelled (formally, not musically) upon Ravel's *Bolero* — a single melody repeated again and again, remaining essentially unchanged throughout, but subject to perpetually renewing variation in harmony and orchestral texture. This is the exact musical counterpart of the action — the representatives of the various provinces may be diversely costumed, but they are united in motive by their pledge of fealty to Aurelius. This is one of Tiomkin's most magnificent flights of fancy, a real compositional *tour de force*. The appearance of the 'Bolero' theme in the closing stages of the film is subtly ironic, since the undermining of the Pax Romana is already well in evidence, and with it a foreshadowing of the eventual disintegration of the Empire.

Another symbolic interpolation is a reference to the funeral procession of Marcus Aurelius. Less obvious is a simple folk-song-like melody that earlier had provided a mutedly elegiac background to shots of the havoc wrought by invading barbarians, the blackened smoking ruins of villages left in their wake. The final shot is of a massive conflagration in the Roman Forum, with clouds of billowing black smoke obscuring all from view. The two scenes are linked by the appearance of this theme, now more expressively scored and fully harmonized: it prefigures the fate of the Eternal City itself at the hands of the approaching marauders.

The *Roman Empire* score offers at least one instance of a dilemma in which most film composers find themselves at one time or another. For there are times when the composer will want to throw the cinematographic paraphernalia overboard and allow free rein to his inspiration; a particular incident or situation having fired his imagination, he longs to be the sole possessor of his musical material, to devlop it in his own way without reference to the stopwatch. Tiomkin was aware of this problem when working on *Roman Empire*:

> . . . naturally I would have preferred to write music before *Roman Empire* was made and ask the producer to film a picture round it but, alas, the picture was already complete . . . in the beginning I had a strange desire to develop my themes in a more complex and interesting manner, and when it was time to put the music to the film, with stopwatch, I found myself in conflict with myself.

This is particularly noticeable in the Forum scene where the music runs continuously for some six minutes. Up to the last few seconds the music exists both as a suitable complement to the visual images and as a composition in its own right. It is organized along sonata-rondo lines with two basic themes, the periodic recurrence of which is separated by free variation and development in the traditional symphonic manner. The first theme depicting the bustle and hum of activity in the Forum is vigorously extrovert and given to the brass, whereas the second is a lyrical, sweeping, Borodin-like melody for high strings which reflects the gleaming white of the temple crests against an azure sky. All is well until there is an abrupt cut to the interior of the Temple of Jupiter. The music is forced to make an equally abrupt transition and within seconds to tail out altogether: we feel that the flow of the composer's invention has been arbitrarily stemmed. And many other marvellous musical scenes bear testimony to the fact that this invention has been at work at high-voltage level throughout the score — one of which is the enormously protracted, sunlit, sylvan calm which precedes Ballomar's first barbarian attack (the Roman army has earlier marched into the woods to an almost jauntily tramping fugato); another, the 'laughter of the gods', which Commodus 'hears' in the Temple of Jove. This 'laughter' exists only as a figment of his brain, so only the

music can give it utterance. And Tiomkin also leaves us in no
doubt that the film's real romance is not between Livius and
Lucilla but between Livius and Commodus (the ecstatic
character of the music tells us it is real). The tremendous
finale — the all-consuming conflagration in the Roman
Forum with organ, orchestra, brass band, the full turn-out —
is 'epic' music in the strict sense: 'having to do with
epoch-making events in an elevated style'. That is Tiomkin to
a T.

Tiomkin's third Oscar-winning score, *The Old Man and the
Sea* (1958, with Spencer Tracy as the Old Man) is also, in a
sense, an epic — man against nature. Any objection that
Tiomkin's music is too lush for the prevailing plainness and
sobriety of Hemingway's prose can be countered by pointing
to the fact that, visually, the film adaptation itself is lush.
James Wong Howe's camera seeks out a variety of gorgeous
sea- and skyscapes which the composer enhances in impressionist tone-colour and rhythmic texture. These are incidentals, however: what undoubtedly appealed to Tiomkin was,
again, the story's quality as myth or folk-tale. Again the
familiar theme of man battling with nature; he gets
bruised and battered, but wins — it cannot be coincidence
that this theme is common to nearly all the scores
chosen (chosen not to chime in with any pre-conceived theory
but simply because they seemed to me to represent Tiomkin at
his best) for discussion in this chapter. The main theme has
lyrical warmth, certainly; but it also accords with Tracey's
portrayal of the Old Man's quiet, simple dignity and heroism.
The 'Faust' theme in Liszt's *Faust Symphony* and
Tiomkin's theme convey a similar feeling of aspiration. The
profile of this theme informs several scenes with the Old
Man's undemonstrative grandeur; it also punctuates both the
quasi-Cuban folk music in the tavern at Casablanca where the
Old Man and a negro spend two days and nights each trying
to force the other's hand down on to the table, and the fight to
the death with the great marlin for which the Old Man needs
to summon all his strength and powers of endurance. When he
makes his first attempt to hook the fish, the music alone is

responsible for describing its pull on the line — the camera focuses exclusively on the Old Man's face and we do not see the fish.

The other important motifs are a scherzando theme for the Boy (Felipe Pazos), a rhythmic tuba theme for the predatory sharks, and a nostalgic melody that survived independently as a song ('I am your dream') for the Old Man as he dreams of the lions playing on the long, golden beaches of Africa. A poetic mood-picture is born of an authentic Portuguese fishing song which Tiomkin himself had collected. In the days before *Lost Horizon*, Frank Capra used to take him for car rides along the Californian coast. 'I was filled with wonder at the magnificence of colour and the abstract immensity where ships sailed out to nowhere', he recalls in *Please Don't Hate Me*. 'Frank also took me fishing . . . in the early morning, at sunrise, our boat would put out from harbour amid a swarm of the boats of Portuguese fishermen. There was a Portuguese colony down the coast. Their outboard motors chugged and they sang; it was like a chorus of boats, the sound drifting across the water. Their chant was lilting and lyrical, with a sweetness, yet a darkness, often found in Iberian music.' The memory of the fishermen's song came back to Tiomkin, and he incorporates it in the scene of the fishermen's early-morning departure and also briefly in the finale. The deep, dark, distant sound of the men's voices is evocative in a true Hemingway manner.

The 'black-and-white' Tiomkin of contemporary dramatic features and thrillers is less familiar to us; yet some of his best work is contained in this genre such as *Dead on Arrival*, *The Steel Trap*, *Jeopardy* and *36 Hours*. We would do well in this regard to examine his three Hitchcock films, all of which are constantly being screened in retrospectives and elsewhere. Tiomkin first worked with Alfred Hitchcock in 1944 on *Shadow of a Doubt* in which the score's main function was to provide a distorted, phantasmagorical version of the 'Merry Widow' waltz. Next came *Strangers on a Train* in 1951. Hitchcock told François Truffaut that in this film he was unhappy with Farley Granger's performance as Guy, the tennis star whom the madman Bruno (Robert Walker) tries to coerce into murdering his father. Ideally Hitchcock would have liked somebody stronger to play Guy's part. This is interesting inasmuch as Guy's theme, and the music that accompanies him throughout the score, is a faithful reflection of the character as he is played by Granger, i.e. somewhat passively and anaemically. Had Hitchcock expressed to Tiomkin his reservations about Granger's performance, the composer could have strengthened the actor musically. As for Bruno, Tiomkin always associates his madness with a specific tone-colour as well as with a theme, namely the weird, thin, glassy sound of high violin harmonics. Bruno's theme and Guy's (in a rhythmic, athletic transformation) are alternated to spectacular effect in the tennis-match scene, in which Guy has to race against time to finish his game and prevent Bruno planting incriminating evidence against him. Here the music not only increases the excitement and suspense but also, as in all scenes where one sequence of events is constantly being intercut with another, supplies continuity. A similar case is the beginning of the picture, with its alternating shots of the two pairs of legs walking towards each other. It would be premature to differentiate between them musically at this point, and Tiomkin invents a cheerful, catchy motif for which developments do not permit him to find further use.

I Confess (1952), Tiomkin's most substantial Hitchcock score, is set in Quebec and concerns a priest (Montgomery Clift) suspected of a murder he did not commit. He knows who the real murderer is because the latter has confessed to him; but, bound by the inviolability of confession, he can make no move to clear himself. The dead man had been blackmailing the priest on account of an affair the priest had had with a married woman before his ordination; and this explains both the lyrical character of the main theme and Tiomkin's unusual mode of presenting it. We hear it time and again as a soprano solo, but with the sweet, innocent-sounding singer very distantly recorded — so distantly, in fact, that the words are barely distinguishable. The effect is of a poignant reminder of long-lost happiness. The main title treatment is poetic. The credits are superimposed on a distant panoramic view of Quebec in silhouette against the evening sky, and the music — *pianissimo sempre* — is an illustration of the lyrics:

> While the town is sleeping tight
> Comes the music of the night.
> One can hear its lonely beat
> On each dark deserted street.
>
> The dreams and hopes of yesterday
> Sigh and slowly drift away;
> All the sounds of earth unite
> Secretly in the night.

The magic of the distant solo voice, the velvety, deep-purple key of D flat major associated with the song throughout the score, the slow, sighing, descending drifts of its melodic profile, the whispered *tenebroso* orchestration: all add up to an evocative tone-picture in miniature, the intent of which is patently to lull the audience rather than place them on the alert. The shadowy, nocturnal mood is sustained through the opening scene in the darkened church but assumes a quite different character as Clift hears the fatal confession: the unmistakable outline of the 'Dies Irae' shapes and repeats itself in the murk with ritualistic *sotto voce* relentlessness. A similar sense of fatalistic implacability lies behind the score's finest dramatic sequence: Clift's decision to give himself up to the police for the crime he did not commit. He walks through the town heading for the police station; the picture suggests an image of Christ bearing his cross and the music realizes it in the form of a massive, monumental *marcia funebre*. What we see is Montgomery Clift walking; what we experience, thanks to the music, is both his agony of mind and his integrity, his willingness to sacrifice himself rather than betray his calling: a true *Via Crucis*.

A later memorable moment when Tiomkin engages our sympathy for Clift follows the courtroom scene. The jury acquits him due to insufficient evidence, but the verdict is unpopular: a hostile crowd in lynching mood surrounds him outside. The passionate music again expresses his bewilderment and that of the real murderer's wife, an unwilling party to her husband's evil. That the latter's mind is giving way during his last confrontation with the priest and the police is subtly insinuated by Tiomkin's use of the soprano saxophone; another subtlety is the motif for Vilette, the blackmailer, whose unusual (for Tiomkin) 5/4 metre characterizes his malevolent persistence. This comes as the climax of the long retrospective montage in which Anne Baxter relates to the police the history of her liaison with Clift. Here the music's function, as always in a montage, is that of binding veneer. It embraces all the diverse elements — young love, dancing in a night-club, the outbreak of war and enforced parting, joyful reunion to the sound of bells in the music, the storm, the encounter with Vilette, the blackmailing — intensifies their momentary significance as they pass, and unifies the narrative.

By contrast *Dial M For Murder* (1954), being more or less the equivalent of a filmed stage play, offered little scope for music. Again in the main title, after a declamatory *tutti* of very brief duration, Tiomkin deliberately disarms his audience by wooing them with a seductive, tuneful salon waltz which plays no part in the ensuing drama. The only important musical sequence in which music really comes into its own is that of the murder itself. Ray Milland plans to have Grace Kelly dispatched by a hired killer while he himself is establishing his alibi at his club. Split-second timing is involved, and Tiomkin responds by turning the orchestra into a monster clock: shades of *High Noon*, (although the musical texture and design are quite different), and of Mussorgsky's *Boris Godunov*. Dense, bunched chords in the low registers of strings, woodwinds and pianos, played very softly but recorded at an abnormally high level, create a potent atmosphere. The deep, cloudy, reverberant sonorities are a Tiomkin hallmark.

No account of Tiomkin's would be complete without the 1959 *Rhapsody of Steel*, a cartoon documentary produced by the U.S. Steel Company and recorded in Pittsburgh with the

Pittsburgh Symphony Orchestra. *Rhapsody of Steel* offers a whistle-stop history of steel from the discovery of meteoric iron by primitive man, through the era of structural steel to the Space Age. The film has disappeared completely, but the music is easily available on record. The subject-matter of the first part — the growth and development of steel through the Iron Age, up to modern techniques of processing steel — allowed free rein to the lyrical dynamism of his characteristic style. There is some affinity too with Prokofiev's 1927 ballet *The Age of Steel*; in the same 'steely' singing quality, the same antiseptic exhilaration. It is likely however that Tiomkin evolved his eminently Russian-sounding *style mécanique* independently rather than directly in the wake of such exemplars of Soviet musical 'realism' as Mossolov's *Iron Foundry*. The 'steel' theme is an ascending four-note figure whose simplicity lends itself readily to a process, typical of Tiomkin, of repetition-with-variation which holds much sway through the first part: listen for it, for example, enfolded deep in the bosom of the orchestra towards the end of the glimmeringly evocative, dawn-of-time music which immediately precedes the falling of the meteor. Of course, the exotic element in Part 1 appealed, and the sinuously seductive veil dance with its languourous melodic charm and colourful ornamentation, is the highlight of a richly evocative sequence.

   Part 2, a scherzo is based on a nonchalant little tune ('I feel wonderful for no particular reason') the first phrase of which is merely the first phrase of the steel theme turned upside down. Here the animation depicts the part played by steel in a busy, modern urban community, and the music is a playful set of variations on 'I feel wonderful'; a big jazz chromium-plated climax is built up in which all the sights and sounds of a seething metropolis seem to converge, among them taxi horns and police whistles. Its eupeptic spirit is similar to that of the rowdier parts of Gershwin's *An American in Paris*, and perhaps should be dubbed 'A Russian in New York'. The finale mirrors the nobility of man's aspiration to a wider knowledge of the universe in a fugato which describes ever-widening circles of movement and energetic endeavour and which, though fraught with a heroic lyricism, is devoid of grandiosity or hollow rhetoric. The astronauts take wing into outer space where meteorites are born; 'Perhaps in the not too distant future', concludes the narrator, Gary Merrill, 'Man will set about shaping his civilization on earth as carefully as he has shaped the metal that takes him on the greatest journey in all history. The progress of man is the progress of STEEL'. These final moments recapitulate the opening music to form an exultant coda.

Tiomkin was a composer whose invention, once activated, flowed freely. Ideas poured forth, bursting clumsily in a kind of smoky blaze. His sketches bear interesting testimony to the way he composed: at breakneck speed, at the piano, using a heavy black lead pencil that makes his manuscript curiously like a visual representation of the way his music actually sounds. The sketches are hard to decipher at first but one comes to terms with them remarkably quickly and realizes, just as quickly, that all the music is *there*. Every note is his and his alone;[11] he composed pianistically (his textures had to be translated into orchestral terms) and super-abundantly. He liked to fill his pictures chock-full of music, his music chock-full of notes. When inspiration failed he had nothing to fall back on; with the result that his failures are as spectacular as his successes. It is all part of the Tiomkin phenomenon — which, once we start teasing out the *real* man, the responsive, responsible musician behind the media image, shows us a balance sheet of which any composer might be proud.

NOTES

1   See Dimitri Tiomkin and P. Buranelli, *Please Don't Hate Me* (New York, 1959), pp. 253–4.

2   Herbert Stothart of MGM frequently interlarded his scores with excerpted Great Masterworks, feeling that the cinema was a useful means of introducing the general public to classical music. My own experience bears this out. As a boy I first heard Beethoven's Seventh Symphony in a Tiomkin film (*The Long Night*) and Debussy's *Nocturnes* in *Portrait of Jennie*. Miklós Rózsa has always thought of the cinema as one of the world's greatest music teachers.

3   See Christopher Palmer, *Dimitri Tiomkin: A Portrait* (London, 1984) for a fuller biographical account; also *Dimitri Tiomkin: The Man and His Music*: NFT Dossier no 1 (London 1980).

4   Few of these wartime documentaries contain much original Tiomkin (most are compilation scores based on 'classical' composers in the manner of silent movie procedures) and those that do are for the most part of negligible interest. *Battle of San Pietro* is a notable exception, though even here the emotional core of the score is really the 'Agnus Dei' from the Fauré *Requiem*.

5   It is worth remarking that the lushly 'exotic' Russian music of Borodin survived well its transmogrification into a Hollywood musical (*Kismet*); whereas the clear-air, cold-water music of Grieg — which lies at the other end of the emotional spectrum — did not (*Song of Norway*).

6   The latter piece, like the riotous 'Fiesta' in another Tiomkin Texan Western, *Strange Lady in Town*, originated as one of the composer's numerous contributions to the repertoire of the Albertina Rasch Dancers in the 1920s.

7   Aside from the river symbolism implicit in their titles, *Red River* and *Rio Bravo* have this in common: that their heroes' relationships

with women are of an incidental, platonic and almost perfunctory nature. In *Rio Bravo* this is reflected in the music inasmuch as Angie Dickinson's slinky saxophone theme stands in marked contrast both texturally, melodically and instrumentally, to all other music in the score.

8   The enormous popular success of the *High Noon* theme-song has often been blamed for re-activating the efforts of producers to make music boost the financial returns of the film. Tiomkin certainly was a willing participant: most of his scores after *High Noon* are geared to some new attempt to hit the popular jackpot (which in fact he succeeded in doing on more than one occasion), This does not, however, invalidate the basic concept of *High Noon* itself, which is brilliant.

9   In its basic monothematicism, *High Noon* has a distinguished Hollywood antecedent in David Raksin's *Laura* (1944); a detective thriller based on an unusual premise: the detective, Mark McPherson (Dana Andrews) gradually becomes obsessed by Laura, the woman whose apparent murder he is investigating (Gene Tierney). Until she turns up in the second half of the picture still very much alive, Mark is in fact falling in love with a ghost-like presence. It is the music's responsibility to make this presence real and felt. Understandably, once the real Laura has materialized its support is no longer required and, for a few brief cues, it is dismissed the screen. For the first 45 minutes, however, Laura, in the shape of her own haunting theme, is everywhere. No distinction is drawn between commentative and realistic music. As the titles come to an end Raksin breaks off his melody in mid-sentence, just before the last phrase, and replaces it with an ominously expectant pedal-point, over which Waldo Lydecker's (Clifton Webb) soliloquy begins; fragments of the theme are heard on the stifled tones of bassoon and cor anglais under a haze of high string harmonies which evoke the heat of a New York midsummer afternoon and make us almost visually aware of 'the silver sun streaming through the windows like a huge magnifying glass' which we do not see on the screen, but which the music has to realize for us. Next, McPherson is examining Laura's apartment; he turns on the radio and her theme is heard — the fact that it is 'her' theme is made clear by Lydecker who rebukes the detective and makes him switch off the radio. Then Lydecker and McPherson go to lunch together; they sit at Laura's table, and Laura's theme is being

played on violin and piano in a salon-type arrangement. Full strings take over as Waldo starts to reminisce about the first time he ever set eyes on Laura, but the song subsides once more into *schmaltz* — true 'background' music — as the flashback begins and we see Waldo at his table being approached by a tentative, apologetic Laura and requested to endorse a pen.

These fluid transitions between commentative and realistic music — and several other short scenes are underscored with 'Laura' — are all designed to prepare us musically for the crucial scene — the one with the longest single musical cue — of McPherson's encounter with the still-living Laura. McPherson is left alone in Laura's apartment at night, and the music begins in the style of a nocturne. The detective is restless, irresolute, and edgy. The theme is developed symphonically on strings with an almost Bergian intensity as he paces about arbitrarily examining Laura's possessions. Only when he goes to the portrait and looks at it is the theme heard clearly for the first time. Throughout this scene the music attempts to convey McPherson's confusion, torn as he is between conflicting emotions — his feeling for Laura, awareness of his own idiocy in falling in love with a corpse, awareness also of his responsibility as a police officer. The music resumes, still in nocturnal garb, after Lydecker has come and gone, and finally McPherson sits down in the armchair, leans back and starts to surrender himself to sleep. Here the theme is played on Raksin's favourite alto saxophone in a mood of serenity and repose. The music fades into nothingness as sleep begins to exert its sway. Then silence as the door opens and Laura walks in. A less sensitive composer might have greeted her entry with a crashing *fortissimo* rendition of her theme. Instead it is as if the music, having once invoked the past and brought a dead girl back to life, deems its duty done and quietly retreats. Its tale is not quite told, however. The theme returns as realistic 'background' music for the party to celebrate Laura's 'homecoming' (each time it recurs in a realistic context it is scored for a contrasting combination of instruments), and at the end of the picture makes a final subtly-graded transition. Lydecker's attempted murder of Laura, the arrival of McPherson, and Lydecker's own death all coincide with the end of Waldo's radio broadcast on the subject of 'love' which Laura had been listening to minutes before. When Laura's theme wells up at this point, we unconsciously accept it as the signature tune of Waldo's radio programme. If anything it is the signature tune of the film itself, for it now leads directly into the end title. The theme is an essential part of the introfilmic fabric.

10 When Tiomkin did the music for the 1960 documentary *A President's Country* (scored for small orchestra plus a few 'western' accessories like harmonica and guitar) he rounded up all his 'Western' classics — *Red River, The Big Sky, High Noon, Giant, Rawhide, The Alamo* — and replayed them in a kind of medley and thematic catalogue which was both spontaneous and pleasing.

11 He rarely indicated specific orchestral colourings in his sketches, but regularly played the latter through to his orchestrators (most of whom worked with him over many years) and made his intentions clear enough in general terms.

ROY WEBB

'Roy who?! Roy *Webb*? Never heard of him!'; a predictable reaction on the part of most *cinéastes* who might also be surprised to find, in a book purportedly devoted to the Hollywood all-stars, a chapter on a composer with whose work even film-music buffs tend to be unfamiliar. He wrote no hit song, no symphony or opera, and passed virtually the whole of his working life in the employ of one studio. So why Webb? I write about him for three reasons. First, because he was, or could be, a good composer. Second, because he worked on a remarkably large number of good films. Third, because he was the first film composer with whom I made personal contact. This was in 1965 when I was 18.

Fascinated by his music and by the frequency with which his name appeared on television, I had written to the Screen Composers' Association endeavouring to learn something about him. Was he still alive? If so, why was he apparently no longer active? Why wasn't he in *Grove*? Had he ever written any 'serious' music? Eventually a letter came back from the composer himself:

Dear Mr Palmer:

As a member, I was present at the last Screen Composers'
Meeting about a week ago. I was proud and happy to be
shown the contents of your letter to the Secretary of our
Association. I am very pleased to be alive and able to
answer your questions about me.

When RKO dissolved I was over 65 and retired on a good
pension. But I kept myself busy as a 'freelance' writing
scores for Warner Bros, (*Blood Alley, Sea Chase*) Paramount
and several other studios, completing over 300 scores since
starting at RKO. Finally I wrote for TV (*Wagon Train* and
Shirley Temple Story Book). I still would have continued, but
had the misfortune to have my home, together with all my
musical efforts, burned to the ground in Nov. 1961. I had
many serious compositions among my losses, but after the
disheartening devastation of my home did not have the
heart to proceed further. Maybe I'll continue in the future
— who knows?

I once had the pleasure of having a concerto for piano,
written for a picture called *The Enchanted Cottage* (with
Herbert Marshall, Robt. Young & Dorothy Maguire),
played at the Hollywood Bowl. Unfortunately my only
copy was lost in the fire.[1]

I will try to get your letter to Mr Bakaleinikoff and Leigh
Harline.[2] Both are wonderful musicians and good friends of
mine and I am sure will be as pleased and honoured as I
am.

If you ever come to California please look me up. If I
have moved from this address, the Screen Composers'
Assn. will have the right one. I would love to talk to you.

With all my thanks and best wishes,
ROY WEBB
Charter member ASCAP and SCA

I started a regular correspondence with him which ceased
only when, in the early 1970s, he became too ill to answer
letters. I met him only once, on my first visit to Hollywood in
1974. Already his memory was failing, but, tactfully
encouraged by his wife Jean, he was able to provide some
reminiscences, and I even recorded him playing some of his

own themes on the piano, a recording good enough to use in a BBC radio portrait I later compiled. Although he was to 'live' for another eight years, there were no more breaks in the silence. He died in hospital in Santa Monica in December 1982 at the age of 94.

Webb was born in New York City on 3 October 1888. The main musical influence in his life was his mother, who frequently took him as a boy to the Metropolitan Opera; and an uncle who was a well-known Gilbert and Sullivan favourite ensured that he had a thorough grounding in comic opera as well. Webb was also gifted as an artist and studied drawing and painting at the Art Students' League in New York for five years. After high school he enrolled at Columbia University where he was fed a diet of Bach and Beethoven: his teacher used the Bach fugues as a basis for his instruction, and Webb would later have cause to be grateful for the rigour of this early training when, years later, he faced the problem of writing 'symphonic' music for films. For the time being, however, his chief interest was light music, and he and his brother Kenneth[3] produced a number of Varsity shows for which Roy composed, arranged and conducted the music, doing, as he put it, 'what came naturally'.

His first professional engagement and Broadway debut came when he was still a student at Columbia with the invitation of Herbert Stothart (later of MGM) to work on *Wildflower*. He was soon an artistic director at the New York Players' Studio and Victor Baravalle booked him to conduct the Fred Stone musical *Stepping Stones*, which ran in New York and on tour for two and a half years. Baravalle, now Musical Director at RKO, then invited him to come to Hollywood to help orchestrate the score for *Rio Rita*. Also at RKO at this time was Max Steiner, Webb's almost exact contemporary. They had met while Webb was conducting Richard Rodgers's *Connecticut Yankee* — Webb had known Rodgers as a gifted 13-year-old at Columbia: 'even then he was composing beautiful songs, but had no idea of how to put them down on paper.' Webb showed him how, and some sixty years later Rodgers paid a charming tribute to his early teacher in his autobiography *Musical Stages*. Steiner was conducting You-mans' *Hit the Deck* just round the corner, and so began a friendship and professional association that was to last over forty years until Steiner's death in 1971.

Webb arrived in Hollywood in 1929 and spent virtually the remainder of his working life in the employ of RKO until the early fifties when the studio ceased production and was sold to Desilu TV. Over a period of some twenty-five years he worked in one capacity or another on a total of over 300 films. His career paralleled Steiner's in that he was involved with musicals in his early years, but gradually, as he began to develop as a composer, became monopolized by feature films. He still did the occasional musical — *The Marines Fly High* (1940), *Let's Make Music* (1941) and shorts such as the 1935 *Metropolitan Nocturne* (based on music by Louis Alter), *Singing in the Air* and *Swing Fever* (1937). He also composed the Florida surfing and aquaplaning sequences in *This is Cinerama* (1953). Occasionally, too, he wrote songs, as in *Bombardier* (1943) and *Rachel and the Stranger* (1948); and his Broadway experience enabled him to handle comedy and light drama: *Quality Street* (1937), *Bringing up Baby* (1938), *Vivacious Lady* (1938), *Love Affair* (1939), *Kitty Foyle* (1940), *Tom, Dick and Harry* (1941) and *Magic Town* (1947). But we can see in *The Last Days of Pompeii* (1935) and *The Last of the Mohicans* (1936) and prototypes of colour and spectacle on the one hand (*Sinbad the Sailor* [1947], *At Sword's Point* [1952; UK title: *Sons of the Musketeers*], *Underwater* [1955]), and of tension and emotion on the other — *The Locket* (1947), *Blood on the Moon* (1948), *The White Tower* (1950) and *The Raid* (1953) are good examples. Webb's real *forte*, however, was the genre known as *film noir* as it evolved in the 1940s.

The *film noir*, the gangster film, the thriller, the horror film; all individual flowerings from a common stem, all intricately interrelated, and all informed with the macabre spirit of the nineteenth-century 'doomed' romantic movement of Poe, Blackwood, Collins, Nerval, Baudelaire, Bertrand and many others. Enhanced through contact with pre-war French and German Expressionist cinema, such films attained a peak of

Notorious: 'Troubled Mind'

Roy Webb in the 1940s

excellence in the Hollywood of the forties. The metropolis was central to the concept; the urban milieu served both as background and as an extension of the violence and brutality of the underworld and its protagonists — a nocturnal world of shabby, ill-lit boarding houses (*Crossfire*), deserted office blocks (*Farewell My Lovely*), dark, wet streets (*Sorry, Wrong Number*), and the claustrophobic interiors of trains, elevators and crowded, sweaty night clubs. Musically we have already encountered a basic obstruction: namely that the general idiom of Hollywood composers, basically nineteenth-century-orientated, was not attuned to the mood and feeling of films of this type. Individual scores of great merit were certainly written — Hans Salter's for *Phantom Lady* (1944), Hugo Friedhofer's for *The Woman in the Window* (1945), Leigh Harline's for *Nocturne* (1948), Cyril Mockridge's for *Nightmare Alley* (1947), Leith Steven's for *Beware My Lovely* (1952), Max Steiner's for *The Big Sleep* (1946), David Raksin's for *Force of Evil* (1949), Franz Waxman's for *Night and the City* and *Dark City* (1950); and Miklós Rózsa's outstanding achievements in the genre remain to be discussed. However Webb, throughout the forties, showed consistent sympathy with the world of *film noir* and skill in translating its nuances into musical terms — largely through a wide spectrum of modern harmonic resource and an understanding of the atmospheric properties of orchestral colour, of texture, and of understatement. If Webb lacks Steiner's melodic distinction, harmonically he is more sophisticated. In his use of chords built up of fourths and in the linear orientation of much of his music, Webb's idiom grows closer to the neo-classical austerity of Hindemith than to romantic prototypes. So it is that the crudities and commonplaces of conventional 'horror' music are completely and remarkably absent from Webb's. So it is too that equipped with a special way with chords and colours, Webb is unusually dexterous in his handling of dialogue scenes. In this regard all his best films show him exerting a species of manipulative control arguably unrivalled among Hollywood composers for its subtlety and nuance. By its very nature this is not the kind of technique to draw much attention to itself, but a crash-course in Webb is definitely recommended to all would-be composers interested in melodrama in the strict sense, i.e. the relationship between music and the spoken word.

Webb's most interesting work is, like the man himself, curiously untouched by Hollywood. His feeling for the particular type of mood — urban, nocturnal, half-lit, understated, mutedly dissonant — associated with *film noir* is well demonstrated in Edward Dmytryk's celebrated *Farewell My Lovely*, the film that first established Dick Powell as a 'straight' actor. Conventional fanfares herald the RKO Radio emblem; then, abruptly, the full orchestra drops out leaving only soft trills. The camera slowly closes in on the lamp-lit table around which are seated Philip Marlowe (Powell) and his police interrogators, and the music subordinates all to ambience. Everything takes place either at night or in darkened rooms, and there is rarely clarity or precision of any kind.[4] Mists, smoke, fog, general murk: these are the protagonists, these create the blackly romantic iconography that is so important a factor in the film's appeal, and this is where Webb's feeling for atmospheric nuance — harmonic and colouristic — stands him in good stead. The music he wrote for the city lights under Marlowe's first narration was omitted from the finished print (much to its detriment), but for the murder of Marriott in the fog Webb exploits the bitonal or multi-chordal textures of the main title to good effect. Bitonal harmony — sounding two opposing concords simultaneously, thus creating a well-defined dissonance — when wedded to the appropriate colour and tempo must by its very nature create a certain quasi-Impressionist textural confusion, and this is the ideal here. A much increased norm of dissonance embraces the montage of Marlowe's three-day ordeal at the hands of Amthor's (Otto Kruger) interrogators in which he is pumped so full of narcotics as to induce hallucinations of nightmare violence — monster faces, a monster syringe, a whole galaxy of locked doors, a terrifying vortex that sucks him at lightning speed towards its centre. The music is a black cloudy chaos of discordant brass, high screaming woodwinds (jabbing minor seconds as Marlowe feels the harpoon-like syringe bury itself in him) and high trilling strings to create a swirling effect as his body falls into the bottomless abyss. Essentially the same kind of texture in a milder variant persists during the following scene. Again, as in the montage, we see everything from Marlowe's point of view (hence the screen is smothered in smoke) and so the music must make us *feel* everything from his point of view too.

Thematically, Webb is concerned to link the two potential lovers (Marlowe and Anne) together early in the picture. After the murder of Marriott a girl approaches Marlowe as he lies stunned in the quarry, shines her torch on his face and asks him if he is all right. We do not see the girl's face, and anyway we do not at this stage know who she is; nor does Marlowe. Only later in the picture, when we have met Anne Grayle and associated the theme with her, do we realize that the music in the quarry scene told us who she was all the time. To add to the mystery Webb introduces the theme even earlier, as Marlowe leaves Mrs Florian's apartment and returns to his office — where he finds Marriott awaiting him with the quarry assignment. So we hear this theme through twice without understanding whom it is supposed to represent: the music is playing its own detective game. We hear it again as Marlowe is recovering from his drug ordeal, by which time it should be telling us that the girl in the quarry is the same girl he is now thinking about. Finally the love theme is brought back to close the picture as the pair finally make proper contact in the back of the car driving Marlowe home.

Moose's three-note motif is also imaginatively handled. Moose has an unnerving habit of suddenly looming up massively from nowhere — which generally bodes no good for whomever he looms up behind or in front of. It is the music's duty always to prepare us for his approach — just before we see his reflection in the mirror in Marlowe's office, just before he materializes in front of Marlowe after the latter's escape from Sonderborg, finally just before he bursts his way into the beach house where Velma (Claire Trevor) is lying, murdered by her elderly husband.[5]

Webb made a valuable contribution to the series of low-budget horror films produced by Val Lewton — films acclaimed by James Agee and others since then as masterpieces of the genre. Webb was the Lewton composer *par excellence; Cat People* (1942), *I Walked with a Zombie, The Leopard Man, The Seventh Victim* (1943), *The Curse of the Cat People* (1944), *The Body Snatcher* (1945) and *Bedlam* (1946). Webb's 'horror' music is, as we shall see, the precise aural equivalent of Lewton's half-heard sounds, half-seen shadows, and atmospheric lighting. It is possible that in a close-knit team such as existed at RKO where Webb worked alongside cinematographer Nicholas Musuraca (a specialist in this idiom), art directors Albert D'Agostino and Walter Keller, and editor Mark Robson, the work of one member of the team would be influenced by that of another and begin to assume some of its characteristics. One of the more positive aspects of the studio system was that it encouraged this type of artistic cross-fertilization. (On the other hand, however, it did not provide for any closeness of collaboration between director and composer since the former would, in the normal course of events, be already engaged on another picture by the time the latter was called in). Lewton is known to have put his personal stamp on almost every aspect of his productions, and it is more than likely that, having discerned Webb's gifts in the treatment of musical *chiaroscuro*, he requested him specifically.

The lyrical, even 'musical' qualities of Lewton's films, rendered them particularly susceptible to music. His masterpiece is generally reckoned to be *I Walked with a Zombie*, described by Tom Milne as 'a nightmarishly beautiful tone-poem of voodoo dreams, dark moonlight and somnabulist ladies in floating white'[6], and Joel E. Siegel refers to the walk to the Houmfort in the same film as 'a symphony of graceful movement'.[7] The latter sequence, being so 'musically' self-contained, does not need the support of actual music; in fact, one of the virtues of Webb's musical handling of

Lewton's films is that, at a time when overscoring was the rule rather than the exception, his placing or 'spotting' of music is so judicious. Lewton's practice was to eschew the crude visualization and Grand Guignol tactics commonly regarded as indispensable flesh-crawling expedients.[8] Horror is implied and suggested, never brought out into the open. Evocation takes the place of literal depiction. This is precisely the technique of Webb's 'horror' music as developed through harmony and timbre: every note is weighed carefully and with an eye for evocative effect. Furthermore, Webb was essentially an urbanite and adept at evoking the Lewton city's varied moods. He evolved a style of orchestration characteristic of murk and shadow whose muted colours perfectly complemented the black-and-white Impressionism of Musuraca's camera, both in these films and elsewhere.

The musical protagonist in *Cat People*[9] is particularly interesting in that the idea came from actress Simone Simon who plays Irena, the Cat Woman. She sang a little French nursery tune ('Do, do, l'enfant do') to Webb, who agreed that it could serve as the score's thematic basis.[10] First heard over the credits, it is hummed by Irena to Oliver (Kent Smith) in one of their early scenes together, and is used in many variants. It haunts the film just as Irena becomes haunted by the fear that she will turn into a cat and kill the man she loves. Its most horrifying transformation comes at the climax when Irena does literally turn into a huge black panther and murders her psychiatrist Dr Judd (Tom Conway). The very sweetness and innocence of the original tune intensifies the dark horror of the harmony that distorts it: the tune turns into a monster along with Irena. Two more inspired musical images: the celesta motif for Irena's perfume — we cannot smell it so must *hear* it instead! — and the sinister measured tread of *pizzicato* cellos and basses padding their stealthy and unmistakably feline way through the whole score.

Both Simone Simon and Webb showed unconscious foresight in selecting 'Do, do, l'enfant do' for it fits with singular aptness into *Cat People*'s sequel, *Curse of the Cat People*, despite its title, a delicate and poetic fantasy of childhood.

Other musical survivors of the earlier film are the main title music, Irena's theme, and the sinister four-note cat motif — which, incidentally, Webb could not resist the temptation to quote *fortissimo* in his introduction to William Wellman's superb *Track of the Cat* made some ten years later. Clearly the excellence of Webb's scores for *Cat People* and its sequel caused him to be regarded as something of a cat specialist. *Track of the Cat* is set on a snowbound ranch in Northern California which is being terrorized by a mysterious black panther. The score broods and crouches and is an important factor in making the lurking menace of the panther more real to us. The film owes not a little to Lewton's prototype inasmuch as the monster is never actually seen, only suggested. The music identifies itself both with fear of the cat and with the elemental forces of nature with which the cat is identified: white snow-logged mountain panoramas, not evil in their outward appearance but made so by the music — granite-like blocks of opaquely glowering sound — which shoots them through with an evil omniscient presence. As in *Cat People* the music instils a feeling of ubiquitous danger. If we were there in person we would sense the danger for ourselves. As we are not the music must realize it for us, and does so most forcibly in the early scene where Arthur (William Hopper) is attacked on horseback by the unseen panther, and later in Curt's (Robert Mitchum) final confrontation with the monster in a blizzard.

The music also, however, covers the opposite end of the emotional spectrum: in a tender theme for Tab Hunter as the repressed boy Harold and Diana Lynn as the girl who strives to liberate him. The music draws them together. Moreover, the aggressive burst of brass that opens the main title ('monster' music) gives way to a long-spanned lyrical theme of American innocence. In this form the theme recurs only once — at the end, where the hateful forces, both actual and symbolic — have been overcome. Then the theme is free to give eloquent expression to a new-found serenity and release.

In *Curse of the Cat People* the music's responsibility is to turn quite another kind of fantasy into reality. 'Do, do, l'enfant do' is all-important during the first scene in the garden when

lonely, sensitive little Amy (Ann Carter) first wishes for a
'Friend' to love and understand and share her life with her.
The screen darkens, showers of petals rain upon the garden
and the tune, scored with a gentle translucent beauty, tells us
not only that the Friend has arrived but also (if we remember
it from *Cat People*, of course) who she is. So too when Amy calls
for her Friend in her nightmare, the limpid pastel tones tell us
that the Friend is there to comfort her, although at this stage
she is still invisible to us. The result is that when Simone
Simon actually appears for the first time we have been aurally
prepared for her. The film's climax is reached when Barbara
(Elizabeth Russell), a murder-bent harpie consumed with
jealousy and hatred, is transformed in Amy's eyes into the
gentle and kindly Friend: 'My Friend!' The music dissolves
into the main theme and Amy's life is saved. Another musical
sleight-of-hand is in the Christmas scene when carollers are
singing 'Shepherds shake off your drowsy sleep'; Irena
appears to Amy and sings the French carol 'Il est né, le divin
enfant' which somehow is woven in counterpoint with the
English. Through the medium of music the 'Friend' is made
into a living presence for Amy, and therefore for us; just as,
through the same agency, the old lady's (Julia Dean)
recounting of the 'Legend of Sleepy Hollow' becomes a
nightmarish eruption of hunting horns and headless horse-
men. Incidentally, the score's real ending — *pianissimo* —
comes a few bars before the bombastic final cadence, tacked
on merely in conformity with end-title convention.

Two other Lewton films call for brief comment. The great
set-piece in *The Seventh Victim* is a nocturne — the heroine's
menaced walk home through a deserted Greenwich Village at
night. The music — discreetly complementing acting and
photography — is heavy with fears and forebodings and
sudden alarms, and explodes in a climax of racing panic. *The
Leopard Man* main title[11] begins with strident trumpets,
putting us in a receptive frame of mind for what in fact turns
out to be the most conventional of Lewton's horror pictures.
However, we are immediately struck by the abnormally loud
sound of castanets. The music has a Spanish flavour (the

setting is a small New Mexico town) and so castanets are expected; even so they are obviously larger than life. Only later is this explained: the castanets belong to one of the chief characters, Clo-Clo the night-club singer who moves through the first part of the film clicking them before meeting her death at the hands of the Leopard Man: a subtle use of naturalistic sound in what purports to be a purely *musical* context. (The castanets would, of course, have been recorded on a track of their own, thus enabling the mixer to amplify them exaggeratedly at will.) So in truth, while the quasi-Mexican title music is commentative, the amplified castanets that accompany it belong more to the realistic category — an interesting example of the way music may serve to alert the audience, to puzzle them even. Why, we ask ourselves, is the sound of these castanets so intrusive? Then later we realize that this sound is a powerful catalyst to the atmospheric presence of the picture — particularly in that castanets normally carry connotations of sunlight, brash colour and breathless activity; but here they are associated primarily with dark empty streets, night stillness and unseen malevolent forces.

Much influenced by Lewton — and by German expression-ism — is Robert Siodmak's *The Spiral Staircase* (1946), one of the best *films noirs* of the forties, and one of Webb's best scores. Professor Warren, the murderer in this film (George Brent) feels himself obliged to rid the world of any young females who are maimed or imperfect; an intended victim is Helen, a mute girl, played by Dorothy Maguire. In an early scene we see him watching her in a mirror; her face swims out of focus, the dumb mouth is replaced by a blur. This is what activates the killer. It may also have activated the composer not to give one theme to the murderer and one to the girl, but instead to make the one a distorted or maimed version of the other. The distortion is aided by an electronic instrument that Webb was among the first to introduce into films, the theremin,[12] whose weirdly oscillating sonority is an apt image of mental derangement. The theremin part was recorded on a separate track in order that, where necessary, it could dominate the orchestra and sound as if in an echo chamber. We hear it in this form in the main title where it is supplemented mainly by a battery of storm sound-effects; immediately it is established as a symbol of terror, just like the spiral staircase itself. Thereafter it identifies on every occasion with the murderer waiting to pounce, with the camera diving deep into a screen-sized eye. Its *alter ego*, Helen's theme, reveals itself as a graceful melody first heard in idyllically romantic vein as she and Dr Parry (Kent Smith) are driving home in a buggy after the murder in the movie house;[13] at the very end when she has finally regained her speech; and, most memorably, when she, in a reverie, imagines herself dancing with Dr Parry in a flower-bedecked ballroom. Here the theme is turned into a sweeping waltz; it dissolves into an impressionistic haze of high strings and celesta surrounding a dim-focused reference to the *Lohengrin* Bridal March as, day-dreaming still as his bride to be, she comes downstairs arm-in-arm with Parry.

Musically, the most intricate sequence is the first. An audience (Helen included) is watching a flickering bioscope display to the piano accompaniment of Beethoven's *Pathétique* Sonata. The camera pans upward to the room above where a lame girl is changing her clothes; the piano can still be heard tinkling faintly in the distance. The girl goes to a closet and takes out a dress, and at this moment the 'commentative' orchestra enters unobtrusively in the same key as the 'realistic' piano. The murderer is lurking deep in the closet; the theremin theme towers above all as the camera plunges into the eye. Then the girl is struggling into her dress, her hands above her head. We focus on the hands, and only their sudden sickening claw-like gesticulations — together with the music — tell us she is being strangled. The music is the strangler! Then the end of the murder happens to coincide with the end of the movie downstairs: a good touch. We cut back, the orchestra disappears and the last few bars of the *Pathétique*'s first movement (piano only, of course) ends the scene.

In cases like this where violence is not explicitly stated

visually, the composer must explicitly state it musically. So, too, Helen being dumb, the music often has to speak for her, particularly in the suspense-ridden *dénouement* when she finds herself at the killer's mercy. After discovering Blanche's body she locks the professor's brother in the cellar, rushes up the spiral staircase and distractedly tries to telephone Dr Parry. She cannot, of course, because she cannot speak; and the music articulates her terror and frustration. Here Webb deals in harsh harmonies, nervous thrusting rhythms and sharp-shooting polyphonic lines, often moulded from distortions of Helen's theme. From here to the end, the music plays almost continuously, with one important exception. Professor Warren's pursuit of Helen is interrupted by the arrival of the local constable with a message from Dr Parry. The music cuts out as we see Helen at an upstairs window vainly trying to attract the constable's attention by battering on the pane. By this time a terrific storm is raging, and he mistakes the noise she is making for the sound of a gate banging. As a final desperate measure she hurls her lamp through the window-pane; but again to no avail. At this point the music puts in a dramatic, almost malignantly exultant reappearance, as if saying to us, 'That's it; there's no further hope for her; her destruction is inevitable' — and, of course, voicing Helen's unspoken (and unspeakable) thoughts to this effect.

Webb's most famous film was *Notorious* (1946), in François Truffaut's view the 'quintessence of Hitchcock'. Webb described his score as one of which he was 'very proud', and with good reason. He takes an original stance right from the first. Many Hollywood films of the period opened rhetorically, but in a bad sense: pompously and self-importantly. The *Notorious* score also begins rhetorically, but in a good sense: with a strong, meaningful dramatic gesture. The discordant trumpet alarms that announce the main titles are splendidly attention-getting, and the shapely love theme for American agent Devlin (Cary Grant) and his aide Alicia (Ingrid Bergman) is a fine lyrical inspiration. It is also a highly effectual musical *dramatis persona*. In the last scene, as Alicia lies in bed hopelessly enfeebled through the slow arsenic poisoning administered by Sebastian (Claude Rains) and his mother, the theme returns in a tortured chromatic guise. What the music tells us is that in her extremity of sickness and confusion her mind is full of Devlin, from whom she is estranged, and of their equivocal, tempestuous relationship. The same variant accompanies Devlin as he walks up the stairs of Sebastian's mansion to rescue Alicia and so deliver Sebastian to the questionable mercies of his fellow Nazis. The music speaks a truth that the lovers themselves are struggling not to recognize.

There is little music in the first half of the picture. The first significant cue comes when Devlin proves German-born Alicia to be an American patriot in spite of herself. He plays her a recording on which she is heard expressing deep abhorrence of her father's pro-Nazi, anti-American activities. Alicia, who has up to now aggressively resisted Devlin's request that she undertake a secret mission for the American authorities, is suddenly rendered defenceless. It is the music that, entering unobtrusively at this moment, helps us feel its significance and her emotion — as so often, it acts as the 'communicating link' between screen and audience. Were we actually in the same room as Alicia, we would have no need of any music to experience the emotion. As we are not, we need the music to help us, to create the missing dimension of reality.

In *Notorious*, Hitchcock hinges all his suspense scenes around two objects, the key to the wine cellar and the fake wine bottle; the music does the same, reinforcing the unity and simplicity that are the picture's great strength. After Alicia's marriage to Sebastian we are first aware of music when she discovers a locked closet and asks Joseph the valet for the key; and then again when she steals the key of the wine cellar from her husband's key-ring. Music enhances the expression in Sebastian's eyes when finding the missing key replaced confirms his suspicions; and there follows one of the most important musical sequences of all. Sebastian goes downstairs and lets himself into his wine cellar. At first everything seems to be in order, but then he notices first the stained sink, then the stained floor. Panic seizes him and he examines the row of bottles. 1937 . . . 1937 . . . 1937 . . . 1937 . . . then the bottle dated 1940 which Devlin had earlier substituted for the one he had accidentally broken. There is no dialogue: the drama is enacted solely by Claude Rains's actions, his facial expressions, and the music. The music must express what is passing through his mind, first as his suspicions are aroused, then when his worst fears are confirmed. It sustains the mood and follows him slowly through the deserted house still sunk in the half-light of dawn, up the staircase to his mother's room. Again it expresses his unspoken thoughts — that he is a ruined man, that he has betrayed his country, his mother and himself and that if he is found out he will pay for it with his life. It would be easy to assign Hitchcock and Rains all the credit for this magnificent piece of cinema and to forget that another crucial element is the music.

Eventually Alicia realizes that she is being poisoned through her coffee: she collapses and is taken upstairs to bed by her husband. The music powerfully enhances the tension through a repeated chromatic figure on tremolo strings. These tremolo strings are also the musical protagonists in the finale as Alicia, still in a state of drugged collapse, is helped downstairs by Devlin. The strings hang over the scene rather like a veil of bated breath, enveloping as much Sebastian and his mother and their terrified whispered conversation as Devlin and Alicia themselves. Then, as Sebastian walks back up the steps of his house to meet his nemesis at the hands of his fellow conspirators, the music swings to, like the huge front door, with an air of black and terrible finality.

In *Crossfire* (1947), one of the supreme achievements of RKO in the forties, much less music is employed than in *Notorious*, but not a note is wasted. It is a film about violence but not a violent film (it was in fact, the first American film to treat frankly the subject of anti-semitism). The violence is perpetrated not on the screen but in the introductory music. The main title is one of Webb's starkest. The first part is based on the *basso ostinato* principle with a recurrent eight-note bass figure battering its way through an electrically-charged full orchestra texture. Then half-way through the *ostinato* yields to a recurrent short sharp rhythmic idea for brass that almost assumes the character of a series of bullet-like fanfares. Webb does not fade out his title music — he brings it to a strident *fortissimo* conclusion, and there is powerful contrast between the violence of this music and that of the first scene (the murder of Sammy) which is played in shadow *without* music. The title music has given us a taste for blood; the shocked silence when the blood starts to flow is the more harrowing.

Thereafter commentative music is applied to two major sequences only. The first is when Mitchell, stricken as much by panic and confusion as nausea, staggers out of Sammy's apartment, leaving him alone with Monty (Robert Ryan) and Floyd. He regains the street and a music of string trills closes in on him suggesting as much the metaphorical fog in his mind as the literal fog in the street. The mood is abruptly shattered by the raucous blare of a jazz trumpeter flutter-tonguing in Ginny's (Gloria Grahame) nightclub. The second sequence is the montage of suspense that culminates in hunted Monty's decision to seek out Floyd (whom actually he has already killed, though he has been persuaded otherwise) and destroy him. As he lies on his bed the music has to tell us of the tormenting thoughts rampaging through his brain and of his eventual decision to snatch at the bait that (unknown to him) is being proffered by Inspector Finlay (Robert Young).

One sequence involves an original use of realistic music. Mitchell hides from the police in a cinema where a movie with music is playing. His friend Kesley (Robert Mitchum) brings him his wife (Jacqueline White) who protests her love for him and her faith in his innocence. In the cinema they are reconciled; and Webb artfully ensures that the music playing realistically for the movie in the theatre is at one and the same time playing commentatively for the real-life love scene. A final subtlety — and an in-joke — is that the music is in fact an extract from Webb's own *Enchanted Cottage* Concerto, which in the film of the same name was concerned with a different, though equally painful, husband/wife situation.

Fritz Lang's *Clash by Night* (1952) was another picture with an arresting main title and sparing use of music elsewhere. The former is a miniature tone–poem of the savage sea which Lang dwells on fascinatedly before embarking on the quasi-documentary montage that precedes the entry of the central character, Mae (Barbara Stanwyck). The music quietens gradually as the fury abates, and the opening scene — a calm sea, hundreds of fishing boats at anchor, flocks of seabirds settled in all directions — is beautifully evoked: high violins etch a distant horizon, the dark sonorous tone-quality of the cor anglais shades in colour in the foreground.

In 1948 Webb scored *The Window*, a film now recognized as a masterpiece. Much of it was shot on location in New York's East Side, and Webb's title music contrives a panoramic quality without (for once) Hollywood's mandatory reference to Gershwin — the mixed-in tone-qualities of saxophone and trumpet are quite evocative enough. It tells the story of the 'boy who cried wolf' — but from the boy's point of view (Bobby Driscol plays Tommy's part with remarkable clarity and insight). Webb's music contributes much to the success of director Ted Tetzlaff's attempt to understand the child's actions and motivations. There is a puckish humour in the music accompanying the opening children's sequence, and, later in Tommy's breathless run to the police station: we can hear the composer entering the child's mind as the music comments on his sudden loss of heart when confronted by the intimidating facade of the station building. In the fire escape sequence the music first conjures up the oppressive heat of the New York night (which Webb, as a native New Yorker, knew well) and then, as Tommy seeks cooler sanctuary outside the Kellersons' apartment, the music enables us to share the boy's perceptions. It continues until Tommy becomes aware through the half-drawn blind that something unusual is happening inside the Kellersons' apartment — then it is slowly faded out, just as the outside world withdraws from his consciousness as he becomes intent only on what the camera is concentrating on. A simple device, but this is how film music works.

Pictures such as George Stevens's *I Remember Mama* (1948), John Cromwell's *The Enchanted Cottage* (1945), and *Rachel and the Stranger* (1948) appealed to a warmly romantic, even sentimental streak in Webb's nature. The framework of *The Enchanted Cottage* (after a play by Pinero) is musical in the first instance — an elderly blind composer (Herbert Marshall) invites some friends to hear his latest composition, a tone–poem for piano and orchestra inspired by two young friends of his (Robert Young and Dorothy Maguire) who have found love in the 'enchanted cottage'. Young returns badly disfigured and embittered from the war; Maguire is frowsy and unattractive. Yet through the spell of the cottage with its centuries-long tradition of happy love-struck honeymooners, they find beauty in each other's eyes, and mutual fulfilment. It is, of course, the music's business to create this enchanted, transfigured atmosphere, for music's powers of *evocation*, of making the invisible and intangible a powerful, sensible force, are unrivalled. Nowhere is this better demonstrated than in the early scene when Dorothy Maguire is left alone in the cottage for the first time. Music floods the scene like a dreamy reminiscence of bygone days and brings the haunted atmosphere to life. Webb was clearly moved by the film — as well he might be, for it is beautifully realized — and suffuses it with warmth and tenderness; the main theme itself is singularly lovely. In *I Remember Mama* the music adds a powerful emotional dimension to this story of homely, family love and life set amid expatriate Norwegians in San Francisco at the turn of the century. Again, too, the film is good, and brought out good qualities in the composer — warmth, tenderness and humour (a delightful cameo for the arrival of the two aunts). The picture opens musically not (as per convention) with a pompous fanfare but in a burst of radiance, and closes not (as per convention) with a bombastic *fortissimo* but drifts out in an exquisitely-graduated *pianissimo* as Katrina's narration comes to an end and mists of time close in on the night-bound city. Also interesting — but in a totally negative way — are the various signs of meddling on the part of director George Stevens: music dubbed so low as to be practically inaudible (and therefore distracting, better deleted) on some scenes, some music drafted into the picture from other sources (still Webb's, perhaps, but stylistically incompatible with the simplicity he cultivates in this score), various awkwardnesses emphatically not represented in the composer's autograph. Other composers, notably Waxman (*A Place in the Sun*), and Newman (*The Greatest Story Ever Told*) were to encounter serious problems with Stevens, and it seems a pity that so gifted a director should have been musically fallible.

Webb's music for *Rachel and the Stranger* — a story of life in the Northwest Territory in early pioneering days — has a formal clarity, an easy melodic grace at one moment folksy and unsophisticated, at another quasi-classical in complexion. The orchestral textures are simple and clear-cut, reflecting the tenor of the Daveys' day-to-day life in unspoilt natural surroundings. Sentimentality or knowingness in the music could easily have thrown the delicate machinery of the picture out of gear. Only brief moments of natural splendour, such as winter dissolving suddenly into spring amid much breaking up of ice floes in the mountain torrents and a sunset over the hills, are scored in a lush romantic manner. The result of this simplicity and restraint is that the two occasions on which the full symphony orchestra and an uncompromisingly contemporary idiom *are* brought into play — first when Rachel (Loretta Young) shoots the panther, then the Shawnees' burning of the Daveys' home — are thrown strikingly into relief.

When RKO was disbanded in 1955 Webb continued to work as a free-lance; and, happily, one of his post-RKO pictures turned out to be one of the biggest successes of the fifties, and Webb's last major score. This was *Marty* (1955). The screenplay by Paddy Chayevsky is about two ordinary people in New York who fear being lonely and unloved — an unprepossessing though sensitive butcher resigned to bachelorhood (Ernest Borgnine), and a schoolteacher equally resigned to spinsterhood (Betsy Blair). The music discreetly and sympathetically 'shadows' their relationship. The 'happy ending' is disclosed during the main title in the form of Harry Warren's cheerful theme song 'Marty' heard instrumentally; this now becomes the basis of the score but acquires lyrics only for the end title when a men's chorus joins the orchestra. Webb's use of it in the interim is worth examining.

Constant pressure is put upon Marty by his mother to get married, and little is needed to exacerbate his awareness of his own loneliness and unattractiveness. He and his mother receive a visit from his cousin and his wife, the purpose of which is to dispose of a troublesome relative in their direction. After they have gone music enters to voice Marty's unspoken thoughts; 'My cousin is happily married — but I am not.' However, there is no bitterness or envy in Marty's heart, just sadness, and this the music underlines. Then Marty phones a girl acquaintance in the hope of fixing a date, and is given a polite brush-off. Again the music, musing wistfully around fragments of the theme song as he sits down at table with his mother, makes us feel how deeply he has been hurt, and helps us sympathize.

Ever hopeful, Marty goes the same night to the Stardust Ballroom. There he meets Clara; and, as he first makes contact through asking her for a dance, the band which up to now has been playing various popular tunes in period jazz arrangements imperceptibly moves into the 'Marty' theme in a similar guise. The music continues to mark the various stages in their relationship: Clara's advice to Marty to buy the butcher's shop (which marks the beginning of a true intimacy), and as they stroll through the New York streets (no dialogue) the music comments on their feeling for one another; harp and solo cor anglais sing with the leaves on the street trees waving in the breeze as they walk homeward (Webb always composed well for pictures set in his home town).

Music plays gently under the love scene that follows, easing and warming the atmosphere, shading the varying nuances of feeling (e.g. when Marty falters in mid-sentence the music says for him what he cannot say himself) rising to an expressively tender climax at the first kiss. In fact the music acts almost as a benevolent unseen presence through whose agency we are permitted to eavesdrop on very intimate and personal scenes. Marty sees his girl home, and as she goes dreamily upstairs the music reflects her rapt mood. Then we see the hero of the hour swaggering home triumphant, hands thrust deep into trouser pockets and swinging his legs; he knocks into a bus stop, dances over the street to hail a cab and is nearly run down in the process. The music communicates all his new-found glee and exhilaration; the climax with its unexpected final chord is splendid.

For a complete account of Webb's career many other pictures and isolated sequences would need to be discussed, e.g. the enormous score for *Mighty Joe Young* reminiscent of Steiner; Anna's flight in *Hitler's Children*; the oriental-romantic *Sinbad the Sailor*; the tiger-fish music in *The Americano*; the eloquent music for Robert Mitchum and the deaf-mute garage hand at the end of the now-celebrated *Out of the Past (Build My Gallows High)*; the spectacular watermill music of *They Won't Believe Me*, the film's dramatic crux; the brilliant, quasi-phantasmagorical treatment of 'Here comes the Bride' in the end-climax of *The Locket*, a a real melodramatic *tour de force*. Webb was immensely prolific. In the final analysis he was one of that band of sound, versatile and sensitive craftsmen who went about their business not in any way conscious of posterity, still less of claiming any special credit for the work they produced. They simply had a job to do and they did it to the best of their ability. Webb was a shy, gentle man, modest and self-effacing to a fault; but the quality of his best work can compare favourably with that of many of his more fêted colleagues.

NOTES

1 In fact copies of most of Webb's scores are preserved in the RKO Archives in Hollywood, including *Enchanted Cottage*.

2 Constantin Bakaleinikoff (1898–1967), head of the RKO Music Department, 1941–55. He receives credit as 'Musical Director' on most of Webb's pictures, and generally shared the conducting with the composer. Webb explained in a later letter, 'I conducted those sequences which were important to me.'

3 Kenneth later became a writer and advertising executive in Hollywood, the most famous film on which he worked being the Astaire-Rogers *Gay Divorcee* (1933). He died in 1966.

4 Some of the music originated in the 1940 *Stranger on the Third Floor*, an expressionistic exercise in paranoia set almost exclusively in the urban night-jungle. The music — Webb the urban night owl in his element — contributes materially to the feeling of claustrophobic, clammy fright.

5 This motif is re-used to identical effect in a scene in Val Lewton's *The Seventh Victim* when the private detective emerges from the room he has been investigating in the cosmetics company and is murdered.

6 *Focus on Film* no. 7, p. 53.

7 *Val Lewton: the Reality of Terror* (London 1972).

8 For an absorbing account of an expert Hollywood musician whose speciality was a more conventional type of horror music, see Preston Jones, 'The Ghost of Hans J. Salter', *Cinéfantastique* vol. 7 no. 2 (1978), pp. 10–25.

9 All these vulgar lurid titles — *I Walked with a Zombie, The Body*

Snatcher, etc. — were forced on Lewton by RKO executives and in no way represent the nature of the films themselves.

10   This traditional tune was also made playful use of by Debussy in 'Jardins sous la pluie' (the third of his *Estampes* for piano), and also in the piece in *Children's Corner* entitled 'Jimbo's Lullaby'.

11   This, like most other RKO films of the period, begins with Webb's RKO Wartime Fanfare, a paraphrase on the 'V for Victory' motif of Beethoven's Fifth Symphony.

12   Technically, Rózsa was first with *Spellbound* (1945), but interest in the instrument was obviously prevalent in Hollywood at this time.

13   Something of an unsolved mystery attaches itself to this melody, since in this very scene Parry hums it to Helen (the orchestra pausing discreetly in a suitable key) and then asks her if she knows the words — implying that it is a popular song. Whether or not she does know them, *we* today certainly do not, nor are we enlightened later in the picture. Most probably an earlier, explanatory scene has been cut.

MIKLÓS RÓZSA

Miklós Rózsa is the complete professional, and without doubt
one of the great musicians of our time. Displays of 'artistic'
temperament, pretentious 'behaviour' and all the other
stratagems by which lesser men seek to draw attention
to their talents, play no part in his scheme of things
— although he has his own way of dealing with them when he
encounters them in others. His concern is with getting the job
done as efficiently as possible. In a professional relationship
he can be a stern taskmaster, but the demands he makes on
others are always exceeded by those he makes on himself. He
thinks and feels naturally through his instruments, and insists
on the closest possible relation between what is in his head
and what goes down on paper. He hates trivial technical talk,
amateurs and *poseurs*. He makes no parade of his knowledge,
but he *knows*, and views his art in the wider perspective in
which cultured Europeans of his generation grew steeped. As
the late Bronislau Kaper (composer of *Red Badge of Courage,
Lili* and *Mutiny on the Bounty*) put it: 'Rózsa as a composer,
historian and art collector represents a sadly vanishing
generation of the highest culture and professionalism.' Other
friends have remarked on the other aspects of Rózsa's

character: courtesy, charm and elegance of manner; kindness, generosity and loyalty (friendship for him is sacred); nor should we forget his ready but never cutting wit and his renowned abilities as a raconteur. But let me emphasize the plainness and simplicity which is a feature of both the man and his music and which, I believe, is a concomitant of greatness.

Rózsa was born in 1907 in Budapest. His father was a land-owning industrialist with a country estate at the foot of the Mátra mountains in Northern Hungary. There Rózsa was exposed at first hand to the authentic Hungarian peasant music, folksong sung by the village people at work in the fields, in the home, at festivities: real folksong — not the pseudo-Hungarian gipsified folk-music represented by the Liszt Rhapsodies and the Brahms Hungarian Dances. This music, strong in expression and fascinating rhythmically, preoccupied young Rózsa and was to exercise a controlling influence over his musical development.

The two pioneers of folksong collecting in Hungary were Béla Bartók and Zoltán Kodály, and Rózsa's interest in their activities might have led him to enrol as a pupil of the latter. But he disliked the musical atmosphere in Budapest and elected instead to study at the Leipzig Conservatory. He was a brilliant student and in 1929 received his diplomas *cum laude*.

In 1932 Rózsa moved to Paris where he lived for three years, during which time he enjoyed his first international success. The *Theme, Variations and Finale* op.13[1] was premiered at Duisburg in 1934, whereafter it received many performances in Europe and later America. In 1935 Rózsa went to London and wrote a ballet, *Hungaria*, for the Markova-Dolin company. One of those who went to see it was the film director Jacques Feyder. He liked what he heard and invited Rózsa to write the music for his next picture, *Knight without Armour*, which he was directing for Rózsa's fellow-expatriate, Sir Alexander Korda. The score was much admired and the composer was put under contract to London Film Productions.

In 1938 Rózsa's score for *The Four Feathers* was well received internationally, and when in 1939, following the outbreak of war, Korda was obliged to transplant the entire production corps of *The Thief of Bagdad* to Hollywood, Rózsa accompanied them to finish composing the music. There being little incentive to return to wartime Britain, Rózsa decided to stay in Hollywood. During and just after the war he worked chiefly for Paramount, United Artists and Universal, but in 1949 he joined the music department of MGM, where he remained until his contract expired in 1961. He won the Academy Award three times — for *Spellbound* (1945), *A Double Life* (1948) and for *Ben-Hur* (1959). He always devoted a part of each year to non-film music. His *Three Hungarian Sketches* were acclaimed at their 1938 Baden-Baden premiere, and of his later works the Concerto for Strings (1943), the Piano Sonata (1949) and the Violin Concerto (1953, composed for, premiered and recorded by Jascha Heifetz) are among the most important. Of recent years he has written less for films and more for himself, notably four more concertos (piano, cello, violin-and-cello, viola), a *Tripartita* for orchestra, a second String Quartet, and a series of sonatas for unaccompanied instruments. However classical in conception his concert works may be Rózsa is fundamentally romantic, and his film work has emphasized this aspect of his musical personality. It has in no way done violence to his style, which was set long before he came to films, but has merely drawn out its latent lyrical qualities. Rózsa's is no ordinary romanticism. His lyricism is strong, intense and elegiac. Its basis is Magyar peasant lamentation, intensified through personal involvement. For Rózsa has been in exile for over fifty years; in August 1974 he set foot on Hungarian soil for the first time since the early 1930s. Yet in his music he has never ceased to sing of his homeland; and his music really does *sing* because of its origins in the archetypal melodic formations of folksong. Rózsa states in his autobiography, *Double Life*: 'I have always tried in my work to express human feelings, assert human values . . . tonality means line; line means melody; melody means song, and song, especially folksong, is the essence of music because it is the natural, spontaneous and primordial expression of human emotion.' So perhaps Rózsa's folksong orientation brings him into more basic and immediate contact with human drama; perhaps this accounts for his music's special input in a film context, the special intensity of response it often appears to invoke.

Rózsa gives of himself unsparingly in his music. Pain and compassion are voiced eloquently. His melody is now rhetorical, now intimate, but essentially alien to the world of commercial romanticism, except when it has to be (e.g. *The Strange Love of Martha Ivers*); but his muse is essentially tragic. In 1951 he scored *The Light Touch*; ironically, because lightness of touch is one quality his music has never possessed in abundance. We do not look for the best of Rózsa in *The Divorce of Lady X* (1938), *Ten Days in Paris* (1939), *Lady on a Train* (1945) or *Adam's Rib* (1949), although each has its attractive moments. Rather do we find it in Bogart's compassion for the Italian prisoner Giuseppe in *Sahara* (1943); the farewells of Emma and Nelson in *That Hamilton Woman* (1941; UK title *Lady Hamilton*); Peter Lawford's anguish at seeing the girl he loves hauled away in a cartload of prisoners destined for repatriation to Soviet Russia in *The Red Danube* (1949); the two lovers whose brief but passion-filled existence amid the ruins of war-torn Berlin in *A Time to Love and a Time to Die* (1958) ends in tragedy; the lepers' search for the Christ in *Ben-Hur* (1959); the healing of the lame boy in *King of Kings* (1961).

Rózsa needed a number of years to adjust himself to the exigencies of the film medium, and there are early occasions (e.g. in *The Squeaker* [1937; UK title *Murder on Diamond Row*]) where, doubtless for safety's sake, he sacrifices individuality to movie-making convention. However, there are many fine moments in nearly all the early Korda scores, notably in *Knight without Armour*, Rózsa's first film. James Hilton's novel was the source for this evocative portrait of post-revolutionary Russia in which Robert Donat plays an English translator who becomes involved in the Revolution, falls in love with a Countess (Marlene Dietrich) and helps her to escape. The score called for authentic Russian folk-

The Naked City: finale

Miklós Rózsa

material, and Rózsa spent much time studying it. However, his advantage here was that his own idiom, having been fired by Hungarian folk music, was well-equipped creatively to assimilate elements from other folkcultures. For instance, in the scene in the Siberian convict settlement where Fothergill (Donat) is confined during the war, the melancholy cor anglais theme sounds like an authentic Russian folksong: Rózsa cannot now remember if it is, or if it is a melody of his own. His dramatic instinct is revealed in the scene where Dietrich, dispossessed by the Revolution, bravely confronts a pack of power-drunk, revenge-hungry peasants in the grounds of her estate; and in the first of Rózsa's great screen love scenes. Fothergill escorts the Countess Alexandra to Petrograd, and *en route* they are obliged to spend the night in the deserted railway-station of Saratursk. To beguile the time they recite poetry to each other: he, as the love theme sings first on a solo cello, then rises through all strings, chooses lines from Browning; then a plaintive Russian folk tune for two clarinets takes over as Alexandra quotes from a Russian poem:

> I have grown weary of my little dreams
> And have outlived the hour of my desire. . .

The music floods the scene with warmth and sweetness. The actors are good, but the music makes them seem even better (a real asset, of course, when the actors are not good).

The Four Feathers (1938) contains an important musical sequence in which Ralph Richardson, scouting for some enemy dervishes in the Sudan, loses his sunhat and kerchief and is blinded by sunstroke; but a notable characteristic of these scores of the late 1930s is the paucity of music employed. In fact, in *The Four Feathers*, *The Spy in Black* (1939) and *On the Night of the Fire* (1939), there are long sequences where we feel the absence of music. No such criticism can however be made of the masterpiece of Rózsa's early period, *The Thief of Bagdad*. All Rózsa's Korda scores have an aura about them; but none glows more radiantly than this one. *The Thief of Bagdad* has a wonderful freshness and agelessness, a childlike spirit of enchantment and wonder. It must be a part of everyone's cinémusical past. It glimmers in our consciousness like a fairy castle in the distance: 'This is the land of legend, where everything is possible when seen through the eyes of a child. We are the remnant of a Golden Age, before men ceased to believe in the beauty of the impossible' — the words of the Old King in the Golden Tent scene. Rózsa brings to life the Land of Long Ago as it is 'seen through the eyes of a child'.

An important visual stimulus was the sets and art direction of Vincent Korda[2], which in their stylized evocation of Arabian fantasy are in perfect accord with the musical fantasy of the score. Another collaborator on the picture was Sir Robert (later Lord) Vansittart, eminent diplomat and spare-time poet, who provided the lyrics for the songs.[3] All three elements contribute to the opening scenes. The fanfares of the title music represent Prince Achmad (John Justin) in his regal capacity, but then the same phrase blossoms into a full-hearted lyrical melody — the song of Achmad the lover. We plunge into a tumult of excitement as a galley with rust-red sails cleaves its way into Basra harbour through a blue-green sea. This galley belongs to Jaffar, the villainous Vizier (Conrad Veidt), whose tritone-based theme shortly comes into prominence. Sailors are heard singing at their work, and one of them tells of his love for the sea with its blessed freedom from human contact.

Abu, the little thief (played by Sabu) is introduced in a brilliant scherzo-like episode: in the busy market place of Bagdad, he profits from the general preoccupation with buying and selling by stealing and evading his pursuers at every turn. This borders close on cartoon territory, and the music is obliged to illustrate each detail of the action (the xylophone clattering nimbly up and down flights of stone steps is a nice touch). The director originally wanted to record the action to the music, with the actors moving in strict synchronization to the pre-composed score. The results were chaotic, and after days of work the sequence was re-shot and the music fitted to the filmed action.

A striking feature of *The Thief of Bagdad* is its range of orchestral colour.[4] Much of the scoring is cast in the Franco-Russian-Oriental tradition of Rimsky-Korsakov's *Sheherazade* and Stravinsky's *Firebird*, an idiom which Rózsa handles with great skill. The Princess (June Duprez) enters to the strains of a delicately-scored *marche orientale*, preceded by an extended stereophonic alarum for brass and drums which sends the whole of Basra scurrying for shelter (the penalty for looking on her is death). She comes into view on a pink elephant: Achmad sees her: the love theme swells and makes the characters real people. A similar translation from fairy-tale to romance is achieved in the pool scene: in the shimmering noonday heat the Princess rocks in a kind of suspended divan whose swaying is exquisitely synchronized with the dove-like humming of the female chorus, while an old nurse (Adelaide Hall, a favourite Duke Ellington vocalist) sings a love song which must rank as one of Rózsa's most beautiful inspirations. Suddenly all scatter to seek the freshness of the pool. Achmad's reflection appears in the surface and he is taken for a *djinn*. Alone with the Princess he declares himself, and they vow eternal love one to another, the banalities of their dialogue being transformed by Rózsa's music into the language of Romeo and Juliet.

Other 'magic' elements bring Rózsa's orchestral imagination alive. One famous sequence is the Flying Horse Galop. The Old Sultan (Miles Malleson) is an avid collector of toys, and we see his collection being put through its paces in a section fastidiously scored for chimes, marimba, glockenspiel, harp, celesta and *pizzicato* strings. Jaffar, to humour the old man, has brought him what he knows will be an irresistible addition: a clockwork horse which, when wound up, comes alive and flies like Pegasus. After the winding of the horse (flute, clarinet and rattle), the Sultan's aerial tour of Basra begins — a feast of melodic and colouristic delights, with an original effect in the whinnying of the horns as the animal's motor runs down. Here, as in the later animated sequence in which the multi-armed Silvermaid stabs the old

King to death, the action directly depends on, and is articulated by, the music.[5]

A broader spectrum is displayed in the storm-at-sea scene. Jaffar has abducted the Princess and is taking her back to Bagdad by boat. During the voyage he espies Achmad and Abu in pursuit on a tiny raft, and summons a mighty tempest to shipwreck them. The music — always founded on Jaffar's theme with its 'diabolic' tritones — depicts the fury of the elements with graphic realism: the howling winds, the first few drops of rain, thunder and lightning, pandemonium. A climax yields to a sudden calm: Abu is washed up alone on an unknown beach. This scene was photographed around Tintagel in Cornwall, and Rózsa's music enhances its visual beauty in a changing play of colour and light. On the beach Abu finds a bottle containing a *djinn* imprisoned by King Solomon; when released he can expand to monstrous proportions, but can also retract to the size of an insect. He performs both feats for Abu's benefit, and both are realized in the music. Then the *djinn* tells Abu of 'the highest mountain of the world, where earth meets the sky', to which they must fly. The music accompanying their flight (with wordless choir) suggests awe and vastness. The backgrounds were shot on location in the Grand Canyon, one of the mightiest spectacles in the world; no wonder Rózsa was moved to compose music of quasi-visionary splendour.

The longest single musical sequence depicts Abu in the skeleton room with its mouldering remains of previous intruders (xylophone and celesta); his death-defying duel with the monster spider, an orchestral *tour de force* in which every department is called upon to give a virtuoso performance as if in emulation of Abu's efforts. Rózsa's particular gift for depicting animals in music, already glimpsed in the flying horse scene, is much in evidence here and was later to enhance his scores for *The Jungle Book* and *Jacaré* (both 1942), *The Lost Weekend* (1946) and others. After Abu's victory (with the spider hurtling chromatically to his doom) and, finally, his wresting of the all-seeing eye from the Goddess of Light, Abu's theme is free to soar amid flickering trills and tremolos until a monumental climax, the film's turning-point, is reached with the entry of the great gongs and the wordless men's choir.

Rózsa calls upon another set of colours in the Golden Tent scene. Transported to a land of infinite shining distances, Abu is acclaimed by white-bearded patriarchs as the Messianic innocent who can regenerate them. Spread harp and celesta chords accompany the old King's discourse, and the floating melismas of the female chorus (derived from Abu's theme) add their own dimension of magic timelessness. Here the music is suffused with a quality which Elmer Bernstein has called 'unsophisticated mysticism'.

The Korda films assured the success of Rózsa as film-composer, and his vein of exotic fantasy was once again successfully mined in *The Jungle Book* (which has survived in the form of a concert piece for narrator and orchestra, first recorded by Sabu — the first commercial recording of an American film score). *Lydia* and *Lady Hamilton* (both 1941) have a youthful exuberance and ardour which largely disappears as Rózsa's music grows older, stronger and more individual. By the time of the two Billy Wilder classics — *Double Indemnity* (1944) and *The Lost Weekend* (1946) — a new maturity is in focus. The startlingly new subject matter of these films demanded a complete change of style from fairy-tale romance.

Rózsa's work in *film noir* and in 'psychological melodrama' was innovatory. *Double Indemnity*, with its many asperities of harmony and texture, brought the wrath of the studio's musical director down upon the composer's head; for the former café violinist a G natural clashing with a G sharp one octave below constituted a dissonance of the type which had no place in a movie studio. Fortunately director Billy Wilder and the then head of Paramount, Buddy de Silva, disagreed, and a major musical breakthrough was accomplished.

Both the form of the titles and the music which accompanies them are unorthodox. A limping man moves slowly towards the camera and into ever clearer focus. The main theme is immediately identified with this figure, who turns out to be the man whom Walter Neff (Fred MacMurray) first murders and then impersonates. It is recognizably a Rózsa theme, stark and angular with bitter harmonic clashes. During the titles it is played by the horns and trombones in octaves to lugubrious and ominous effect, and underpinned by a steady, almost funereal drum-beat synchronized with the dragging steps of the limping figure. Music and picture have joined forces to pose a question for the answer to which we are kept on the alert.

At the end of the titles the music explodes in an aural complement to the neon lights and panoramic surge of the Los Angeles night-scene. Here Rózsa fuses a chaotic impression of big-city nightlife with Neff's inner turmoil as he drags himself to his office to make his confession. The main theme with its steady pulse returns and underlines the whole montage — Neff enters the building, mounts the stairs, looks at the huge open-plan office, enters his own office and begins to speak into the dictaphone. At this point the flashback begins and the main theme gives way to a running figure for strings which is to characterize each of Neff's narrations and so help move the drama on. This motif is neutral in character, in contrast to the main theme which returns at peak moments of tension — notably when Neff first realizes how inextricably he has been caught within Phyllis Dietrichson's (Barbara Stanwyck) web of intrigue — 'the machine had started to move and nothing could stop it'. After Mr Dietrichson has metaphorically signed his own death-warrant in the form of what he believes to be a motor accident insurance policy, and when Phyllis assures Walter over the phone that she has been able to arrange the murder in accordance with their plans, this theme is given so rancid a harmonization as to impress upon us the full force of her evil. Music of this kind is never associated with Neff himself; Rózsa emphasizes the fact that it is Phyllis who is vicious, cold-blooded and almost devoid of human feeling, both here and in the scene where Walter is breaking her husband's neck in the back of the car. We do not see the murder, the camera fixes on Phyllis's face throughout its duration, and the music freezes on a dissonant unresolved chord which helps us to implant the close-up in our memory and to refer back to it when Lola tells of the look on her stepmother's face both when she had very nearly succeeded in murdering her husband's first wife and when, in gleeful anticipation of her husband's death, she was trying on a black veil in front of a mirror. In these and similar passages we receive intimations of how Rózsa's film-style is to approximate to his concert-hall style in later *films noirs*.

Charles Higham has stated that *Double Indemnity* is a film 'without a single trace of pity or love'. This is not strictly true since there are at least two such moments, both enhanced by music. When, during the *dénouement*, Phyllis pulls a gun on Walter in a darkened room, she wounds him but is unable to fire a second time to kill him; they embrace, and as they do so their love theme, which hitherto has been merely hovering rather uncertainly in the background, comes in on a solo cello and then blossoms for the first time — but tragically, for at the height of their embrace Walter shoots Phyllis with the gun he has just taken from her hand. The second moment is at the end, when Barton Keyes (Edward G. Robinson) lights a cigarette for Neff, who is lying helpless on the floor like a wounded animal, and assures him of his genuine sympathy. The music builds the main theme over its drumbeat to a climax and ends the picture in a way that intensifies the audience's feeling of sympathy.

The Lost Weekend, a realistic study of alcoholism, was one of Wilder's and Rózsa's best films. Throughout we can sense Rózsa's involvement — he feels the pity of Don Birnam's (Ray Milland) mania for drink, his creative paralysis, the depths of degradation to which he falls. The main theme embraces the starkness of the tragedy: hard outlines and harsh monochrome scoring to match. The theme develops in an impassioned soaring manner but the first phrase always returns to clamp down and hold the victim fast in his prison. After the titles euphonious and lyrical music tracks with the camera across the New York skyline, but as we fix upon

Birnam's bottle dangling by a cord outside his window the weirdly ululating theremin contaminates the scene with a new theme associated with Birnam's craving for alcohol. The theremin twists and turns it chromatically so as to suggest a loss of equilibrium, and variations and elaborations on this insidious motif grow to control the score, just as Birnam's passion for liquor controls him. They underline the hopelessness of his efforts and the distemper of his mind. A graphic demonstration is when Birnam sits down in front of his typewriter and attempts to write; a low flute with a nagging muted brass rhythm in the background comments on his lack of success. Then he remembers that he has hidden a bottle somewhere in the flat but has no idea exactly where. He starts to search frantically, and the alcohol theme with theremin and a crazily-rolling *ostinato* above it mirrors his increasing desperation. He turns the apartment upside-down to no avail; and as he finally collapses into an armchair in an abyss of despondency the music reaches a climax with a drunkenly-distorted trumpet variant of the alcohol theme and a snare-drum rhythm which hammers and bites like a toothache or migraine.

The most powerful scene musically is that in which Birnam trudges along New York's Third Avenue with his typewriter and finds every pawnshop he comes to shut and barred — it is Yom Kippur, a Jewish holiday. Rózsa's music is a *via dolorosa* of mounting anguish and despair. Starting with the main theme, it conjures up the big-city ambience — the unending soulless streets, the steely, tawdry magnificence of the skyscrapers and overhead bridges, the midday sun beating mercilessly down. But it also synthesizes these impressions with Birnam's agony of mind and body as the alcohol theme takes over and overwhelms the orchestra. In other words, the music intensifies both what is clearly visible on the screen and what is not: it is at one and the same time illustrative and interpretative, as it is in the scene where Birnam is assailed by *delirium tremens*. Here the music both characterizes the giant bats and the rat he thinks he sees in his room and points his terror-stricken reactions to them.

Movingly handled too is the final scene where, as in the beginning, the camera tracks across the impassive stare of the skyline. The music here has the spacious lyrical feeling of the *Naked City* finale: 'And out there, in that great big concrete jungle, I wonder how many others there are like me, poor bedevilled guys on fire with thirst — such comical figures to the rest of the world as they stagger blindly towards another binge, another bender, another spree.' These are Birnam's final words, and from them the music takes its cue as it closes the picture on a compassionate, distressful yet optimistic note.

The theremin was first heard on a motion-picture soundtrack in Hitchcock's *Spellbound* (1945). Hitchcock asked the composer for a special sound for Gregory Peck's amnesia-paranoia, a tone-quality that would impress itself upon the audience by virtue of its unfamiliarity. Rózsa hit on the theremin, the exact musical complement, in fact, of the dream-sequences designed by Salvador Dali. Hitchcock said he wanted Dali to do the dreams because of the architectural sharpness of his work; the theremin has a vertiginous, swooning quality which well suggests a dream-like ambience, but it is also able to articulate a melodic line with great clarity. The four dream-sequences with the theremin contain some of the best music in the picture.

We are made familiar with the theremin and its theme within the first few seconds of the main title, after the Selznick trademark music.[6] It then recurs dramatically for every manifestation of Dr Edwardes's (Gregory Peck) obsession with the colour white: when he is upset by Constance (Ingrid Bergman) drawing lines with her fork on a white tablecloth, when his eyes catch her white dressing-gown and — the tensest scene of all — when he is distracted from his shaving by the colour of the washbasin, goes in and stands beside the sleeping Constance with an open razor in his hand, then downstairs to where her former professor (Michael Chekhov) is asleep in a chair. The music, with the chromatic theremin theme thrown into strong relief by the nervous snare-drum figure, symbolizes the inscrutable force which controls him.

The love theme for Peck and Bergman is associated

with one of the loveliest moments in Hitchcock: the opening of the doors following upon Peck's and Bergman's first kiss. Earlier, Constance has discovered she cannot sleep, and the love theme on a solo cello has told us it is for thinking of Edwardes. The theme flares up when she sees the light under his door; but rarely does Rózsa wear his heart on his sleeve so unreservedly as in the burst of technicolour musical glory with which he spotlights the climax, the opening of the doors. 'Cymbals!' ordered producer David O. Selznick, which Rózsa interpreted figuratively rather than literally. A subsidiary theme has a warm simplicity intended no doubt to serve as a foil to the voluptuousness of its companion; as Gregory Peck comes into the restaurant where Bergman is dining with her colleagues and sees her for the first time, this secondary theme makes us feel 'the light of her eyes into his life/smite of a sudden' even before the camera takes them both in together. We sense their eyes meeting in love at first sight even while only Peck's face is on the screen (Hitchcock found this music intrusive). Later, on the hair-raising ski-ride in Gabriel Valley which serves to reveal the source of Peck's guilt-complex, the (original) music's concern is to underline his quasi-murderous feelings towards Bergman, which seem to be gathering momentum as they hurtle down the slope together;[7] and in the moving group of shadow-shots following Peck's arrest, the music is full of compassion and mercy.

After the enormous success of *Spellbound* and, the next year, *The Lost Weekend*, the composer was 'typed': 'Call Rózsa, he's the one for nuts!' A crop of similar films came his way, all somehow related to the 'psychological melodrama' genre, among them *The Strange Love of Martha Ivers* (1946), *The Macomber Affair* (1947) and *Kiss the Blood off my Hands* (1948). The two best scores are those for *The Red House* (1947) and *The Secret Beyond the Door* (1948). In the latter Rózsa collaborated with Fritz Lang — a true collaboration in that composer and director were careful to plan each scene with a view to avoiding all unnecessary duplication between music and picture. Lang told Rózsa that when Michael Redgrave displays his weird collection of murder rooms for his guests, he would like to have something unusual on the soundtrack.[8] By this time Rózsa's audience had become inured to the sound of the theremin, so that was discounted. Then Lang remarked that whenever a soundtrack was run backwards in the projection room the result was always unnerving; and this gave Rózsa the idea of writing his music for this sequence in the usual way but then to have it copied backwards for each member of the orchestra and to record it in this form. If the recording thus obtained were then to be *played* backwards, the music would come out forwards — i.e. as it had been originally written, but somehow unnatural. This was long before the days of electronic music and *musique concrète*, when such techniques became common practice, and the idea caused unimaginable confusion in rehearsal; but Lang, it seems, enjoyed himself hugely.[9]

It was a natural transition from such films to the gangster melodramas which dominated Rózsa's career in the late forties,[10] several of them belonging to the *film noir* genre. *The Killers* (1946) was one of a trilogy of underworld dramas produced by Mark Hellinger for which his friend Rózsa wrote the music, the other two being *Brute Force* (1947) and *The Naked City* (1948). Today, films with an urban or metropolitan setting usually attract a jazz-based score, but in Hollywood films of the 1940s the expressive norm was still the standard symphony orchestra; though Rózsa, remaining within the confines of a glossy, basically 19th–century medium, produces from it a very 20th–century sound. The music is heavily scored and the dynamic idiom of concert works such as the Concerto for Strings (1943), with its hammer-blows of accents and splintered rhythms, is called into play. It is music of the asphalt jungle, impartially and professionally brutal, evoking a dark, tortured and delirious world whose rawness is rarely tempered by display of human feelings.[11] The overtures both to *The Killers* and *Brute Force* are typical; jagged rhythms, sharp accents, pulsating *ostinati*, bitonal harm-ony, flurried snatches of theme, iron textures, repetitive figures and phrases. Utterly characteristic is the opening sequence of *The Killers* which (like that of *The Asphalt Jungle*) is propelled solely by the music. A boy is seen running through the dark streets of the town to warn the doomed man, Swede (Burt Lancaster) at his rooming-house. The music creates a feeling of havoc, panic and imminent disaster. Swede remains smoking in the darkness, stoically indifferent to the boy's pleas that he should escape. Now the music tells us that the killers are approaching: a sustained, dissonant chord, prolonged almost to breaking-point. Since we know that the dissonance cannot last, that something must happen to break the tension, the suspense achieved so simply is impressive. Yet in all these underworld films there are moments of lyrical relaxation whose cool elegiac beauty is the more affecting for the hot neurotic violence of the prevailing musical temper — Swede's nocturnal musings in the penitentiary in *The Killers*, the flashbacks in *Brute Force* and the *Naked City* finale.

The Naked City was Hellinger's last film, and the composing was shared between Rózsa and Frank Skinner. The story goes that on the day before his death Hellinger, aghast at an earlier score provided by a hack composer, rang Rózsa and said simply, 'Would you?'. Rózsa said he would, and we feel that the noble, magisterial epilogue is an 'in memoriam' (not exactly a threnody, for its tone is heroic, not elegiac), a personal tribute. The music begins quietly under Hellinger's final narration: 'It's two o'clock in the morning now . . . This is the city . . . these are the lights . . . there are eight million stories in the Naked City, and this has been one of them.' The melody has a calm spaciousness — Copland-like in feel, though not in actual sound — and as it develops in great girder-like shafts of tune, the ambience of the big city in summer by night is superbly evoked. Rózsa subtitles this epilogue 'the song of a great city', and perhaps nowhere else is the singing quality of his music better illustrated. The composer hymns the skyline of New York; but with the voice of one to whom the Lord said, as to Abraham, 'Get thee out of thy country and from thy kindred, and from thy father's house, unto a land that I shall shew thee'. Rózsa has made of his nostalgia something strong and life-enhancing. In the unhurried inevitability of its unfolding, the music achieves a quality of Greek drama, a poetry of the modern city. Apart from this, Rózsa's contribution to the score lies chiefly in his fugato for the chase up the Brooklyn Bridge after the killer, markedly Hungarian in melodic profile. Its development reaches a nerve-shattering climax as the wanted man is shot down by the police.

Rózsa's last film in this genre was John Huston's *The Asphalt Jungle* (1950), which dealt with the planning, execution and retribution of a million-dollar jewel store robbery, but struck a more coolly realistic, less histrionic tone than most of its predecessors. Dramatic music was restricted to two major episodes only — a prologue and epilogue — and Rózsa was asked by Huston to match in his music the kind of humanizing restraint he had tried to exercise in his direction. Accordingly the music for the main titles and opening scene — a bleak cityscape with prowling, preying police-car — irradiates tension in terms not of volume but of complex, agitated rhythms. All around those mean and desolate streets, the music tells us, a world is waiting to pounce: the 'jungle' is already thrusting upwards, and its rhythms are accentuated by the 'jungle' sound of tom-toms. The finale called for a different type of commentary. Dix, the killer (Sterling Hayden), mortally wounded in a fight with the police, reaches his Hickory Wood Farm in Kentucky where he lived as a boy; and the music intensifies the pathos as Dix falls lifeless on the grass and the horses he talked so much about, and lost all his money playing, trot towards him and encircle his body. The end title music, which follows without a break, acts as a kind of emotional prolongation of this final image.

Double Life, the film which not only won Rózsa his second Oscar but also gave him the title of his autobiography, deserves mention here, since for the most part — despite the fact that the film is not about gangsters but about a highly civilized actor (Ronald Colman) who lets the part of Othello and the emotion of the 'green-eyed monster' overwhelm him — the music is in Rózsa's big-city vein. The setting is New

York and, clearly, Rózsa's mind was to convey the stresses and tensions of urban life — and life in New York in particular — exacerbated as they are to the *nth* degree in the case of an actor prey to intense and passionate neuroses. The music has to collaborate with Colman in creating a sense of the manic jealousy which masters and finally destroys him. A striking moment is the scene at the party after the first night where the piano is so insistently and harrowingly blotted out by Rózsa's mania-music that finally Colman can stand it no longer and slams his hands to his ears. In other words, this music is not merely an aural *representation* of the mania — the offstage voices rhythmically repeating 'we must hide our loves' over and over in a crescendo of cacophonous malevolence is a fine touch — for a moment it actually *is* the mania. Elsewhere Rózsa adapts some Venetian music by Giovanni Gabrieli (developed in symphonic style) as musical scenery for the stage-production of *Othello*, then lifts it deliberately out-of-context with weird orchestration to represent the role's gradual intrusion into Colman's personal life.

Rózsa's move to MGM in 1949 inaugurated a new era in his film music. True, there was fresh exploration of already familiar territory, but also interesting new departures. One of the earliest was *Adam's Rib* (1949), with one of the composer's rare comedy scores. *Tribute to a Badman* (1956) was an equally rare Rózsa western, but if his folksong orientation could embrace Hungary, the Orient and the Ancient World, why not the American West? Even less typical are *Crisis* (1950), a political melodrama set in South America with a score for two guitars, and *Something of Value* (1957), set in Kenya and exploring relations between blacks and whites. Here Rózsa studied Kenyan folk music and absorbed its essence with the same sureness of touch he was later to bring to Vietnamese music in *The Green Berets* (1968).

The pivotal score of the 'forties — and for Rózsa's whole MGM period — was *Madame Bovary* (1949). Up to then, choice of subjects had been bringing his film-music idiom closer to that of his concert works; but *Madame Bovary* opened the summer gates of his romanticism, and caused his talent for encompassing an intensity of personal emotion within the confines of a period stylistic convention fully to flower. Odd shadows of the old dark world still lurk here and there, but the emphasis now is veering to richness of texture and lyrical warmth.

This we can hear at once in the main theme, which tells us that the history of Emma Bovary is going to be tragic; and a note of impassioned desperation represents Emma's striving for the unattainable. Her first extra-marital affair is with the solicitor's clerk Léon Dupuis (Christopher Kent), whose theme is one of Rózsa's loveliest; it is first heard as a cello solo, then taken up by all the strings as Emma responds to his advances. But the mood of the relationship soon darkens (as the return of Emma's tragic theme from the titles suggests) when Léon and Emma both come to realize the sordidness of clandestine meetings in a dingy hotel.

Emma's life is transformed when, invited to a ball in a country château, she meets Rodolphe Boulanger, wealthy, handsome and aristrocratic. The dance music in this scene (including such period pieces as Passepied, Quadrille, Polka and Galop) demonstrates Rózsa's talent for recreating the spirit of popular music both old and new. But the most spectacular set-piece is the Waltz, an elaborately choreographed sequence in which Emma is literally swept off her feet by Rodolphe as action, camera and music fuse and interpenetrate in masterly fashion. This was possible only because the music was written first, recorded in a temporary version for two pianos, and the action planned and shot to suit — precisely the routine of a choreographic sequence in a musical (the director, Vincente Minnelli, is remembered today more for his musicals than for his dramatic features). The waltz begins in what is ostensibly a formally elegant vein, but the orchestration already has an unnatural flush, and the contours of the main theme are unusually wide-spanned. Little by little the momentum increases as Emma and Rodolphe become oblivious of all the other dancers, the two main strains of the waltz being developed in symphonic style. A simple but telling modulation which has the effect of the ground giving way underfoot[12] marks the real turning-point, and from then on the music accumulates, not a savage hysteria as in Ravel's *La Valse*, but a reckless, intoxicated, all-submerging ecstasy. The air grows so hot that all the windows in the ballroom are broken (cymbals), but the dance swirls madly on, *sempre accelerando*, to reach a fever-pitch of excitement which has been known to provoke a spontaneous outburst of applause when the film is screened. It is one of Rózsa's finest moments.

Emma subsequently persuades Rodolphe to elope with her. Their plan is that his coach will stop in Yonville to collect her at dead of night. In the event the coach arrives but drives straight through, with devastating effect on Emma. The musical strategy is well-planned. Two motifs are employed, the first sombrely in formal quasi-Hindemithian fugal style, the second introduced almost incidentally as part of a poignant passage for string quartet (Emma in the nursery). But once it is established, this second motif gradually becomes an *idée fixe* as the scene darkens and Emma's mood becomes one of nervous anticipation. As an *ostinato*, it ultimately becomes identified with the sound of horses' hooves in the distance; the coach draws nearer and nearer, and the two motifs — the one rhythmic, the other melodic — are united to drive the music to a hysterical climax.

Misfortunes rain upon Emma, and she begins to grow demented. To a ghostly, distant and disordered echo of the waltz she relives the moment when she first met Rodolphe; then we hear the approach of L'Heureux, the money-lender, who has come to present Emma with an ultimatum. The music builds on a four-bar *basso ostinato* timed to the relentless rhythm of his footsteps. Emma decides to end her own life by taking poison. The deathbed scene follows her agony in compassionate detail.

In retrospect, the significance of *Madame Bovary* in Rózsa's output lies not so much in his handling of individual characters and situations — impressive as this is — but in marking the first of a series of scores in which Rózsa recreates a historical period with a depth of imaginative insight which puts his work into a class of its own. It is worth examining his approach in more detail.

The mid-nineteenth-century French setting of *Madame Bovary* required, as we have seen, dance music in an authentic period style. But many of his later excursions into the past called for a musical character which could only be authentically recreated from specialized and sometimes very limited source material. In each case Rózsa sought out and studied what music was available and achieved a synthesis of elements of the older style within his personal idiom. This ability to express the past in music of the present is a rare gift. The success of Rózsa's historical music stems from the fact that he never tries to be artificially or self-consciously archaic, merely to be himself, musically speaking, at a variety of points in times past. He absorbs the spirit of a period style and then recreates his own musical personality within its frame of reference. All Rózsa's historical films bear witness to this unique chemistry of the creative process, the secrets of which are known only to a select band of initiates. Rózsa is one, Stravinsky another; but in Rózsa's 'time-travelling' emotion and feeling are the touchstones.

We can hear this chemistry at work in *Young Bess* (1953) and *Diane* (1955), where the music supplies precisely that element of genuine historical resonance which often tends to be missing in Hollywood films with a European historical setting. In both all the dramaturgical musical material is original Rózsa. But in *Plymouth Adventure* and *Ivanhoe* (both 1952) he incorporates borrowed material which research had established to be germane. *Plymouth Adventure* is the story of the Mayflower's journey from Plymouth harbour to Plymouth Rock in 1620. Rózsa discovered that when the Pilgrim Fathers sailed they took with them one book with music: *Henry Ainsworth's Psalter*, printed in Amsterdam in 1612. One of the melodies it contained was a sturdy setting of the 136th Psalm, which Rózsa found an ideal choice for his main theme. It opens and closes the picture in a choral-orchestral setting and (in the orchestra alone this time) crowns an impressive climax as the Mayflower's sails billow in the wind and she starts her course toward the unknown region.[13]

Elsewhere, as in *Diane* and *Young Bess*, Rózsa works the stylistic trick William Walton used in *Henry V, Hamlet* and

Richard III. To create a tolerably authentic period atmosphere he adopts certain conventions of phraseology and texture but does not always conform to harmonic practice. In other words, he preserves the contemporary musical spirit, but not in every respect its letter, and the emotional stuff of the music is his own. An instance in *Plymouth Adventure* is his treatment of Dorothy Bradford's suicide. Dorothy's tragic theme, like those of Winslow, John Alden and Priscilla and little William Button, is superficially reminiscent of the style of the seventeenth-century English lutenists, yet it is not pastiche but living tissue. In the scene where Dorothy decides to throw herself overboard, the harmonic temperature gradually rises, and twentieth-century orchestral sonorities begin to intrude until the climax is reached.

In *Ivanhoe* Rózsa reached back to the music of the troubadours and trouvères of Norman France in the interests of twelfth-century Saxon England — for later Saxon culture was inevitably influenced by that of the invading Normans. Rózsa's own feeling for modality enables him to assimilate authentic melodic fragments of the period — a Ballade actually composed by Richard Coeur-de-Lion (who is, of course, one of the characters in the film) and the theme for Lady Rowena and Ivanhoe, which is a free adaptation of an old popular song from the north of France. The rhythmic theme representing the Normans derives from a Latin hymn by a thirteenth-century troubadour. As for Rebecca, daughter of Isaac of York, her theme may have been suggested to Rózsa by medieval Jewish sources, but again he made it his own.

For *Knights of the Round Table* (1954) Rózsa wrote ninety minutes of music in six weeks. The film was undistinguished, but Rózsa's imagination was fired by the colour, warmth and splendour of the Arthurian legends on which it was based and which have been celebrated in a wealth of literature. Rózsa read his Malory, his Tennyson, ideas proliferated, and the resulting music, like Whitman's Mystic Trumpeter, makes pass before us all the pageantry and poetry of the early feudal world. *Lust for Life* (1956), the Van Gogh 'biopic' based on the novel by Irving Stone and featuring Kirk Douglas as the great painter, offered a challenge of a different order. Impressionistic elements had always been endemic in Rózsa's style, as they were in that of Bartók, Kodály, Vaughan Williams and other composers weaned on folksong (many aspects of musical impressionism are derived from folksong) and Rózsa felt a certain affinity between the early style of Van Gogh and Debussy's so-called 'impressionistic' language. The 'impressionist' musical episodes are mostly decorative. They are prominent in the scenes around Van Gogh's father's country home and in the first of the picture-montages showing the evolution of the painter's mature style, where Rózsa intensifies the impact of the Provençal sun and colour. This is Van Gogh the artist. The *man* is portrayed in Rózsa's own strong, characteristic style. Van Gogh's theme is akin to those of King Arthur and the Cid; its upward-striving melodic shape reflects his yearning and all-consuming aspiration. It twists itself into a distorted atonal variant to depict his mental instability and incipient madness in the scene where he holds his hand in a candle flame as proof of his love for his cousin Kay, and traumatizes the climax as he hacks off his ear with a razor. By contrast the theme of joy in artistic creation is a glowing melody first heard as Vincent speaks of his desire to capture the poetry latent in 'a man or woman at work . . . some furrows in a ploughed field . . . a bit of sand, sea or sky . . . suddenly so different, so beautiful. . .' It activates the creation of the 'Sunflowers' and other works in the heat of the burning Southern sun at Arles, and returns to close the picture on a note of ecstasy as we hear Van Gogh (voice-over) talking of the figure of death in one of his paintings: '. . . it's not a sad death . . . it happens in bright sunlight, the sun flooding everything in a light of pure gold. . .'. This theme is actually developed from a segment of the theme of Van Gogh, the man. Both are complementary facets of the same personality.

The best of Rózsa's non-historical MGM romances was the tripartite *The Story of Three Loves* (1953), two of its segments directed by Gottfried Reinhardt ('The Jealous Lover' and 'Equilibrium'), the other ('Mademoiselle') by Minnelli. 'The Jealous Lover' is the story of a young ballet dancer with a heart condition (Moira Shearer) who dances the dance of her life before James Mason and then collapses and dies when she reaches home. The choreography for this sequence was by Frederick Ashton, and Rózsa originally suggested that he use the love music in César Franck's symphonic poem *Psyché*. In the event Rachmaninov's *Variations on a Theme by Paganini* for piano and orchestra was chosen instead — happily, since it is perfect ballet music — and in an early scene both conductor Rózsa and the pianist, Jacob Gimpel, can be glimpsed briefly on screen in the pit as we view the final moments of the fictitious ballet *Astarte*, which Moira Shearer dances to her own choreography in Mason's apartment. Then, as the realization dawns on Mason that he has found here the dancer — and the love — of a lifetime, Rózsa begins to weave his own variations on Rachmaninov[14], reaching an impassioned climax as Mason bursts into the room where Shearer is supposed to be changing, finds her gone and sees her from the window flying up the street. This is the only licence taken with Rachmaninov.

Music of the bells and fountains of the Eternal City[15] introduces 'Mademoiselle'. In the opening scenes Leslie Caron as a young, pretty but harassed French governess is reading French poetry to Tommy, her sullen, unresponsive and ill-mannered American charge. The music, with solo violin and prominent harp, vibraphone and celesta, enhances the beauty of the verses, ignoring the nasty, brutish interruptions. Tommy escapes to the hotel bar (where the salon orchestra is playing the *Madame Bovary* waltz), but is ejected on account of his age and meets the mysterious Hazel Pennicott (Ethel Barrymore), who promises to turn him into a man for four hours. The spell will only work if he presses a piece of red ribbon to his temple and repeats the words 'Hazel Pennicott' in the manner of an incantation. As the clock begins to strike, a xylophone picks up the rhythm of its ticking and a celesta the rhythm of Tommy's reiterated 'Hazel Pennicott'. There follows a fantastic jangling counterpoint of chimes and bells, and Tommy's new-found manhood (in the person of Farley Granger) is signalled by a little quasi-Hungarian tune which gradually increases in pride and confidence while 'Hazel Pennicott' continues to sound rhythmically in various departments of the orchestra. And now Farley Granger meets Leslie Caron in the moonlight, finds the poetry-book from the first scene, and the enchanted music returns to the words of Verlaine's 'Il pleure dans mon coeur'. It is a lovely scene and the responsibility for enveloping the audience with the aura of moonlight and roses, magic and romance is primarily the music's. Minnelli directed this segment with his customary painter's eye for composition. In its fluidity and grace of movement, and in the importance of the music as a textured element, this fantasy is just like a scene from one of his musicals.

'Mademoiselle' as a fantasy is heavily dependent on music. In 'Equilibrium', however, the story of a trapeze artist (Kirk Douglas) dogged by ill-fate, and a younger girl (Pier Angeli) embittered by wartime experiences in a concentration camp, needed a more selective approach. The only scene where music is crucial is where Kirk Douglas banishes his unnecessary guilt complex through helping Pier Angeli banish hers; and here the music supplies the all-important quality of compassion. The end title neatly engages the lyrical theme alongside the first phrase of the Rachmaninov 18th Variation: the famous one, used as the climax of Moira Shearer's dance.

In 1869 the young Henry James, overwhelmed by his first experience of Rome, wrote: 'From midday to dusk I have been roaming the streets . . . At last — for the first time — I live! it beats everything — it makes Venice — Florence — Oxford — London — seem like little cities of pasteboard. I went reeling thro' the streets in a fever of enjoyment'. And as surely was Rózsa conquered when he first visited the Eternal City in 1950 for the purpose of writing the music for *Quo Vadis*. Since then many roads have led him back to Rome, both literally and metaphorically; it is his favourite European city and one in which he has done some of his best work. *Quo Vadis*, in fact, was the occasion of a kind of spiritual homecoming and a turning-point in the composer's film career.

It is worth remembering that it was in Italy that the most highly-evolved form of music-and-drama — i.e. opera —

originated. Many of the greatest composers have been Italian — Monteverdi, Rossini, Donizetti, Bellini, Verdi, Puccini — and Rózsa's unreserved admiration for Puccini gives some food for thought. It is hard to speak of direct influence, for Rózsa has had enough originality to absorb his nutrients without producing any effect of imitation, or even of eclecticism. We may, however, draw some interesting parallels. There is in both a passionate sincerity and a feeling for strong emotion; a sure sense of theatrical effect; a love of sensuous beauty (the *de luxe* quality of orchestral texture, with its glowing, shifting colours, bespeaks a powerful sensual drive). The symphonic element (sustained use of definite ideas) is marked. But above all there is melody. Rózsa sings (instrumentally) because he needs to express human emotion and effect human values, and this he can only do through melody, tune, line, song. Here is, I hope, the real point of bringing in Puccini. *His* power of pervasive, persuasive melody has never failed to hold an enormous public throughout the world. Rózsa's public is far greater, but it is for the most part unaware that it is being held; *his* 'operas' have no words and, for the most part, no singing voices, yet it is the same power of persuasive, pervasive melody that does the holding, in the more subtle and insidious context of a filmscore. There are times when the very endlessness of melody, the ceaseless surge and influx of wonderful ideas, almost overwhelms: I think of *Turandot*, the first act of *Madam Butterfly*, and then of 'Madamoiselle' in *The Story of Three Loves*, and the *King of Kings* Entr'acte. Melody and ideas: nothing in Rózsa's eyes is more important in music; and for over fifty years his work has possessed these qualities in abundance.

While Rózsa's finest hour came in 1959 with Wyler's *Ben-Hur*[16], those qualities which contributed to its sensational success are already present in more than embryonic form in the first of his 'epic' spectaculars. Unlikely as it may seem, the success of his scores both for *Quo Vadis* and for the later — and greater — super-spectacles on which he worked, may be explained at least partly in terms of the grounding of his music in Magyar folksong. For the roots of Hungarian peasant song are in the church modes and the pentatonic scale, its predominant intervals are the fourth and the fifth and therefore suggest a harmonic treatment derived from those intervals, i.e. parallel chords of superimposed fourths and fifths. Now these are precisely the means whereby an atmosphere of antiquity may be conjured up for western ears; and, furthermore, there is an element of exotic decoration endemic in Hungarian and all East-European folksong which can also lend itself readily to an evocation of the Orient of the Ancients. So there was no need for Rózsa consciously to assume an archaic-sounding idiom: the prerequisites were already inherent in his own style. An interesting example occurs in the *Siciliana Antica* played 'realistically' during Nero's banquet. The performers are slaves and the music would therefore be music from their own countries of origin — Babylonia, Syria, Egypt, Persia and elsewhere — and a bagpipe episode is therefore acceptably authentic: Nero is known to have been fond of bagpipes. But the bagpipes form also a very lively part of Hungarian folk music tradition, and to write in their idiom is second nature to Rózsa anyway. See, for example, his *Kaleidoscope*, the finale of his Piano Sonata and the 'Danza' in *Three Hungarian Sketches*. In this way Rózsa's score for *Quo Vadis* has a ring of *inner* authenticity which complements the *outer* authenticity for which he strove in its general substance and presentation. *Quo Vadis* is in fact a landmark not only in Rózsa's career but also in film-music history: for neither before nor since has any composer taken so much trouble over the preparation of the *materia musica* for a film of this kind. He supervised the reconstruction of all the ancient instruments which actually appear realistically in the film. He then divided the realistic music to be composed into three distinct categories: the Romans' music (Nero's songs, the sacrificial hymns of the Vestals, marches and fanfares); the Slaves' dances; and the Christians' hymns. Finally, there was the problem of the functional music, which had to be so fashioned as to reduce stylistic incompatibility to a minimum.

As no Roman music has survived, and Roman culture was heavily influenced by that of the Greeks, Rózsa drew on

Grecian sources for Nero's song 'The Burning of Troy', an adaptation of a Greek drinking song; for the slave-girl Eunice's song, and for the 'Bacchanal' in 5/8 time at Nero's banquet. Of the other dances performed at the banquet, 'Syrian Dance' (*Allegretto Orientale*) credits no borrowed material, but the *Siciliana Antica* has a sinuous melody of Sicilian origin which bears broad signs of Arab influence. All these songs and dances are given simple modal harmonizations (with liberal use of fourths and fifths) which renders them acceptable to the contemporary ear but does not harm their original character. With respect to the instrumentation another compromise is reached, in that latter-day approximations to the instruments of antiquity are employed wherever practicable. Nero and Eunice accompany themselves on the clarsach, a small Scottish harp whose timbre, however, is closer to that of the lyre than the modern harp. In the dance-music, cor anglais and bass flute impersonate the 'aulos'; cornets add a stridency and roughness characteristic of the Roman 'salpinx' and 'buccina'; modern percussion — tambourines, jingles, drums and gongs of various sizes, antique and ordinary cymbals — is similar to that of the Ancients. Bowed strings would, of course, be anachronistic, but where a larger, fuller sound is needed *pizzicato* strings, guitars and mandolins reinforce the main body of the orchestra. The hymns for the Christians' scenes — St Paul baptizing new believers in the catacombs, the martyrs burning as human torches on crosses in Nero's gardens, the massacre in the arena — are all culled from early Jewish and Greek sources, the fountainhead of Ambrosian plainchant and Gregorian hymnody.

Rózsa is successful in avoiding stylistic confrontation between the realistic and commentative musics, again because of the common ground between his own musical speech and these acquired elements; and mindful of this he takes particular care to ensure that the commentative music should respect the norm established by the realistic. The main theme of the former is modelled on the Gregorian 'Libera me domine', but the themes for Lygia and Petronius are Rózsa's

own. Both are simple and modally inflected: Lygia's has a cool
serenity and Petronius's stresses the nobility of the patrician
author of the *Satyricon* rather than his cynicism. In conjunction
with an agonized harmonization of Eunice's song it gives
in-depth emotion to the scene in which the two cut their wrists
and die together rather than face the wrath of Nero. In
complete contrast comes the theme of Marcus Vinicius as
heard in the 'Triumph' march, 'Ave Caesar' — brash and
assertive and shot through with a spirit of pagan heroism.
This splendid march exemplifies Rózsa's way of creating an
ambience of period pomp with the minimum of rhetorical
bombast — it is a true symphonic march in that the melodic
material changes and grows as it proceeds. The main reason
for the proven staying-power of this music — and of *Ben-Hur*,
King of Kings and *El Cid* — is surely that Rózsa writes in the
grand manner because he *thinks* in the grand manner.

Two particularly striking sequences in *Quo Vadis* are the
main titles and the finale. The former neatly pits the two
protagonists one against the other — behind the massive,
confident swing of the Christians' motif, we are continually
aware of the clamour of Roman 'buccinae' (trumpets). The
finale — Marcus and Lygia passing the spot on the Appian
Way where St Peter has been vouchsafed his vision of Christ
— begins with Lygia's theme, heard through a trickling harp
figure. Shimmering chords (high string harmonics) recall the
mystical light of Peter's vision, and his shepherd's crook, still
standing where he put it, is seen to blossom miraculously. As
the travellers move on, the chorus, singing as the voices of
humanity, ask the question of the main theme: 'Quo Vadis,
Domine?'. The voice of Jesus answers them: 'I am the Way,
the Truth, and the Life' — a striking use of choral speech,
difficult to realize in recording as the words, spoken *sotto voce*
by the massed chorus, had to be audible. This leads into a
fully harmonized version of the hymn the Christians had sung
in the arena; in the closing bars the violins can be heard
excitedly reiterating a motif reminiscent of the 'Alleluia' from
Rózsa's motet *To Everything there is a Season*, and orchestra and
chorus together produce the effect of a paean of bell-ringing.

Joseph L. Manckiewicz's *Julius Caesar* (1953) demanded a different approach. Rózsa elected to regard the production not as a historical pageant but as 'a universal drama about the problems of men and the fates of dictators, and I wrote the same music I would have written for a modern stage presentation: interpretative incidental music, expressing in my own musical language, for a modern audience, what Shakespeare expressed in his own language for his own audience 350 years ago'. The result is one of his best-integrated scores. In the title music Brutus' and Caesar's themes are intertwined, just as Brutus' and Cassius's are after Caesar's death. This anticipates the extraordinary musical construction of the finale, when Brutus meets his nemesis. This employs the then novel technique of stereophony, with the orchestra divided into two distinct groups: woodwind, brass and percussion (the marching armies of Antony and Octavian), and strings (Brutus). The one is the exact antithesis of the other in every respect, and they are recorded on separate tracks: the march in the far distance on one, Brutus' theme in the foreground (since his is the tragedy being enacted in front of us) on the other. The armies draw nearer to each other, and the march music based on Caesar's theme braced by a field-drum rhythm is faded up. The two orchestras converge, each steadfast in its purpose, the march building inexorably over its steady field-drum rhythm, Brutus' elegiac theme stoically indifferent to Clitus' pleas: 'Fly, fly my Lord! There is no tarrying here'. The climax is reached with the arrival on the scene of the enemy armies — by which time the march has overpowered the strings — Brutus' running on his own sword. Here Caesar's theme (horns *fortissimo*) is invoked, of course, by Brutus' dying words: 'Caesar, now be still: I kill'd not thee with half so good a will'. The *marcia romana* becomes an oppressor which crushes the calm modality of Brutus' theme beneath its feet and drives home the *dénouement*, the fate of Brutus, as deadly sure as that of any character in classical tragedy.

Rózsa's treatment of other scenes in *Julius Caesar*, while

personal as always, is similarly imbued with the objective universality of tragedy. There is a classical austerity and restraint about the themes notwithstanding the emotionally-charged nature of Brutus'. The result is that the spareness of the women's dirge, in the manner of a *nenia*, at Caesar's funeral, and of Dowland's 'Now, now, I needs must part' for Lucius in Brutus' camp, do not jar against the commentative music, but seem a natural outgrowth of it. The music for the scene outside the Capitol is similarly born of the stark objectivity of catastrophe. Its block chording helps to give it a portentous quality, but its real intimations of doom are contained in the dissonant horn chords which, over a repeated bass figure, gradually gather momentum and rise from the depths in hooded menace as Artemidorus reads the letter of warning, and Caesar and the Senators arrive.

The difference between the classical and romantic approaches can easily be demonstrated by comparing Rózsa's music for the ghost scene in *Julius Caesar* with Shostakovich's for the corresponding scene in the Russian *Hamlet* (1964). Shostakovich helps his ghost strike terror into the hearts of those who see or hear it: a giant figure in full armour, its cloak billows behind it as it stalks the battlements to the accompaniment of an imperious full-blown theme for heavy brass *fortissimo*. Rózsa evokes in an impressionistic way the spectral glow in which the apparition is enveloped: first high strings clusters in harmonics, then vibraphone and celesta emit a kind of blue light, a cold, glassy, shimmering sound; while down below the cellos and basses pronounce the distorted Caesar motif.

Ben-Hur (1959), Rózsa's magnum opus, has an impact and commitment which may be ascribed for the greater part to the fact that, as in the case of *Quo Vadis*, inspiration came to the composer in Rome itself. 'I walked long afternoons in the Forum Romanum on the Capitoline and Palatine Hills, imagining the old splendour of the buildings which are in ruins now, and the excitement of the multitude in flowing togas in the Circus Maximus where I wrote the music for the Circus and Victory Parades . . . I was fortunate enought to be connected with it from its very inception and I felt instinctively that, with its sweeping human drama and flamboyant pageantry, *Ben-Hur* needed music which grew naturally from its atmosphere and became an integral part of it.' In fact what Rózsa achieves here is a synthesis of his contrasting approaches to *Quo Vadis* and *Julius Caesar*.

Ben-Hur begins with a prologue showing the Nativity, and the apparition of the Morning star is signalled by a chorale-like melody, its harmonies shaded by a wordless chorus, that later becomes Balthazar's leitmotif. This yields, in the stable, to a charming carol with woodwind skirls which director William Wyler finally came — reluctantly — to prefer to his original idea of 'Adeste Fideles'. The titles are superimposed on Michelangelo's *Creation of Adam*; the full title of the film is *Ben-Hur — A Tale of the Christ*, but the opening music leaves us in no doubt as to the true protagonist, with its *fortissimo* statement in full regal splendour of the Christ-theme. This is generally heard in the form of soft organ chords with high string harmonics, punctuated by a bell-like figure for cellos *pizzicato*, harp and vibraphone. Two scenes depend on this theme: the first is when a thirst-crazed Ben-Hur, one of a party of convicts on their way to the galleys, is given water by a carpenter's son in the village of Nazareth. The tranquil shimmer of the Christ theme comes as an almost physically experienced relief after the brassy dissonant turmoil of the desert music, like the cool pools and green leafage of an unexpected oasis. The party begins to move off and Ben-Hur's own theme returns; but above it the bell-like part of the Christ theme can be heard as a counterpoint in flutes and glockenspiel. Then as Ben-Hur turns to look back over his shoulder at the carpenter of Nazareth, the Christ theme *in toto* swells to a mighty peroration in a manner which foreshadows the miracle scene. The relationship is encompassed in the music.

Many years later in Jerusalem Ben-Hur offers water to a young condemned criminal on his way to be crucified who collapses under the weight of his cross, and whom Ben-Hur

seems to remember having met before. Here again the Christ
theme brings solace in the midst of strife, but is this time
interrupted by a snarl on the muted brass as Ben-Hur is thrust
aside, and Christ lashed on his way. The theme has to convey
something of the spirit of the Sermon on the Mount, witnessed
by Ben-Hur at the instigation of Esther, his betrothed; and
just as we do not see Christ's face or hear his voice, so in this
scene the Christ theme is alluded to (by soft brass and high
string harmonics) rather than explicity stated. In the final
scene, at the climax of the thunderstorm which coincides with
the Crucifixion, Ben-Hur's mother and sister realize that they
have been cured of their leprosy. Dissonant chords (with
sharp tearing figures on the high strident E-flat clarinet)
suggest the pain of the cure; then an exultant transformation
of the Christ theme — high strings and horns — leads to music
of rushing mighty waters, blood trickling down from the cross
mingling with the torrents of rain flowing past on the ground.
It all culminates in a great outburst — showers of
glockenspiel, bells, chimes, general jubilation — marked
(untypically for Rózsa, who generally prefers more matter-of-
fact expression-marks) 'luminoso ed estatico' — which is, in
fact, a symphonic elaboration of the *second* part, the bell-motif,
of the Christ theme. The tumult quietens for the cut to the
House of Hur. The film's main themes pass in review: Ben
Hur's, Esther's, finally his mother's. A shepherd in the
foreground drives his flock past the three crosses sharply
etched against a darkling horizon, and the Christ theme
complete closes the picture as a peal of Alleluias rings out.
Always and immediately, the theme's character evokes a
presence too: a brief shot of Christ as a youth walking in the
hills around Nazareth — 'Oh, he's working', says Joseph to a
critical neighbour — of a stream of blue water (just before the
Sermon on the Mount); and Ben-Hur labouring over his oar
in the galleys and thinking back to the unknown young man
who had shown him unexpected kindness. Ben-Hur's own
theme is a noble march and the Ben-Hur/Esther love theme a
simple tune with a light exotic inflexion. Ben-Hur's mother
Miriam's theme is an austere and passionate melody, Hebraic

in character, used movingly in the scenes where she implores
Esther not to reveal to her son that she and her daughter are
lepers, and later when Ben-Hur follows Esther to the Valley of
the Lepers to rescue them. Another melody with a strong
undercurrent of Jewish feeling[17] is the woodwind theme
depicting Ben-Hur's longing for his homeland: in the scene
showing his return voyage to Judaea it is projected against a
rising and falling bass figure (cellos) to suggest the calm swell
of the sea.

The ambivalent Ben-Hur/Messala relationship is subtly
handled. The warm, manly theme which represents their
early friendship is first heard in the emotion-filled scene of the
boys' first meeting as young men (the scene with the spears),
and shortly after, against a gentle, orientally-coloured
background as Ben-Hur, his mother and sister entertain
Messala at their house. But as the Roman iron in the latter's
soul begins to reveal itself, there arises a venomous theme,
rearing up from the depths of the orchestra. Its first
appearance comes after Ben-Hur's refusal to betray his own
people to Messala: 'In that case I am *against* you, Messala'.
Yet, in the 'Parade of the Charioteers', to which all the
competitors in the race march round the arena of the circus at
Antioch, here is this same theme transformed into a ringing
march, sharing equal honours with Ben-Hurs's own. Then,
for Messala's death scene (witnessed by Ben-Hur), both
Messala's and the 'friendship' theme return in slow and
disfigured guise; and — a poetic moment — as Ben-Hur
stands in the vast, deserted amphitheatre in the irony of
the afternoon sunlight, a distant muted trumpet sounds a
reminiscence of one of the fanfares which had preceded the
race and then been drawn into the march around the arena.

Triumphal marches abound in the score: the 'Bread and
Circus March' played before and after the chariot race (from
Quo Vadis), the 'Victory Parade' for Quintus Arrius and his
new-found 'son', Gratus' entry into Jerusalem (developed
from a period fragment in *Quo Vadis* associated with the
burning of Rome). 'Parade of the Charioteers' and 'Victory
Parade', like the 'Ave Caesar' march in *Quo Vadis* and Pontius

Pilate's entry into Jerusalem in *King of Kings*, are both effectively realistic and good well-made marches in their own right. And as in *Quo Vadis* other realistic music comes in the form of exotic festal dances — an orgiastic 'Fertility Dance' for African drums and flutes, and a gentle piece for Quintus Arrius' Roman orchestra, coolly scored for modern counterparts of antique instruments — auloi, lyres and Roman percussion. Here again, as in the later *Sodom and Gomorrah* (1964), Rózsa's *Quo Vadis* researches served him well.

Sequences like the rowing of the galley slaves and the procession to Calvary are self-contained enough to function as musical compositions almost independently of any programme. The former is a remarkable four-minute sustained rhythmic *accelerando*, the relentless *basso ostinato* of the timpani marking the rowers' gear-changes from rowing to battle to ramming speed.[18] It is interesting to compare the 'Procession to Calvary' with the 'Via Crucis' in *King of Kings*. The latter is more personal and inward-looking, focusing attention directly on the physical and mental sufferings of Christ, specific rather than general in reference. In *Ben-Hur*, however, we view the tragedy in perspective. There is a monumental, 'classical' quality about the music. Both marches opt for a *basso ostinato*, which in *Ben-Hur* is simply a heaving two-note figure, rather like the swinging of a huge funeral bell. The music moves to a powerful climax, the agonized character of which is the more effective for the simplicity of the means whereby it is produced. The conflict between the inexorable D minor implied by the fixed *basso ostinato* and the comings and goings of ordinary chords — 'God's chords' is what the English composer Walford Davies called ordinary major and minor chords — in a ceaseless flux of other keys. How simple, how potent, how personal; so often in Rózsa, the dramatic strength lies in the simplicity. The 'gift to be simple' has always been his.

King of Kings (1961) followed hard on *Ben-Hur*. Rózsa cannot have relished the lack of contrast between the new assignment and its predecessor. Having written music for scenes of the Nativity and Procession to Calvary in *Ben-Hur*, he now had to re-compose the same scenes for *King of Kings*. The difference in conception between the *viae dolorosae* of *Ben-Hur* and *King of Kings* respectively has already been outlined. The 'Via Crucis' in *King of Kings* makes an almost physical impact on the listener, chiefly by dint of the close-harmony scoring in the brass. The familiar carol-like *alla pastorale* in 6/8 time having been avoided for the Nativity scene in *Ben-Hur*, Rózsa gainfully employs it here in the guise of a lullaby for small orchestra and wordless chorus — again unselfconsciously simple.

The main *King of Kings* theme bears the full panoply of orchestra and chorus in the main titles. It also makes its point tellingly in quieter contexts, often as a solo oboe over *tremolo* strings: as Christ's eyes meet John the Baptist's in the Jordan; when Christ turns and looks on Peter after his three-fold denial; and when he appears to his disciples by the Sea of Galilee after the Resurrection.[19] A spectacularly different transformation occurs in the scene where Christ is being scourged, and soldiers are preparing the cross. The rhythmic impulses of the flagellum are synchronized to the rhythm of the music, but as the Cross rears its monster-image across the screen the main *King of Kings* theme weighs in *fortissimo* in the heavy brass, with full organ.

The other main theme is a lyrical melody introduced at the point during the Sermon on the Mount when a man in the crowd asks Christ to teach them how to pray. It enhances Jeffrey Hunter's delivery of the Lord's Prayer, moving to an eloquent climax at 'For Thine is the Kingdom, the power and the glory. . .' Thereafter it recurs periodically throughout the score, notably during the Agony in the Garden and the Resurrection scenes. It serves to emphasize the humanity and warmth (not to mention the Hollywood glamour) of Christ as he appears in Hunter's portrayal.

The other principal characters are also given leitmotifs. John the Baptist has a brooding theme which, as Rózsa himself has written, tries to convey 'his passionate sincerity and self-effacing humility'. For Mary a gentle melody for oboe over an undecided, major-minor figure which later, in less sharply-profiled colours, accompanies the scenes at the foot of the Cross, the descent, and Christ's body being carried to the Sepulchre. Satan, and later the man possessed of a thousand devils, are represented by a sinister twelve-tone theme, Rózsa's one and only conscious use of Schoenberg's invention; although we have already seen how the scenes of Van Gogh's diabolical seizures subject the painter's theme to 'diabolical' atonal distortion. Here the fact that the only twelve-tone motif is associated with Lucifer is unequivocally, if privately, symbolic of the composer's rejection of serialism as a viable compositional method (shades of Adrian Leverkühn in Thomas Mann's *Doktor Faustus!*)

There are two major sequences of quasi-realistic music. The first is a Roman march accompanying Pontius Pilate's arrival in Judaea, the second a dance — Salome's (this scene and the music were badly cut in the film but the latter is preserved in its original form on the album), which (in Rózsa's realization) emphasizes barbarity at the expense of lewdness. It is first cousin to the 'Syrian Dance' in *Quo Vadis* and is expertly scored. Beginning languidly with a cor anglais solo of feline seductiveness, it gradually gathers momentum through changing rhythmic patterns until a frenzied climax is reached. Falling midway between realistic and commentative music is the musical cohesion Rózsa brings to the scenes of Christ's triumphal entry into Jerusalem and the rebels' storming of the Antonia fortress. The festive music which accompanies the former is based on a Hebrew melody generally sung during the Passover, just as the music for the elders of the Temple of Jerusalem as Pompey makes his entry into the Holy of Holies is fashioned after examples of Babylonian and Yemenite melodies. The mood changes suddenly as we see Barabbas inciting the people to storm the Fortress. The movement culminates in a granite-like march over a timpani *basso ostinato* which conveys a fine sense of inexorability as the Roman phalanx mows down the retreating Judaeans.

One of the best scenes in all Rózsa is that of the healing of the lame boy. The boy's agony is reflected in a tortured chromaticism which rises ever higher as if in a paroxysm of pain, to be countered by the radiant theme of the Redeemer who passes his hands over the boy's legs. Again the climbing chromatics, but this time secure in the promise of ultimate release, and again at the climax the triumphant *King of Kings* theme as the boy leaves his bed and begins to walk. No help (or hindrance) from dialogue or sound effects. Watching it, we are reminded again of Herrmann's description of film music as 'the communicating link between the screen and the audience, reaching out and enveloping all in one single experience'.

El Cid (1962) remains, to date, the last of the great Rózsa epics, and shows him conforming to his own high standards of historical authenticity. He wanted his music not only to sound real but actually to *be* real; and with characteristic thoroughness he set out to learn as much about the musical mores of eleventh-century Spain as he could. He consulted the late Dr Ramon Menendez Pidal, Spain's greatest authority on the life and times of El Cid. He directed the composer to the *Cantigas de Santa Maria* — a collection of over 400 songs in praise of the Virgin Mary assembled by King Alfonso X (known as 'The Wise') of Castile, described by Gilbert Chase as 'one of the greatest monuments of non-liturgical monodic music that have come down to us from the Middle Ages'. Rózsa studied the *Cantigas*, marked those melodies or melodic fragments which appealed to him, and allowed them spontaneously to suggest motivic material to him; and, as before, the modal character of his own melodic cast of thought enabled him easily to assimilate these *données*. It would be a rash critic who would endeavour to point out where the *Cantigas* end and Rózsa begins. Witness merely the best of the 'set-pieces', the ceremonial prelude to the tournament at Calahorra, where the music sounds as integral a part of eleventh-century heraldry as all the banners, tents, grandstands, knights in armour, ladies in brocades and velvets and the castle of Belmonte (overlooking Cervantes's La Mancha) which serves as backdrop. Much of the melodic profusion derives from the *Cantigas*, and fanfares rocket back and forth with a splendid insouciant grandeur. The musical symbolism at the end is nice: the Cid's fanfare sounds in one key, his opponent Don Martin's in another. The key-conflict is not resolved: that is the responsibility of the 'trial by single combat' which follows.

Other 'set pieces' include the entry of King Ferdinand and his court to hear the charge of treason brought against the Cid, Rodrigo de Bivar (Charlton Heston) by Count Ordonez (Raf Vallone) and the march that leads the Cid's victorious army into Valencia after the siege. This fine march — the 'El Cid March' — is first heard as intermission music, heralded by the same spectacular fanfare which opened the 'overture' played in the theatre before the picture begins.

The Cid's theme is a muscular melody with a tone of heroic aspiration, easily related to Van Gogh's and King Arthur's themes, but capable also of tenderness and a melancholy beauty. This is apparent, for example, in the scene where the Cid is seen trekking into exile across vast stretches of open country, and the theme is passed from one solo woodwind to another over a rocking guitar figure. Chimène's theme, darkly voluptuous, is a corrective to the intransigent theme of the Cid. The main title music presents both, the latter as the climax of the former; its monochrome orchestration suitably complements the murals in charcoal by Maciek Piotrowski against which the credits unfurl, although in fact the music was written before the design was decided upon.

Although the music is often more concerned with historical atmosphere than with human drama, some gestures are powerful. For instance the first part of the tragic duel between Rodrigo and his father-in-law Count Gormaz (Andrew Cruickshank) is played without music. Rózsa's dramatic instinct told him that the crux of the scene is Rodrigo's grazing of Gormaz, which Rodrigo hoped would settle the account between them. Instead it so infuriates Gormaz as to make him pursue the contest in envenomed earnest. Here, then, was the cue for music, not before. The combatants disappear beneath the curve of the stone stairway, and only the music tells us what is happening.

The Cid's theme dominates the climax. The hero has died after being struck by a Moorish arrow at the height of the battle of Valencia. All through his deathbed scene we are conscious of Chimène's sorrowing presence as the music, an elegy, alludes constantly to her theme but never explicitly states it. His death is kept a secret in order not to demoralize his army on the eve of their final stand against the fanatical Ben-Yussef. So the following morning his body is propped up and strapped to his horse, and lance in hand he leads his men to victory *in absentia*. The huge Moorish gates are swung open; light reflected from the dead warrior's shield fills the screen and we hear the narrator's words 'And so the Cid rode forth from the pages of history into legend.' Thereupon the full organ sounds, solo, ablaze with the Cid's theme in all its power and glory. This sudden burst of sound is the more effective for the enormously long tension-fraught silence, broken only by the sounds of wind and sea, the clink of armour and clip-clop of horses, which have preceded it. The organ is engulfed in a fiery sortie of battle-music as the black-robed Moorish hordes are flung back into the sea; but it returns in company with a wordless chorus to close the picture as the figure of the Cid reappears galloping along the shoreline and is finally lost in the immensity of sea merging with sky ('Almighty God, open Your Arms to receive the soul of one who lived and died for Spain, the purest Knight of them all.') It is a grand romantic finale, and one of the greatest in film music.

Rózsa's memoirs remind us that his 'Double Life' has been the story of a creative artist's struggle to maintain his integrity and his self-respect in a world where art is invariably expected to serve the interests of commerce. His relation to the cinema medium is complex and equivocal. There is a strong element of love/hate in it: resentment, perhaps, towards the medium that has claimed so many of the best years of his creative life. I believe that Rózsa *needed* to write the kind of music films demanded of him; it was a side of his musical personality that had to find an expressive outlet, just as a very different side fulfilled itself in terms of non-film-music. Both were part of him, both had to be provided for. He has always, clearly, been driven by some daemon, always taken a very passionate stance. His music is always honest. Right from the first, even in Hollywood, there were people to recognize both the imprimatur of excellence his music stamped on films (often far exceeding their deserts), and the two features common to all Rózsa's composing — its individuality and its quality. In fact it could almost be claimed that his voice is *too* authoritative, *too* individual: when his music plays we have to listen. But Hollywood is so used to encountering and accommodating this phenomenon it has given it a name. In fact it is of the essence of Hollywood. The name is Star Quality.

NOTES

1   In later years Hollywood sensed the dramatic potential even in this early piece of non-film-music, as John Fitzpatrick pointed out in an issue of *Pro Musica Sana*, the journal of the Miklós Rózsa Society (Vol. IV No. 1 pp. 14–15, Winter 1978). The seventh variation, with its characteristic use of the gong, pounding drum, and swirling string figures, found its way into the American *Superman* TV series of the early 1950s. Used in several *Superman* episodes (and at least two other TV series as well), the music is memorably associated with an episode when Superman is threatened by a rampaging white gorilla. Rózsa himself, who saw the episode by chance, noted that his music fitted perfectly, and can provide his own impersonation of the gorilla to prove the point.

2   Rózsa was to be similarly inspired — though with quite different results — by Salvador Dali's surrealist designs for the dream sequences in *Spellbound* (1945) and by the paintings of Van Gogh in the 'biopic' *Lust for Life* (1956).

3   Including one for Rex Ingram as the Djinn which was discarded.

4   This comes up with startling clarity in the pre-war Denham soundtrack, which has a sharper profile than the music in many modern films.

5   This piece is also clearly the prototype of 'Salome's Dance' in the later *King of Kings* (1961), which similarly traces a course from alluring orientalism to a violently orgiastic climax.

6   Composed, like the 20th Century Fox trademark music, by Alfred Newman.

7   Someone else's music was substituted for this scene and the later one where Murchison turns the revolver on himself — probably Roy Webb's, since he himself told me that payments for

Spellbound showed up on his A.S.C.A.P. returns, and the music editor on the picture, Audray Granville, was known to be a great admirer of his. Of course Webb did not specifically compose music for these cues; Ms Granville would have selected 'appropriate' tracks from one of his dozens of RKO scores of the period, and cut them to fit the *Spellbound* footage (a routine exercise in the Hollywood of those days). Why or on whose authority these changes were made is not known — possibly on Hitchcock's, more likely Selznick's. The 'substitute' music is in both cases less overtly dramatic and therefore out of keeping with the rest of the score, which has a high blood-count! It also has a romantic gloss which accords perfectly with the sumptuous quality of the cinematography.

8   By coincidence, Rózsa's fellow-countryman Bartók's opera *Bluebeard's Castle* resembles the present scenario in that Bluebeard also has a collection of rooms each of which conceals one aspect of his past life or nature. When he flings wide the door to reveal the furthest reaches of his domain, here too the orchestra yields to the full organ. Rózsa had never heard Bartók's opera at the time he was writing *Secret Beyond the Door*, so any communication between the two expatriate composers (Bartók had died in New York in 1945) must have been telepathic. Rózsa was to re-work the same idea to spectacular effect in the *El Cid* finale.

9   Daniele Amfitheatrof in his score for *The Lost Moment* (1947) makes use of a similar technique with a choral passage, producing an extraordinary sound as of a person gulping in the process of drowning.

10   Rózsa's last film to date, *Dead Men don't Wear Plaid* (1981) is a Steve Martin comedy which incorporates film-clips from a number of 40s classics, some of which Rózsa had actually scored (including *The Bribe* and *The Killers*). This gave him a unique opportunity to view himself — at a distance of nearly forty years — in a kind of ironic perspective: an esoteric variation on the Hollywood-on-Hollywood theme.

11   This kind of pyschotic musical violence is notably similar in expression to Leonard Bernstein's in *On the Waterfront* (1955); even the 'look' of the score-page is similar (the far-back common denominator is, of course, Stravinsky's *Rite of Spring*).

12   Rózsa recalls in *Double Life* that when Judy Garland, Minnelli's

wife at the time, heard this marvellous effect in the two-piano version used during shooting, she 'gasped in thrilled amazement and goose pimples appeared on her arms'!

13   Another version of the same melody is used by Bach in the final chorus of part 1 of the *St Matthew Passion*.

14   Rózsa had earlier adapted Schubert for *New Wine* (1941), Chopin for *A Song to Remember* (1945) and Rimsky-Korsakov for *Song of Scheherezade* (1947), not to mention Herbert Stothart for *The Miniver Story* (1950). He later adapted parts of his own op. 24 Violin Concerto for Billy Wilder's *The Private Life of Sherlock Holmes* (1971). Conan Doyle's detective was, of course, an amateur violinist, and Wilder's enthusiasm for the concerto gave him the idea of making use of it here. The concerto's opening movement is associated with Holmes's addiction to drugs, the introspective melancholy of the music being strangely in keeping with the 'private' aspect of Holmes's persona. The beautiful theme of the slow movement becomes the love motif of the glamorous lady spy Gabrielle, to whose charms the hero involuntarily succumbs, and the turbulent opening of the third movement suggested to Wilder the supposed Loch Ness monster.

15   The way this music is dubbed enables us to hear little of this brief but beautiful early tribute to Rózsa's favourite European city.

16   In this context one should mention the most recent of Rózsa's major film scores, that to Alain Resnais's *Providence* (1977), as the antithesis of his spectacular style; Rózsa has dubbed it his 'anti-*Ben-Hur*'. The director, with whom Rózsa enjoyed a close and fruitful collaboration, asked for 'une musique grise' — grey music — for this strangely surreal study of an ageing writer (John Gielgud) haunted by thoughts of the past and of the troubled relationships of his family.

17   Although Rózsa is not Jewish, his music often *sounds* Jewish; sounds in fact like Ernest Bloch. The gravity of tone, the intensely elegiac expressiveness — both Rózsa and Bloch lived most of their lives in exile — the vivid sense of the theatre, of flamboyant orchestral colour, speak eloquently for the deep-sunk origins of both their musics in atavistic folk impulse. Naturally in Rózsa this feeling

comes particularly to the fore in his Biblical epics, but it surfaces
frequently elsewhere. For example, a musician to whom I once
played the sunstroke music in *The Four Feathers* suggested Bloch as
the composer.

18 A fascinating insight into the problems of synchronization
besetting a scene like this is contained in a memorandum from
Charles Wolcott (then head of the MGM music department) to
Walter Strohm (an MGM production executive) dated April 21
1958:

> In all rowing scenes to facilitate matching shots from varying
> camera angles to the master shot, we suggest the use of the
> electric metronome (being sent) which can be quickly adjusted
> to the beat of the hortator's gavel after such beat has been
> selected by Mr Wyler for the master shot. The flashing light of
> the electric metronome can be easily hidden from the camera
> eye and yet be plainly seen by the hortator.
>
> Because the script indicates varying faster rowing speeds in
> addition to the normal speed, we suggest that the fastest speed
> (ramming) be ascertained first and the others, battle speed,
> attack speed and normal speed, be scaled down accordingly.
> Obviously, the fastest speed (ramming) must be in terms of the
> physical ability of the men doing the rowing; therefore we
> suggest all speeds be determined at the first rehearsal thereby
> allowing complete freedom for Mr Wyler to shoot in any
> sequence he desires. We suggest the musical technical advisor
> be the one to set the metronome to the desired beat. The script
> clerk, of course, then makes a note of it for subsequent shots.
> This method should be the easiest and quickest procedure for
> maintaining matching beats and is flexible enough to be put
> into operation with little delay. Incidentally, it is possible to
> have an audible click along with the flashing light if desired,
> and if it does not interfere with the dialogue.

Even more complicated problems of timing are created later in the
scene after this *tour de force*, when shots of the rowers at work are
rapidly alternated with those of the naval battle raging outside.

19   The use of soft organ chords for the theme on occasion is (intentionally or unintentionally?) reminiscent of the tradition in Bach's *St John Passion* whereby the harpsichord continuo yields to the organ every time Christ's voice is heard.

BERNARD HERRMANN

I saw more than usual of Bernard Herrmann during the last two months of his life, November–December 1975, for he called me in to help him with the preparation and pre-recording of his blues theme for what turned out to be his last film, *Taxi Driver*. I noticed how excited he became when we did the recording in the Chappell's London studios in New Bond Street, and realized only later — when I saw the finished film the following year — that the idea of using the blues as the thematic basis of the whole score must have come to him then. He finished the music in mid-December and in the week before Christmas flew to Hollywood to record it. Just before he left he gave me the newly-reissued recording of his much-cherished opera *Wuthering Heights* and inscribed it specially. It was a final gesture of friendship. *Taxi Driver* was his first film-recording in Hollywood since the early 1960s, and when he returned the fatted calf was killed in his honour. All through the session days old friends, among them some of Hollywood's most distinguished names (and new ones, one of them a young director called Steven Spielberg) called in or telephoned to pay their respects. Herrmann and his assistant Jack Hayes (of the famous Shuken-Hayes orchestrating partnership) finished fitting the music to the picture on the evening of December 23. He then ate a good dinner with his wife Norma and friends, saw a run-through of *The Seven-Per Cent Solution*, the next film on his agenda (ironically as things turned out it would be scored by John Addison, who years before had replaced Herrmann on Hitchcock's *Torn Curtain*) and retired to his hotel well satisfied. Before dawn, with total unexpectedness, death, not sleep, had been to claim him: suddenly he was gone, and without any leave-taking.

That was nearly 14 years ago; but 'Benny' was unforgettable and has remained unforgotten. To say that his was an animating presence is to understate the case somewhat insultingly. Jerome Morass, who knew him in boyhood, told me that so dominant, so domineering was his personality that the time came when he (Moross) simply had to break away from it.

Herrmann's brusqueness made him many enemies: but friend and foe alike concurred in recognizing both the integrity of the man and the devotion and professionalism of the musician. Most of his 'enemies' — and in Herrmann's case that is really too strong a term for those who found him personally or professionally unsympathetic — were in fact to be found in his own generation or in the one immediately following his own: for to the young of many countries he was an idol to be worshipped.

Yet no idol can be worshipped unless it communicates in some way; and it is difficult to put into words exactly how Herrmann communicated. He certainly made no parade of knowledge or technique; I never once knew him to lecture or talk 'at' me, nor to discuss music in technical terms. He abhorred pedantry, like one of his most admired composers, Delius; and for him, as for Delius, life and music were entirely a matter of emotional response. He would not have made a good teacher in the strict sense for he lacked the gift of direct, lucid, factual expression. He communicated in an 'impressionistic' kind of way, one learned from him about music just as one learns about medieval Latin literature from Helen Waddell's *The Wandering Scholars* rather than from an academic textbook. One may not go away from such a lesson with one's head full of facts, dates and clearly-delineated expositions: one may not even be able to define one's newly-acquired knowledge in terms of clear-cut definitions. One absorbs something of the essence of the subject, its poetic spirit. He transmitted ways of thinking and feeling about music and art, and aesthetic awareness. In terms of substance rather than the show of art, Herrmann was one of the best teachers of all.

Ronald Stevenson once wrote of Herrmann's teacher Percy Grainger that he 'loved culture but hated civilization'. The same in a sense could be said of Herrmann. 'Civilized' in the superficial sense he was not; he made few concessions to social convention. I think it was Voltaire who said that to rise in the world it was not enough to be stupid; one must also have good manners. Herrmann could be irascible and impatient, much given to tantrums should things not immediately appear to be going his way; but there was no nonsense about him, he refused to tolerate it in others, and took no pains to hide his dislike of stupidity or insensitivity, whatever the age of the person in whom it was manifesting itself. Those who met him on a first occasion, or who had only superficial contact with him, often found him uncouth and disagreeable, if not overtly offensive. Interviews were liable to turn into head-on collisions. Yet there was a common thread running through all his antipathies, new and old, like the pattern on an Eastern carpet: the *raison d'être* was always what he considered some betrayal of the cause which to him was the most sacred in the world: music.

He detested most of Hollywood's 'film music composers' — as opposed to composers in Hollywood who also composed for films — because he suspected that their interest in music was financially rather than artistically motivated. He never tired of reiterating that there is no essential distinction to be drawn between composing for films and composing for other media. Stylistically he acknowledged no cleft, and was as generous in his commendation of 'serious' composers who had achieved greatness in film music — Vaughan Williams, Rawsthorne,

Walton, Prokofiev, Copland — as he was forthright in
denouncing those who proclaimed film music to be unworthy
of serious consideration by an artist — 'of course that kind
never get asked anyway.' In fairness it must be said that if a
'film composer's' reputation had pre-empted him Herrmann
was rarely prepared to allow him a fair hearing and too often
dismissed him out of hand — a good composer after all will
write good music whether the incentive be financial or
aesthetic, and in the last analysis the good of the film is the
only criterion. If the end is well served the means need not
concern us unduly. Unfortunately in many cases where sham
composers are involved, the end is anything but well-served,
and for these Herrmann reserved some of his bitterest
invective. Yet Jerry Goldsmith's anecdote is revealing.
Relations between the two composers had never been good
(largely due it seems to a misunderstanding on Herrmann's
part) nor were they improved when Goldsmith, doing one of
his first major pictures for Universal, was publicly excoriated
by Herrmann for working with an orchestrator (a practice
Herrmann abhorred). Then without a word of warning
Herrmann appeared on the sound-stage while a recording
session for that film was in progress. 'But he did walk in at a
very opportune moment', recalls Goldsmith, 'it happened to
be the best piece of music in the score and was quite exciting.
And he [Herrmann] said "Don't use that music — it's too
damn good for the picture! You save it, it's too damn good for
the picture!" The point is that in spite of all his animosities,
prejudices and idiosyncrasies he was a musician to the core,
his musical instincts could not be denied and in that area he
could not help but be honest.'[1]

If Herrmann was often less than generous in his attitude
towards his colleagues in film music, his knowledge of the
work of 'non-film' composers was encyclopaedic, and his
enthusiasm limitless. Many composers seem to be able to
compose only in a solipsistic musical world; indifference to the
work of others is often a prerequisite to the functioning of the
creative mechanism, a spur to single-mindedness. Not so in
Herrmann's case: he throve on the work of others, especially

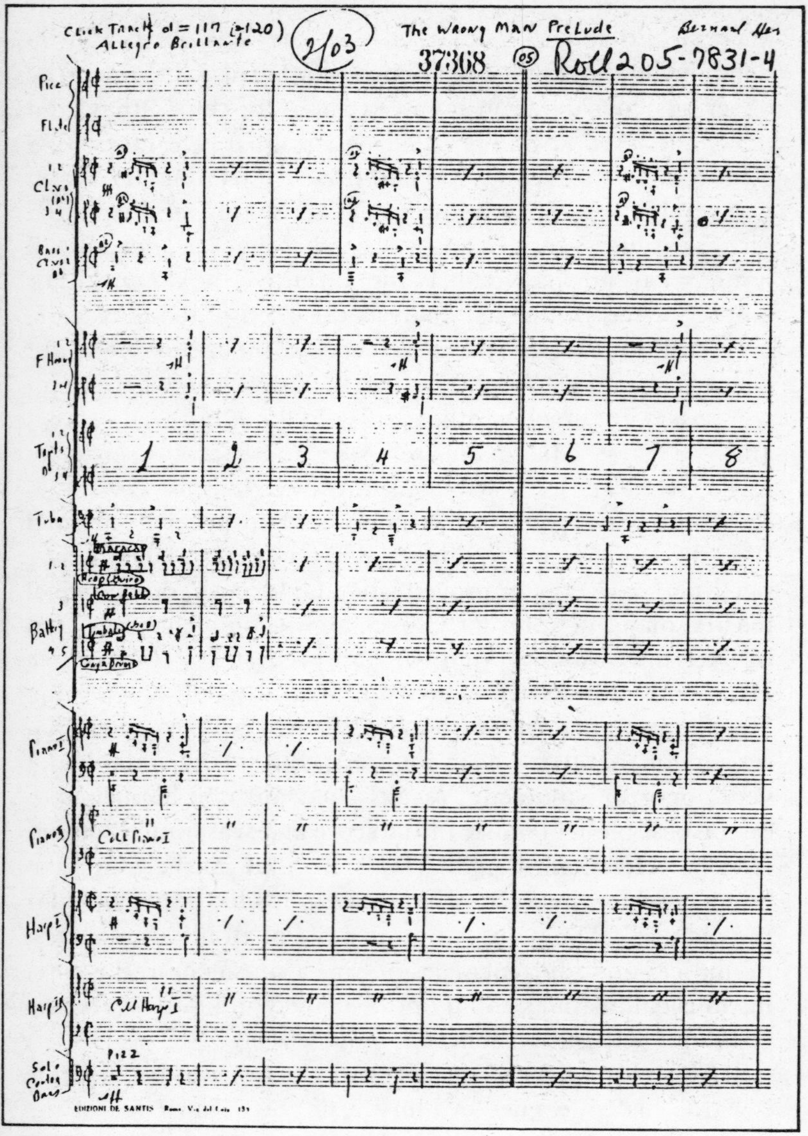

The Wrong Man: Prelude

Bernard Herrmann

those neglected by the Establishment or considered *passé* by the musical world at large. During his tenure of the CBS Symphony Orchestra the volume of unfamiliar music through which he worked his way defies credibility; nor did his knowledge of music restrict itself to what he himself could conduct. He was a musician of immense learning and culture, a fact to which the size and scope of his music library bears witness. Very well, one may say, a library of great size and scope does not itself bespeak erudition; but Herrmann's library consisted as much of books on music and composers as of music itself, and if you took any one of those books down from the shelves you were certain to find the pages interleaved with relevant articles from music periodicals or scholarly journals or with newspaper cuttings, all of which Herrmann had abstracted himself. He was devoted to music — and the range of his sympathies was enormous — wholly disinterestedly, for its own sake, not as a potential showcase for his own talents as an interpreter. Much about his sensibility could be gauged from his preferences. After his own contemporaries in America he was drawn primarily to the English, French and Russian schools: the Austro-German symphonic tradition interested him less. In this he resembles Constant Lambert, and the two have much else in common — not that Herrmann ever squandered his gifts in the way that Lambert did. Both, for instance, took their light music seriously — Messager and Waldteufel could elicit as much enthusiasm from them as Roussel or Puccini. Herrmann's Anglophilia was nowhere more pronounced than in his devotion to English music: he was the friend of Lord Berners, Finzi, Bax, Vaughan Williams and Rubbra, and adored Delius. In America he was one of the first to espouse the cause of Ives, long before he became a cult figure: in Russian music he was drawn to the symphonies of Miaskovsky. Even in the 1960s when he no longer had his own orchestra, he was championing the work of Raff ('when I met Richard Strauss in London after the last war', he told me, 'he spent half an hour talking to me about Raff'). A composer had only to set his face against stereotype and easy respectability and Herrmann was his friend for life.

The same could be said of the artists in other spheres whom he admired: they were always first and foremost *individualists*. Herrmann waged a life-long battle against those whom Grainger described as 'the snobs and prigs of music'. And those who defied convention — in the interests not of iconoclasm but of artistic integrity — always commanded his respect: conductors such as Beecham, Stokowski, Koussevitsky, Barbirolli; composers like Ives and Grainger; directors — Welles, Hitchcock, Truffaut — with whom he formed momentous relationships. Once asked how it was that he had managed to contend with so notoriously 'difficult' a collaborator as Orson Welles he replied, 'I always find difficult people easy. I only find "glad Harrys" difficult . . . those who pretend to be "nice guys" but are in reality vicious and vindictive people'. Of Welles he said 'he was by far the most exciting man to make a film with because of his sheer creativeness. I've worked with other distinguished directors but they're very secretive about their vision. With Welles you always knew what he was looking for. He was precocious, with a great streak of originality . . . he's a great improvisor in the sense that Beecham was an improvisational conductor.' Hitchcock's respect for Herrmann's dramatic sense led him to make a practice of consulting his composer before shooting. Truffaut asked Herrmann for the music of the twenty-first century in *Fahrenheit 451*, having heard in his music that simplicity to which both men felt that music in general would revert in years to come. These were the artists with whom Herrmann felt the kind of temperamental affinity that encouraged him to produce his best work.

Herrmann's breadth of general culture was not of the superficial kind frequently affected by Americans in their anxiety to conform to their own conception of cultured Europeanism. He hated pretentiousness and exhibitionism. Yet in painting and literature his was one of the most discriminating of tastes (even though, oddly, he had no feeling for foreign languages as such). Again, England tended to claim pride of place in his affections: the works of Traherne, Beddoes, LeFanu and Arthur Machen in literature, Samuel Palmer, Whistler, Richard Dadd and Turner in painting were among his constant companions; and at the time of his death he had made a tentative start on a suite for organ each of whose four movements was to be related to a picture by John Martin. His home was a repository of rare and beautiful things, some of which may be seen reproduced on the covers of his records on the Unicorn label — a hand-coloured engraving from his copy of Thornton's *Temple of Flora* for the Symphony (RHS 331); a Currier and Ives lithograph for *The Devil and Daniel Webster/Welles Raises Kane*; a contemporary limoges enamel painting for *A Musical Garland of the Seasons*. Again, Herrmann made no show of the riches he had painstakingly garnered; yet on visits to his home one always knew that, if the omens were propitious, something priceless was likely to be produced, whether a Chopin autograph or a Debussy first edition. Whatever it was one could be sure of one thing: it had been acquired, not out of the collector's mania for rarities, but love of and reverence for the artist.

The same principle applied in Herrmann's relations with his friends. That saw's edge exterior concealed a warm and generous heart and a mischievous sense of humour. Apart from his work, Herrmann's domestic life was centred around his wife and his dog (here we may note that he always proved irresistible to women and was rarely destitute of attractive companionship.)[2] For Herrmann friendship *meant* friendship: he was never interested in other people merely for what they might do for him, rather for what he might do for them. His 'generosity' reached beyond the bounds of ordinary practical things. He was deeply appreciative of any efforts people did make on his behalf, and responded to any admiration of his work he felt to be genuine. In return he was always there to help if help were needed, no doubt mindful of his own early days and of Ives' unstinting munificence. His mind worked in subtle ways: his encouragement was frequently expressed not so much in words as in actions. He had the ability to make you realize that you were capable of more than you thought possible. Of malice or meanness there was not a shred in his character. He was highly-strung and inflammable; few were spared the whiplash of his tongue on occasion, and some received more than their fair share, particularly if they touched unsuspectingly on any of his raw spots, of which there were a great many. But the iron claw was an illusion: all that was there was a velvet glove.

Herrmann was born on 29 June 1911 in New York City into a typical middle-class Jewish family of Russian origin. In spite of this, however, few traces of Russian or Jewish musical influence found their way into his own music, nor was he ever drawn to Russian music any more than to French or English. Neither his father nor his mother seem to have been musically inclined, although his father apparently liked music. Herrmann loved to relate the story that whenever his father went to the opera he would take two seats, one for himself and one for his coat and hat. 'Benny' was given piano and violin lessons as a small boy, although he never became even moderately proficient on either instrument; and in later years the piano in his home was rarely put to any use whatever. He certainly did not compose at the piano: the most he did was intermittently to check out a harmonic progression. Despite his admiration for the Impressionist composers, harmony — the science of chords — never interested him especially in the way that it preoccupied Delius, Debussy and Ravel, who all composed at the piano. Herrmann was drawn more to experiments in pure timbre and colour for which he had to rely on his inner ear.

At 13 he read Berlioz's treatise on orchestration and resolved to compose. On graduating from High School he entered New York University to study composition with Philip James and conducting with Albert Stoessel, although perhaps the most important influence was that of Percy Grainger. He continued studying with Stoessel at the Juilliard School of Music where he also took composition lessons with Bernard Wagenaar. His ambition at that time

was to become a conductor, and with the approval of the
school he and a friend, Charles Lichter, formed a chamber
orchestra and gave student concerts in which they performed
works by themselves and their friends. He had also been
earning something of a livelihood through playing the violin
in the famous New York Yiddish Theatre on Second Avenue,
an experience which may have been significant in the light of
his later interest in dramatic music.

Herrmann's first 'breakthrough' came at the age of 19. He
conducted in public at a concert of the League of Composers
where, among other things, he directed an octet by George
Antheil. Through this performance the two met and became
friends. One day the author and playwright J.P. McAvoy
came to Antheil and asked him compose a ballet for his
forthcoming *Americana* revue. Antheil at the time was busy
writing his opera *Helen Retires* and had to refuse the
commission, but suggested Herrmann in his stead. (Exactly
why Herrmann could never ascertain, since Antheil had never
heard a note of his music!) A meeting was arranged between
youthful composer and producer, and Herrmann got the job.
Incidentally the commission also solved, at least temporarily,
the problem of how to make a living; for McAvoy engaged him
not only to write the ballet, but to conduct it as well for a
twenty-six week period.

During the run of the revue he met Hans Spialek, a
Gershwin arranger. Spialek proposed that they form a
chamber orchestra to perform deserving but unplayed works.
This became known as the New Chamber Orchestra and gave
its concerts both in New York and in the Library of Congress
in Washington, D.C. Spialek urged Herrmann to develop his
talent as an orchestrator of show music on Broadway, largely
in the interests of financial security. This he did and
collaborated with a number of distinguished figures, among
them Vincent Youmans and Johnny (later John) Green.
When Green joined the Columbia Broadcasting System as
conductor he took Herrmann with him as arranger and
assistant conductor, and it was here that the latter's
involvement with serious dramatic music really began. A

fascinating thumb-nail sketch of Herrmann in his CBS days is
provided by his first wife, Lucille Fletcher, in an article
written for *Screen and Radio Weekly* in 1936:

> Bill Robson needed an iceberg. A melting, slithering
> iceberg that would slip down into the ocean with a sad, wet
> sigh. He needed it for his Columbia Workshop programme.
>
> Another sound effect. That's what anybody would think.
> But Bill didn't call the CBS Sound Effects Department for
> that iceberg. He reached for his phone and dialled a little
> office on the sixteenth floor of the CBS Building.
>
> "Hey, Benny?" he called. "Is Benny Herrmann there?
> Oh— Benny? Will you write me out an iceberg please?"
>
> That's what Bill Robson did. And so have dozens of other
> radio producers who have needed similar queer things in a
> hurry. For Bernard Herrmann has raised musical sound
> effects to the status of a fine art. He is a composing wizard
> who can wave a fountain pen and turn six notes and two
> chords into a mountain slide or a fog, in no time at all.
>
> Herrmann's "musical capsules" have graced such
> famous programs as the *Orson Welles Playhouse,* the *Columbia
> Workshop, Men Against Death*, the *Four Corners Theater* and *The
> March of Time.*
>
> Very few of Herrmann's cues are longer than 30 seconds.
> Yet he composes each one as carefully as though it were a
> symphony. Script in hand, he sits down at his office piano
> and puts himself into the mood. Sometimes the cue must
> paint a background — give the effect of rain, or fog or a
> tropical jungle. Sometimes it must be psychological — that
> is, express love, or horror or insanity. More often, it must go
> far beyond these realms and express what no man has ever
> heard. In the last type of cue Herrmann especially shines.
>
> For example — who in the world has ever heard the
> sound of a man turning into a sycamore tree? Yet that was
> one of Herrmann's assignments on the Workshop not long
> ago. It didn't floor him in the least. He thought for a few
> moments — and figured that on the whole turning into a
> tree might be rather a pleasant experience.
>
> "I scored the cues for strings, harp, celeste and flute —
> all delicate instruments — and composed a theme which

wistful, but not too sad," he says. "After all, the man turning into the tree was a postman, and his feet were tired. He was glad to be at peace."

Another difficult hit was the sound of a Revolutionary army playing *Yankee Doodle* inside a bottle. This appeared in a script by Stephen Vincent Benet performed in the Workshop last year. Herrmann solved it by taking a standard orchestration of *Yankee Doodle* and re-orchestrating it for very soft strings, woodwinds and celeste, so that it sounded almost like a music box. On the air he had the whole orchestra placed in a separate studio, and the sound piped through an electrical filter to make the music sound thin, tiny and far away. The result was perfect.

Even a time-clock didn't bother him. He had to compose a music representation of this device last year when Pare Lorentz presented the industrial drama, *Ecce Homo*. Lorentz — who was a guest producer — hadn't heard about Herrmann, and at first he planned to use a real sound effect time-clock as background for the show. His friends talked him out of it.

"Get Herrmann to write you a time-clock," they told him. "It'll make the show." It did. Herrmann has never been inside a factory in his life, but he whipped up a cue cut of a French horn, a couple of Chinese wood-blocks and a piano; and it was better than the real thing.

Herrmann, of course, doesn't dream up every cue he writes. On many he does real research, goes down to the Library and burrows through dusty books to find the authentic flavour of a period or country. Give him a script laid in Bali, for example, and he will give you a perfect imitation of a Balinese orchestra, complete with gamelans and quarter tones. Lay your story during the time of Henry VIII, and Herrmann will turn out musical backgrounds that have all the modal sadness, the strange harmonies of Tudor England. Some time ago the Workshop did an Irish fantasy by John Synge, *The Well of the Saints*. Herrmann composed a lilting Irish score. Two days after the broadcast, he received a letter from a lady named Feeney.

"Your name doesn't sound Irish," it read, "but I'd swear you had a leprechaun somewhere in your background."

Herrmann doesn't remember knowing any leprechauns. But he does know a great deal about music. He is only 26 years old now, and has been composing ever since he was 13 . . .

David Ross, the announcer, he says, was responsible for starting him off on a career of cue music. This happened five years ago. Ross was reading poetry in a weekly series called the Columbia Variety Hour. Herrmann, then a shy, thin lad of 21, was working as Johnny Green's assistant. One day in the elevator, Ross saw him with a copy of Emily Dickinson's *Poems* in his pocket.

"Like poetry?" Ross asked. Herrmann nodded his head.

"Why don't you write me a musical background for my poetry reading?" Ross asked him. He never dreamed Herrmann would take him seriously. As far as he knew, the boy was just a jazz conductor. But young Herrmann went home that night, and in two days turned out a symphonic score for Keats' *La Belle Dame Sans Merci*. It was then his favourite poem. A week later, he was conducting it on Variety Hour as background to Ross' reading.

It was so successful, so different from any other type of musical background then known, that CBS executives promptly commissioned the youngster to turn out many more.

The melodramas were full of cue music germs — effects like the shrill wind or the scuttering of dead leaves in *La Belle Dame Sans Merci*, the moonlight in *Annabel Lee*, the mental loneliness of the sightless kings in *The City of Brass*.

For example, there were such instructions as these scattered through them: "Harp: Place long strips of paper among strings to soften tone." Or "Piano: Place ruler on 12 notes above high C. Put down damper pedal. Play other notes in score with left hand."

They made Herrmann's reputation as a composer, and established him as a man who was as sensitive to words as he was to music. When experimental radio drama came along, he was snapped up right away.

Herrmann was probably the first musician in radio to compose original cues for every radio drama he was asked to score. He felt this was necessary for two reasons — the first being that familiar music tends to distract the listener's attention from the drama itself, and the second, that freshly composed music, inspired by the script, is more likely to hit the nail exactly on the head than music culled from symphonies or operas.

"The cue music composer seldom has more than 30 seconds to gain his effect," he says, "and often a discord will make a quicker impression than a snatch of beautiful melody. Dissonant harmonies also express unpleasant emotions like fear, hatred, melancholy and the like much more effectively than do diatonic chords or square-cut melodies."

Herrmann paid little attention to the tradition that if a symphony orchestra was assigned to a program, the full orchestra ought to play all the cues. He wrote for all kinds of combinations. Once, for a script by Irwin Shaw, he scored his cues for a single harmonica player. On another program, *The Broken Feather*, he used an orchestra composed only of percussion instruments — bells, chimes, marimbas, drums and xylophones.

Probably the oddest combination he ever wrote music for was for an orchestra of saws, hammers and nails. This was used in a script written by Alfred Kreymbourg; *The House that Jack Didn't Build*. It was a play about the Federal Housing Project, and Herrmann conceived the idea of having the rhythm of carpentering substitute for music.

Herrmann and the Sound Effects Department co-operated, too, in a Workshop Production of Lord Dunsany's *Gods of the Mountain*.

The play was about three Indian beggars who disguise themselves and pretend to be three stone gods who sit out in the middle of the desert. The populace feeds and worships them, until suddenly the footsteps of the real gods are heard in the distance, striding over the desert toward the town. Herrmann's job was to express these giant stone footsteps in music. He and the Sound Effects Department did it together by a very ingenious set-up.

Herrmann and his orchestra — fortified for the occasion with a couple of extra kettle-drums and tom-toms — were placed on the twenty-second floor in a studio of their own. Downstairs in another studio, a sound effects man sat, with a huge bag of rocks at his side. But the sound effects man and Herrmann wore earphones which were connected with the main studio where the drama was taking place. At a signal from the producer, Herrmann would bring down his baton, and the orchestra would give out an ominous "rumble" cue. Then, on the off-beat, the sound effects man downstairs would throw his bag of rocks from one end of the studio to the other. Herrmann would pause, and bring his baton down again. Again the rumble would sound, and again the bag of rocks would fly across the studio. On the air, it gave the effect of ponderous feet moving slowly and terribly across the earth.

Three-quarters of Herrmann's musical cues are only partially heard. But that doesn't bother him. In fact, he says, his greatest compliment is when people don't notice the music. He feels with Shakespeare, that "the play's the thing."

As the concluding remark makes clear, Herrmann at the age of 26 had already formulated a musico-dramatic aesthetic from which to the end of his life he never deviated.

In 1934 he was made a CBS staff conductor and started to direct symphonic programmes for 'The American School of the Air' in conjunction with other CBS conductors such as Victor Bay and Howard Barlow. Herrmann felt strongly that since studio concerts did not have to be influenced by box office considerations they could be planned in an unconventional way and feature rarely-heard music, both old and new. Several of Ives's works received their first performances under his direction. His advocacy of the living composer was a major facet of his conducting career, and he was also responsible for having CBS commission new works from High School music students and conducting them over the air. Given this all-American musical environment, with so much first-hand exposure to native, authentic American 'serious' music, the almost total absence of Americanisms in Herrmann's own music is surprising.

In 1940 his career opened out in another direction. At CBS he had met the young Orson Welles who at that time was running an enterprise called 'The Mercury Theater' in collaboration with John Houseman. In order to keep it financially solvent Welles 'leased' the company to CBS to perform a series of radio plays based on well-known novels and short stories. The new series was called *The Mercury Theater of the Air* and in 1936 Herrmann became its musical director. In that capacity he was involved in the famous *War of the Worlds* presentation which terrified the nation, although he did not write any special music for it; the idea was to create the illusion of reality, and so Herrmann and his orchestra played realistic music in the background until Welles interrupted the 'programme' to announce the discovery of the Martian 'spacecraft'. In 1940 when Welles took his company to Hollywood to make *Citizen Kane* Herrmann accompanied him to write the score. No motion picture career could have had a more auspicious beginning. The following year he won an Academy Award for *All that Money can Buy (The Devil and Daniel Webster)* but in 1942 he evidently took the tragic fate of Welles' *The Magnificent Ambersons* much to heart, for he then returned to New York to continue his conducting career. The following year he came back to score *Jane Eyre* which he described as a very important event in his life as it took him into the world of the Brontës and led to his composing an opera based on *Wuthering Heights*. *Jane Eyre* was a 20th Century Fox film, and for the next fifteen years or so Herrmann worked more consistently for Fox than for any other studio: this was due largely to Alfred Newman, the head of the Music Department, who was quick to appreciate Herrmann's exceptional talent. Herrmann never became a prolific composer of film scores, partly because he insisted on a six-week minimum period to complete a score (in order that he might do his own orchestration) and partly because he was in a sense, like Mahler, a 'summer' composer — the greater part of his year was spent conducting in New York, and composing for films had to be reserved for vacations and sabbaticals. In 1955 he began his 10-year long collaboration with Alfred Hitchcock, and in 1966 became associated with one of Hitchcock's greatest admirers, François Truffaut. At the end of his life he was 're-discovered' by a new and enlightened generation of directors including Larry Cohen, Brian de Palma and Martin Scorsese.

Herrmann's dislike of conformity is revealed above all in his approach to orchestration. No film composer thought as directly in terms of orchestral sonority as Herrmann. It is almost true to say that whereas for many composers orchestral colour is a means to an expressive end, for Herrmann it is an expressive end in itself. Every chord has to be individually voiced. A Herrmann fingerprint is that musical backgrounds or 'wallpaper' are often conceived not melodically but chordally, in the form of blocks of chords dissolving one into another. These chord sequences are often scored for low woodwinds, or woodwinds alternating with brass. While a Herrmann score is generally far from stereotyped or predictable in its instrumental demands in whatever departments (another aspect of his individuality) it is generally in the low woodwind area that he casts his net most widely.

Herrmann in his student days learned bassoon, harp and violin and writes for these instruments from an inner knowledge. He can identify instruments with the sounds and movements of creatures in an uncannily realistic manner — the fugato for Mr Scratch in the finale of *The Devil and Daniel Webster* actually *scratches*, the violins peck and jab like birds in the *Psycho* murder scenes, piccolos screech in torment on behalf of the murder victims in *Hangover Square*. He is never averse to diminishing the strings' traditional claim to pre-eminence (no violins are employed in *The Bride Wore Black* or *It's Alive*) or even dismissing it altogether (*Twisted Nerve* and *Journey to the Centre of the Earth* are quite stringless). Yet in the sublime *scène d'amour* in *Vertigo* when Kim Novak emerges from the bathroom to meet James Stewart, the strings bear the burden. They yearn and throb and sing and leave us in no doubt as to Herrmann's admiration for Wagner and to his own loving expertise in writing for strings. Herrmann has described this sequence as 'a long crescendo of emotional fulfilment': there is no dialogue whatever, only the camera and music, and the latter makes abundantly clear that this is the long-awaited climax of the film.[3]

Herrmann's sixty-odd scores run the gamut of emotion and nuance. It is a far cry from the monochrome intransigence of *Kane* to the feasts of colour in *Beneath the Twelve-Mile Reef, The Seventh Voyage of Sinbad* or *Mysterious Island* where Herrmann mixes his palette with the precision and panache of a Ravel or a Rimsky-Korsakov. His music (totally European, non-American, in orientation, and in this at least he outwardly conforms to Hollywood stereotype) is extremely well *composed*, in every sense. It has a certain suaveness and finish that may suggest some Gallic influence — the more so as he is always careful to balance classical poise of form and romantic intensity of feeling. Feeling is uppermost, yet he is rarely prey to the sentimentalities and lapses of taste which ensue whenever it is allowed to proceed unchecked by form. His music is so smoothly processed that all superfluities and impurities seem to have been filtered out; but not to the extent of precluding the kind of startling or sudden musical gesture which comes from a properly human response to drama. Many of his scores are suffused with a bittersweet quality in which aspiration and suffering are transmuted, via his evident delight in orchestral sound *per se* as an emotional vehicle, into musical joy. Intensifying many passages is his sense of life's transience and the need to sustain the purely instinctive, spontaneous responses of adolescence's first awakening. In films such as *The Snows of Kilimanjaro, Tender is the Night, Blue Denim* and *Joy in the Morning* (whose score, exceptionally for Herrmann, is based on a song by Jule Styne) he returns again and again to this area of feeling as a mainspring. Whenever he depicts a strong emotion he does so without cliché, without subterfuge and without compromising its purity — which is not to say that a physical or sexual element is missing. In fact the unforced intermingling of sensuousness and simplicity is one of the most disarming features of Herrmann's music. It is equally vivid and honest when projecting in orchestral sound visions of natural phenomena — the sea and underwater kingdom in *Beneath the Twelve-Mile Reef*, the primeval forests in *White Witch Doctor*, the marvels of the inner earth and their aura of mystical innocence in *Journey to the Centre of the Earth*, the North of England moorlands with their bleakness and savage beauty in *Jane Eyre*. In the latter we begin to approach the opposite end of the emotional spectrum — that which embraces extreme physical violence and mental derangement. Few composers have committed murder as savagely and bloodily in their music, and in so many different ways: the murder in *Blood Sisters* with its screaming Moog Synthesizers is as different as can be imagined from *Psycho*, where Herrmann utilizes merely that instrument of romantic nostalgia *par excellence*, the violin.

Herrmann always cared passionately about films and was never afraid to fight the ravages of mediocrity and illiteracy; nor did increasing years and radical changes in film and musical fashion impel him to retreat.

> I feel that music on the screen can seek out and intensify the inner thoughts of the characters. It can invest a scene with terror, grandeur, gaiety or misery. It can propel narrative swiftly forward, or slow it down. It often lifts mere dialogue into the realm of poetry. Finally, it is the communicating link between the screen and the audience, reaching out and enveloping all into one single experience.

This was Herrmann's own film-music credo, and a more precise definition and evaluation of the function of music in the sound-film can rarely have been put into words. Yet Herrmann, though aware of the composer's importance, never sought his own glory in his film-work; he was too conscious of the nature of film as a co-operative, mosaic enterprise in which music acted as a kind of cement, fusing together all the other component elements. No composer in the cinema was more dedicated to what he believed to be the most durable of all art-forms ('wouldn't you like to see a movie made 200 years ago?'); he once told me that leaving the characters in *Obsession* once the score was completed was like bidding farewell to a part of his life, so intimately had he grown to know and love them.

The secret was Herrmann's refusal to recognize any valid distinction between composing for the screen and composing for any other medium: he regarded the cinema as a viable and valuable creative outlet, a great art form whose full range of potential had yet to be tapped. Some composers perform a kind of Jekyll-and-Hyde act in relation to their film work, keeping one self-consciously 'popular' style for the cinema, another (sometimes just as self-consciously *un*popular) for the concert hall. Herrmann simply wrote what he felt. The only consideration was the good of the film. As he once tersely remarked 'the first step is to get inside the drama. If you can't do that you shouldn't be writing the music.'

Herrmann's first score, *Citizen Kane*, is unique. True, just as Welles at RKO was given an unprecedentedly free hand in the preparation of the film, so Herrmann worked under conditions that must have seemed Utopian to many of his Hollywood colleagues. He was given twelve weeks to compose the score. 'I worked on the film, reel by reel, as it was being shot and cut,' he has written. 'In this way I had a sense of the picture being built, and of my own music being a part of that building. Many of the sequences in *Citizen Kane* were actually tailored to match the music.' As always he did his own orchestration, conducted at the recording sessions and finally supervised the dubbing.

In few other films is music so completely an integral part of the fabric as in *Citizen Kane*. Structurally the score employs a variant of the leitmotif technique, one that Herrmann was

always wary of resorting to, but he realized that in this case
the music's job could not be done any other way. For in *Kane* a
reporter, trying to discover the meaning of Kane's dying word
'Rosebud', meets and talks with several of those most
intimately involved with him: and in a rapid succession of
flashbacks the audience learns something about Kane's
childhood, his character, his rise to power and final downfall.
'Rosebud' is the name of a sled which represents for Kane the
unspoilt world of his boyhood, an ideal the attainment of
which his whole life had, so it seemed, been dedicated to
opposing. So there are two central ideas — 'Rosebud' and its
antithesis, Kane's ambition, his all-consuming lust for power,
which proved ultimately futile. These are the twin concepts
for which Herrmann evolved musical equivalents or leitmotifs, and both are first heard in the opening Xanadu sequence.
Except for the film company's name spelled out in rapid
morse and the title, credits are dispensed with. Instead we are
plunged straight into the dark domain of Xanadu, Kane's
fantastic pleasure-palace; and as through a haze of swirling
mists the camera takes us closer to the outline of the main
tower, the motif of Kane's power sounds softly but ominously
on low muted brass and woodwind. Those familiar
with the plainsong motif sung to the 'Dies Irae' portion of the
Requiem Mass[4] will recognize its outline here; a subtle way of
suggesting the vanity of Kane's ambitions. It is heard clearly
for the first time as we see the massive wrought-iron K at the
top of the main gate. Then through a series of slow dissolves
we are shown some of the fabulous contents of Xanadu — a
cage of monkeys, an artificial lake with two gondolas, black
statues of mythical beasts, an imitation Greek temple with
artificial ruins. When, at last, we have seen the final sequence
of the film in which the identity of Rosebud is revealed, we
realize that somewhere amongst all the paraphernalia
Rosebud lay concealed; and, again wise after the event, we
realize that its presence has in fact been indicated to us by a
new motif which, first heard on the shimmering vibraphone, is
subsequently revealed as the 'Rosebud' motif. It is
heard again very soon as the apparent snowstorm fills the

screen and is thus associated with snow even before it accompanies Kane's dropping the glass snow-toy and comments upon his uttering of the one word 'Rosebud.'

So the music summarizes in its own terms the argument of the film: but on the purely practical level it is also important. Without music the scene seems interminable and fails to communicate. The music negates our time-sense: it distracts our attention from the roving motions of the camera and implants in us a series of unconscious anchors. Without music, the Xanadu sequence presents us with the pieces of a giant jigsaw puzzle in hopeless disarray. With music we may still not be in a position to understand what the pieces mean, but at least we have been shown that they all fit together somehow. The eloquence of the *Kane* music lies in its concentration. It is sparing of the grandiose gesture, the rhetorical flourish; but as the film progresses we realize that it is carrying on its own running commentary on Kane's life and fortunes, and providing clue after clue to the identity of 'Rosebud.'

There are three visual clues — the opening Xanadu sequence, the scene with Thatcher, Charlie Kane as a boy and his parents outside Mrs Kane's lodging house, and Raymond's account of Susan's departure and Kane's wrecking of her room. There are *four* musical clues. Number one, the Xanadu sequence. In the Thatcher scene 'Rosebud' sounds as the sled which little Charlie has been forced to abandon is covered by the falling snow, and eventually dissolves to a fancy new sled, thus confirming the association (intimated in the prologue) of 'Rosebud' with snow, Welles' symbol of innocence. Again the motif sounds as Kane, after smashing up Susan's room in a frenzy, chances on the snow-scene paperweight, utters 'Rosebud!' and, clutching it, staggers down the hall in front of the servants past a series of endlessly reflecting mirrors. These are clues both musical and visual; but the most vital clue to Rosebud's identity is the fourth, the one which is purely musical. When Kane first meets Susan Alexander, for once he forswears projecting his customary image and confides to her that he has just been 'on a sentimental journey. . . in search of my youth'. We learn that he has rescued his mother's belongings stored 'in a warehouse out West' (one of which would have been the sled, Rosebud). 'Rosebud' accompanies the whole of this scene, thus revealing unequivocally that it is connected with the lost innocence of Kane's boyhood.

In all these clue-spots, of course, 'Rosebud' is no more insisted upon than the clues themselves: it is simply there for those who have ears to hear. But in the finale, when Rosebud's identity is for the first and last time made clear for all to see, so 'Rosebud' for the first and last time is brought right out of its shell and fully developed. The camera reaches the end of a long tracking shot over the vast accumulation of Kane's possessions; a workman feeding a furnace shouts 'throw that junk', and flings a little sled onto the flames accompanied by dramatic trills on celli and clarinets. Then the full orchestra — one of the few moments when it is used as such — hurls 'Rosebud' with all its might at the audience as the word 'Rosebud' painted on the sled is clearly shown for a moment, before the heat buckles and splits both paint and woodwork. Music and camera have together fitted the missing piece into the jigsaw.

Very different is the treatment of the motif of Kane's quest for power. There is no need for understatement here. After the prologue the theme is first heard in an ironic nose-thumbing transformation on the cut from Susan's cabaret to the imposing bust of Thatcher in the Thatcher Memorial Library. The irony is pointed by the contrast between the theme's harmonization in open fifths and the zany sound of trumpets playing with wa-wa mutes; the intention is to characterize the officiousness of the librarian who admits Thompson, the reporter.

When Thompson begins to read Thatcher's memoirs, he learns first of the transaction between the Lawyer and Kane's parents. There is a slow dissolve from the manuscript to the snowstorm in which Charlie as a boy is presently descried playing with his sled; the music accompanying this dissolve is a fresh and innocent transformation of 'Power' on flute and celesta heard through a haze of trilling strings. It thus mirrors both the snowstorm itself and the troublefree spirit of Kane as a boy; he has not yet been corrupted by wealth and so there is no indication in this version of 'Power' of the sharp edge it is later to acquire.

The Thatcher-Kane relationship is limned in a series of short, sharp flashes as the years roll by. At one point Thatcher is chiding Kane for having lost so much money on his 'philanthropic enterprise', *The Inquirer*, during its first year's running. Kane, however, is breezily confident: 'at the rate of a million dollars a year I'll have to close this place . . . in fifty years'. But for all his arrogance the next we hear is that he is bankrupt and obliged to relinquish control of the newspaper. The transition is bridged by an ironic reference to the ragtime which accompanies Bernstein's account of the opening of *The Inquirer* office (itself a variant of 'Power'), and by two ominous variants of 'Power' symbolizing the decline of his fortunes.

At the end of the Thatcher sequence Thompson leaves the vaults; wa-wa trumpets caw 'Power' again in its open fifths harmonization, but with a syncopated rhythm which suggests both the reporter's cheery departure and the officious librarian's outraged reaction at his irreverence: '*You're* not Rosebud, are you? Well, goodbye everybody, thanks for the use of the hall!'

Bernstein describes Kane's first day at the *Inquirer* office and their encounter with the editor Carter, a pompous bumbling pillar of bourgeois conservatism; here, as already indicated, 'Power' is transformed into a vigorous piece of early ragtime which typifies the young Kane's iconoclasm. In fact many of the scenes portraying Kane as the early *enfant terrible* and his public activities generally are accompanied by stylizations of dance forms popular in the 'gay nineties'[5]. The *Inquirer*'s campaign against the traction trust is done in the form of a galop; a can-can scherzo blusters its way through the montage showing the *Inquirer*'s increase in circulation, and the ragtime is associated with the explosive start of the paper. The can-can also manages to work in a reference to 'Power' but immediately before this it has sounded wearily as Kane changes the make-up of his front page for the umpteenth time and formulates his 'declaration of principles'.

The most interesting metamorphosis of 'Power' occurs in the well-known 'breakfast montage'[6] in which the break-up of Kane's first marriage is followed in terms of the couple's progressively deteriorating relationship over the breakfast table. The whole sequence lasts only a few minutes and comprises a number of brief scenes ranging from warmth and affection in the first to silence and indifference in the last. Herrmann accompanies each scene by a mini-variation on a Waldteufel-like waltz theme, the variations becoming more and more chilly and less waltz-like as the scene proceeds. The reason for Kane's loss of interest in his wife is, of course, his ambition; and this is cleverly indicated in the music when 'Power' finally appears in the last two variations, and it reveals itself as the waltz-theme turned upside down. In other words as Kane makes plain where his true interests lie, so the music strips the mask from its features too.

After this 'Power' does not re-appear until the seventh main flash-back, Susan's narrative. In the form of a montage we are shown her national tour as an opera star, in which she is metaphorically crushed and trampled by the weight of her husband's ambition and driven eventually to attempt suicide. In this montage, tracks of her voice singing the specially composed opera *Salammbô* are chaotically superimposed on 'Power' which after one statement is reduced to an obsessive rhythmic hammering on drums, as if beating poor incompetent but sensitive Susan into a mental pulp. The climax comes with a visual and aural 'run-down' — the music and Susan's voice disintegrate and a light-bulb filament goes out, both symbolizing the collapse of her career. Then after her attempted suicide we are transported to Xanadu to the sound of a tired, bored-sounding variant of 'Power' presaging the monotonous passing of the hours in the so-called 'pleasure-dome'. So it continues as Kane and Susan argue, she longing for New York and for fun, he insisting that Xanadu is their real home and that there they must stay ('Power' is clearly audible as he pontificates in front of the huge Scottish Stuart fireplace). Then *pizzicato* strings imitate the ticking of a giant clock as Susan pores vacantly over the monster jigsaw puzzle for want of anything more interesting to do. For the opening scene of the 'picnic' — a thread of black cars winding its way mournfully along the Florida beach-line — Herrmann turns 'Power' into a funeral cortège, trumpets injecting a note of jazzy desperation.

Finally, we return to Xanadu for Raymond the butler's account, and 'Power' dramatically points the cut into the massive 'K' over the entrance. Then comes the Epilogue. Thompson and the other reporters prepare to leave, talking among themselves as they move through the crates and packing-cases and admitting their quest to have been in vain. The final crane shot begins, 'the camera rising again', in Charles Higham's words, 'until all the boxes seem like the ruins of a skyscraper city, a vanished empire'.[7] Sombre brass chords, not unlike those of the prologue, lead in with 'Power' which suddenly gives way to 'Rosebud' as Rosebud's identity is revealed in the manner already described; but the real climax comes with a shattering *fortissimo* statement of 'Power' in the guise of a brass chorale as we see Xanadu's chimney symbolically belching forth spirals of thick black smoke — the *Dies Irae* with a vengeance. A sudden hush as we are once again on the outside of the castle, now shrouded again by the impressionistic mists of the prologue; but as the huge initial 'K' in its metal scrollwork commands the screen, 'Power' swells for one final statement on the brass in the major and, in fact, closes the film on a note of triumph. Was this a concession to the Hollywood convention of a happy *fortissimo* musical ending to even the most devastating of tragedies, or does it indicate that Kane's life was not altogether the unmitigated moral and spiritual disaster it has appeared? Does the fact that he was always unconsciously striving after Rosebud, the dimly-focused crystallization of the better life, suggest a streak of nobility reflected in these closing bars? Or does this affirmation strike a hollow note? It seems inconceivable that Herrmann could have paid lip-service to stereotype over an issue of crucial importance.

Citizen Kane is unorthodox in most respects, and its treatment of realistic music is no exception. Few sequences have given rise to more admiring comment and analysis than the two perspectives — Jedediah Leland's and Susan Alexander's herself — from which the latter's disastrous debut as an opera singer is viewed. Herrmann was here beset by a variety of problems. He had to produce a fragment of realistic grand opera which would effectively demonstrate that, while Susan Alexander certainly possessed a voice of a kind, it was particularly unsuited to what she had to sing. Also the music had to reflect both Susan's hysterical awareness of her own inadequacy, her anguish, and the pandemonium around her — noise, dirt, stage-hands rushing to and fro, an ear-splitting orchestra, glaring footlights, the frantic gesticulation of her teacher Signor Matisti. In other words, the realistic music had to serve as a kind of abstract commentary on the dramatic action. Herrmann realized that no excerpt from the standard repertoire could satisfactorily fulfil all these requirements.[8] So he composed a pastiche recitative and aria in the manner of the late nineteenth century Franco-Oriental school but incorporating a number of 20th century elements of harmony and orchestration. The text was loosely derived from Racine's *Phèdre* (the scene where Phèdre implores Hippolyte to stab her to expiate her shame — perhaps a symbolic reference to the Susan-Kane relationship?) and prepared by the playwright Lucille Fletcher (not John Houseman, as has been claimed), who was Herrmann's first wife and librettist of *Wuthering Heights*. The vocal line was pitched high, the orchestral accompaniment so heavily scored that only a powerful dramatic soprano with a strong top octave could make headway against it. A light lyric soprano was then engaged to sing the part, her best efforts so helplessly at odds with the Straussian hurly-burly of the orchestra as to give the impression that she was floundering in quicksands. This produced the desired effect: had the singer performed badly on purpose (as has been claimed) the result might have sounded contrived.

Realistic music exists on various other levels throughout

the film, but is everywhere handled with skill and imagination. The song sung by the dancing girls at the *Inquirer* celebration (lyrics by Herman Ruby to music by Pepe Guizar originally composed for a song called *A Poco No*) recurs as Kane's campaign anthem (in conjunction with a reference to Handel's *See the Conquering Hero Comes*), then as his epithalamium (somehow jumbled up with a quotation from Mendelssohn's *Wedding March*): and, most tellingly, in a poignantly dismal transformation on a street hurdy-gurdy as Leland gets drunk and staggers towards the *Inquirer* building after Kane's defeat at the polls. We barely see the hurdy-gurdy player, we barely hear his tune, but almost subliminally do we remember the words originally sung to it: 'There is a man, a certain man, who for the poor you may be sure will do all he can. . .' The song is heard for the last time, in an arrangement for orchestra alone by Conrad Salinger,[9] over the comic-strip-type credits at the end. This economy is as typical of the score as of the film. Every note is there because it makes a contribution, no matter how small, to the whole. Even the words of the song being sung by the old Negro singer in close-up at the start of the Xanadu picnic scene serve as an unwitting ironic comment on the Susan-Kane relationship: 'there ain't no love/there ain't no true love'. But we have already heard this song *without* words (it is in fact a jazz piece called *In a Mizz* by Charles Barrett and Haven Johnson dating from 1933) as an accompaniment to Susan's first appearance at the El Rancho nightclub, then again later as she finally consents to talk to Thompson. Musically the bridge from the latter scene to the flashback of the singing lesson which follows is cleverly negotiated: as Susan and Thompson are still talking the pianist in the background drifts imperceptibly and in the same key from *In a Mizz* to the song Signor Matisti attempts to teach Susan, Rossini's *Una voce poco fa*. The Rossini is actually upon us *before* the dissolve, almost imperceptibly — a device which may well have its origin in Herrmann's experience as a composer of incidental music for radio. In the latter the responsibility for the transitions rests entirely with the music; the music must tell the listener that the scene is shifting, for the eye cannot. Herrmann uses this technique frequently in *Kane*, in which there are many abrupt time transitions and sharp photographic contrasts.

A final unorthodoxy concerns the newsreel music in the 'News on the March' sequence. The newsreel is an impersonal compilation of footage with no dramatic or emotional significance, so Welles selected the music from RKO files and used it in typical newsreel manner. There are snatches of the Tannhäuser Overture and the Chopin Funeral March, but most of the music was assembled from the scores of contemporary or near-contemporary RKO productions — *Nurse Edith Cavell* (Anthony Collins), *Gunga Din* (Alfred Newman), *Reno, Five came Back, Abe Lincoln in Illinois* (Roy Webb) and others. The newsreel is a fake, but at least a genuine fake.

It is remarkable that *Citizen Kane* marks not the climax of Herrmann's or Welles's professional career, but the beginning. Yet in a sense it *was* the climax in that neither ever really excelled his achievement in *Kane*, which remains a masterpiece of world cinema. Yet at no time did Herrmann or any of his colleagues suspect that they were working on a project of unusual moment. He said simply, 'We were all being paid to do a job and we did it to the best of our ability'. It is tempting to add, echoing a remark of Welles' character Bernstein, that the only difference was, they happened to be the best men in the business.

Herrmann collaborated again with Welles on his next RKO assignment, *The Magnificent Ambersons*, a haunting threnody for a vanished America, butchered by the studio after Welles's departure for Rio in February 1942. There was no need here for the intricate thematic manoeuvering of *Kane*, but the music is no less an integral part. As Charles Higham has pointed out,[10] Welles uses sound *per se* sensitively and evocatively in this film. The sounds of his characters' voices all have a distinctive timbre, and these are contrasted with the sounds of doors slamming in the huge reverberative Amberson mansion, engines revving, horses clip-clopping, trains whistling hoarsely, sleighbells jingling, thunder pealing — and the composer had to find a way of threading his music into his carefully-wrought web of natural noise in such a way that an extra emotional dimension could be established without disturbing the symmetry. As in *Kane*, the impression is that Herrmann's solution was the only one possible. There are two distinct musical motifs, and the main theme is not the composer's own but a waltz, *Toujours ou jamais*, by Waldteufel (a particular favourite of Welles's). Lyrical, gaily wistful, and lightly scored, it is as insubstantial as the world which drifts away before the Ambersons' eyes; and in the various metamorphoses it undergoes from the time of its initial appearance it comes to stand as a symbol of dissolution and decay, as a microcosm of the film itself.

Opening credits are again dispensed with. Instead a montage, a frolic depicting some of the sentimental attitudes and manners of the days when the Ambersons and their environment were still untroubled by any threat of a dawning industrial age, is accompanied by a set of variations on the waltz. 'The Magnificence of the Ambersons began in 1873', announces Welles, whereupon the waltz begins as well on muted strings and harps, 'their splendour lasted through all the years that saw their Midland town spread and darken into a city'. This, then, is the theme, both in sight and sound; and variations on the one are reflected in variations on the other. The first, scherzo-like, follows Eugene's (Joseph Cotten) demonstration of the changing world of men's fashions. Then the mood changes from one of gentle buffoonery to nostalgia: 'In those days they had time for everything. Time for sleigh-rides, and balls, and assemblies, and cotillions, and open house on New Year's, and all-day picnics in the woods. And even that prettiest of all banished customs, the serenade'. As Welles speaks the opening words a new variation begins, tender and innocent-sounding, and as we see the Amberson house covered in snow, the fragile celesta picks out a new melody (Herrmann's own in this case) which recurs later and is always associated with this Wellesian symbol of freshness and innocence. The muted strings and harps return, 'releasing their melodies to the dulcet stars' as Eugene and his friends perform their summernight serenade outside Isabel's window; and, following Eugene's untimely accident with the bass viol, with a brief tongue-in-cheek reference to the waltz, the montage is over.

We hear next the tinkly celesta theme as we move into the Amberson house at Christmas time and see the wind shaking the bells on the Christmas trees: the scene of the ball in George's honour, 'the last of the great long-remembered dances that everybody talked about' where the waltz is heard for the first and only time *as* a waltz in a ballroom context. In the sleigh-scene in the snow the unusual scoring — 3 glockenspiels, 2 celestas, 2 harps, piano, small and large triangles and jingles — give the music a frosty glitter which is faded up for each shot of the sleigh, so pointing the contrast between the noiseless untrammelled flight of the latter and the asthmatic lurchings and flounderings of Eugene's 'horseless carriage' — Herrmann calls this musical sequence, aptly a 'moto perpetuo'. The theme of snow-fresh innocence returns as George and Lucy pick themselves up out of the snow after the sleigh has overturned, a new awareness in their eyes. The later scene in which George proposes to Lucy in a carriage and is rejected is also accompanied by the 'innocence' theme on its last appearance — for now the clouds begin to gather. This is where the Waldteufel-like theme begins its process of dissolution. Barely recognizable is its transformation, in Isabel's death-scene, on a quasi-disembodied vibraphone over very soft, low, dull, numbly-shifting brass chords as Fanny hugs George in anguish and assures him that his mother really loved him; and during Major Amberson's senile ramblings just before his death it sounds on a melancholy, dark-hued viola. By this time there is nothing in the least waltz-like about the waltz. Finally it accompanies the quietly climactic scene in which George walks home slowly 'through what seemed to him to be the strange streets of a strange city. For the town was growing, changing . . . and as it heaved and spread it befouled itself and darkened its skies. This was the last walk home he would ever take . . . tomorrow they were to move out — tomorrow they would be gone'. The

disembodied vibraphone with its ghostly shimmering reverberations again takes the theme over soft, dissonant
muted brass chords, as if twisted by pain. By now the theme is
no more than a wraith of its former self, and one final desolate
reference, as George kneels by his mother's bedside to ask her
forgiveness, brings the saga of the Ambersons (at least as far
as Welles and Herrmann were concerned) to its close.[11]

There is one scene, however, where the waltz-theme is
heard in a fresh perspective. Lucy and her father Eugene walk
through a shower of weeping willows. She has just voluntarily
renounced George and tells Eugene (who has lost Isabel),
quietly and without any visible show of emotion, about the
Indian Prince rejected and sent to his death by his own
people; yet once he was gone nobody seemed quite able to
replace him. Father and daughter talk softly, each aware of
the other's grief but by tacit mutual consent declining to refer
to it directly: and Herrmann accompanies their colloquy by a
variant of the Waldteufel theme played discreetly but audibly
on the organ. The unusual sonority and the emotive quality of
the harmony give the scene a new poetic dimension.
Elsewhere the musical substance is spare, static and frugally
apportioned — a few sinister chords, gauntly-scored, are
sufficient to conjure up the death-charged atmosphere of the
Amberson house at the time of Wilbur Minafer's demise, or to
intensify the tragedy of George's unmeaning but systematic
undermining of his mother's health and happiness.

In *Citizen Kane* the familiar sound of the full orchestra is
avoided except in the opera sequence, some of the ballet
montages and a portion of the finale. Instead we find (for
example) that the prologue is so scored as to produce a darker
sound than would normally be practicable via a standard
instrumental complement: here the tone-palette consists of
three bass flutes, two clarinets, three bass clarinets, three
bassoons, contrabassoon, full brass, timpani, percussion,
vibraphone and double basses. Similarly in *The Devil and
Daniel Webster* (1941) many sequences are scored in the
conventional manner — the toccata-like music for the
hailstorms invoked by the Devil (Mr Scratch) to decimate the

crops of Jabez Stone, the pastoral variations on 'The Ballad of Springfield Mountain' reflecting the beauty of the New Hampshire countryside, the sleigh-ride scherzo for Mr Scratch and his ill-fated victims, the waltz to which Miser Stevens is danced to death and transmuted into a butterfly, the final barn dance with its interpolated fugato which indicates the presence of Mr Scratch among the revellers in search of new clients.[12] But for those who think of electronic sound-effects experimentation and *musique concrète* as the prerogative of the post-war generation, there are passages in *Daniel Webster* to pull them up short. Needing a sound to characterize the first appearance of Mr Scratch to Jabez Stone, Herrmann had the singing of telegraph wires recorded at 4 am, and blended the result with the overtones of C painted on the negative which, when run through the projector, produced a phantom fundamental electronically. This was before the days of radiophonic workshops. In another scene Mr Scratch is seen playing the violin at a hoe-down. Herrmann wrote a series of variations for solo violin on 'Pop goes the Weasel' and had each one recorded by the same player on a separate track. The tracks were then married, resulting in weird combinations of *arco* and *pizzicato*, normally unplayable double and triple stops, glissandos moving in contrary motion, and so on — such as no single 'earthly' player could ever have produced.

This, in 1941, was before the beginning. In 1951, still in advance of the electronic age, Herrmann scored a science fiction feature called *The Day the Earth Stood Still* in which a being from another world (Michael Rennie) lands on earth in a spaceship manned by an enormous robot to deliver a warning to the stirrers-up of strife between nations. Herrmann attempted to give the film a feeling of other-worldliness, and dispensed with traditional strings and woodwind. He substituted an array of electronic instruments — two theremins, electric violin, electric bass, electric guitar — and balanced them against three organs (one pipe and two Hammond), two pianos, two harps, timpani and percussion and brass (no horns) with four tubas for Gort, the robot. The 'outer space' music of the prelude with its glittering textures, feeling of weightlessness and mystical overtones is a musical image which recurs elsewhere in Herrmann's *oeuvre*, and is as different from the conventional Hollywood main title as can be imagined.

Journey to the Centre of the Earth (1939) is even more outlandish: no strings but four clarinets, two bass clarinets, four bassoons, two double bassoons and one serpent (an obsolete instrument resurrected by the composer to depict the giant chameleon, whose sound resembles that of a splenetic bassoon), brass, with three extra tubas, four harps — and no fewer than five organs (one pipe and four Hammonds). Herrmann thus ensures that he has an extraordinarily wide range of tone-colour in the lower regions, and manipulates his outsize forces always with poetic revelance. The five organs are employed in the prelude with the brass to create an effect of neolithic grandeur. The music opens in a *fortissimo* blaze with every instrument at the top of its compass, but we are gradually dragged further and further down into a mass of opaque sound. The picture does not open in the centre of the earth (although the credits veer downwards from outer space); but the music has taken us straight to the heart of the matter, both literally and figuratively. A mirror-image of the same music in the form of a huge crescendo accompanies the party as they journey up the shaft from the middle earth to the centre again. This time the organs hold down a throbbing pedal-point (two notes a semitone apart) beneath a rising many-layered sequence of dissonances (with the help of two bass drums and four suspended cymbals) until a pitch of incandescence is reached. The *pipe* organ ennobles the mountain-top sunrise, but the four *Hammond* organs are allotted a remarkable passage as the explorers come upon the fabled city of Atlantis: they exchange or pass round a series of simple major chords *pianissimo* as accompaniment for a melody picked out by two solo vibraphones, also *pianissimo*. The result is the eeriest of Herrmann's psychedelic dreamscapes.

Herrmann tended to become 'typed' as a fantasy specialist,

and Ray Harryhausen's *Jason and the Argonauts* (1963) is typical. The special visual effects inspired Herrmann to create music that enhances every feature of the monster, mythological survival, natural phenomenon or whatever — its movements, appearance, even its sound. The music lends depth and character to the visual aspect of those creations, and distracts attention from technical imperfections (of which a certain number cannot be avoided). Aural terror is added to visual terror. We may think the music for Talos, the gargantuan bronze statue, enhances its lumbering massiveness and the almost static deliberateness of its motions; in fact the latter are so slow that they become almost unwatchable but for the music which creates the illusion of extra movement, and implants fear. The circular woodwind patterns with their dry wind sonorities reminiscent of Stravinsky mimic the movement and appearance of the harpies that fly down to plague the blinded Phineas. There is chordal music to accentuate the splayed amorphousness of the seven-headed Hydra; the Children of the Hydra's Teeth — fighting skeletons armed with shield and sword — are introduced by the 'Dies Irae' on brass in octaves and then by a wild dance which avoids the almost mandatory xylophones. The brass here prove themselves capable of unsuspected agility.

There is more monster music in the first Ray Harryhausen–Charles Schneer animated fantasy in Dynamation on which Herrmann worked, *The Seventh Voyage of Sinbad* (1958). The scenario, based on a tale from the Arabian Nights, moved the composer to some intriguing flights of musical fancy: the man-eating Cyclops music in which running scalic figures reach ever higher, first on woodwinds, then on the four horns and two tubas; the fight with the Cyclops which is a miniature percussion concerto (two sets of timpani, tambourine, snare drums, two small cymbals, suspended cymbals, three Indian drums, three Chinese temple blocks, tam tam). The dragon's music contrives a visual suggestion of the monster's huge stature by contrasting the high, bright sonority of three piccolos with the subterranean darkness of trombones and two tubas which bray with fiery potency in octave starkness and whose rhythmic stasis (semibreves and minims) sturdily resists the repeated assaults of six timpani playing triplets. Best of all is Sinbad's duel with the skeleton, one of Herrmann's wittiest inspirations, in which the brass section is set dancing to a cha-cha-like rhythm by a clickety-clack of percussion, all wood (two xylophones, two wood blocks, two castanets, and whip).

Mysterious Island (1961) is another Harryhausen score which adds aural 'Dynamation' or gigantism to visual. Here Herrmann calls for eight horns, four tubas and much extra wind and percussion. Apart from the wild Turner-like seascape which constitutes the overture (Herrmann was a great chronicler of the elements in clash and convulsion) the most remarkable music is reserved for the various bird and animal monstrosities encountered on the island. For the Giant Bee, Herrmann, by combining all the various techniques of string *tremolo*, woodwind trills and flutter-tonguing in the brass, effectively turns the orchestra into a monster buzzing-machine. Those who heard electronically-amplified bird cries in *Psycho* might well be misled here. Is there a real buzz — or only a simulation of one? Herrmann's film-world is full of such ambiguities, and in a sense his music for the Giant Bird is the biggest fake of all. For the bird in question — a prehistoric phororhacus — was supposed to be centuries old, and this suggested to Herrmann the use of some 'centuries old' music. Perhaps the sheer grotesqueness of this masterly Harryhausen creation reminded Herrmann that one of the shades of meaning of the term 'baroque' is outlandish, extravagant, grotesque. Whatever the reason, a baroque organ fugue by J.L. Krebs (whose very name, meaning 'crab', fits felicitously — if surrealistically — into this context), admirably suited the composer's purpose. He orchestrated this lively 18th century strict fugal exercise in a manner approaching the phantasmagorical, deploying all the resources of his amazingly constituted orchestra with a virtuoso fearlessness.

Orchestral virtuosity is endemic in many of Herrmann's

best scores. One of them is a tone-poem of the sea, *Beneath the Twelve-Mile Reef* (1953), which is also a concerto for nine harps.[13] The film spins elements of conventional melodrama into a quasi-documentary study of sponge-fishing in the Atlantic. Hence the insistence on harp tone-colour, the aquatic potential of which had first been explored by Debussy in *La Mer*, in 'Sirènes' (*Nocturnes*) and by other composers of the Impressionist school. Harp arpeggios suggest trickling water, glissandos the surge of waves, rapid figurations on the low resonant bass notes the swell and rhythm of moving water — all enhanced by the naturally reverberative properties of the harp strings which make for a characteristic haze, a film or mist as of water and light. The main title shows a series of seascapes in changing perspectives, and the first upward glissando of the harps (each harp starting on a different note and so producing a nine-part chordal glissando) sweeps us into the drama like a tidal wave. The score can almost be listened to as a sequence of mood-impressions of the sea. The harps are present constantly to liquefy the textures: in the undersea forest scene, for example, their low registers maintain a shadowy, murmurous continuum against which drums, low winds, electric bass and organ pedals heave and writhe as if to resist the enormous pressure of the water. In the same way the music increases the menace of the octopus — the harps' sinister pedal glissando (one low note smeared into its neighbour and back again) as the monster is sighted, then, as it rears and splays itself, glissandos in the low brass and timpani (centering on the 'diabolic' interval of the augmented fourth) and downward harp glissandi played with picks. The burst of sea-sound which opens the picture and which recurs at intervals throughout features a grand theme now heroic (horns), now lyric (strings against an intricately-woven tapestry of harps): and the folksong-like melody which announces the boat's safe return to port has the tangy flavour of one of Herrmann's favourite works, Vincent d'Indy's *Symphony on a French Mountain Air*.

We now come to the momentous collaboration with Alfred Hitchcock, which began in 1955 with the composer's nearest approach to a comedy score, *The Trouble with Harry*. (Herr-mann's orchestral *Portrait of Hitch* was largely based on this music). Then in the same year came the remake of the 1934 *Man who Knew too much*, the climax of which is a piece of harmonic/instrumental colouration throughout is bare and shoot a politician in the Royal Albert Hall during a concert; he is to fire precisely at the moment when the score calls for a climactic cymbal-clash so that the noise will drown the sound of the shot. Here, as in the first version, the work being performed is Arthur Benjamin's *Storm Cloud Cantata*, com-posed to a text by Wyndham Lewis. Herrmann refurbished the scoring somewhat and appears as conductor in the Albert Hall sequence; the remainder of the score is his own original work, notably a virtuoso display piece for brass and percussion which accompanies the credits and reappears briefly at the end. The climax of this piece, as of the cantata, is a *fortissimo* cymbal clash for which the camera focuses on the player; as the reverberations die away and the two massive metal plates are held quivering aloft, we read a caption to the effect that such a cymbal-clash can change the course of an American family's life. Hitchcock later told François Truffaut that ideally, for the Albert Hall scene to produce its maximum effect, the audience should be able to read a musical score. The cymbals' role at the end of the credits ensures that everyone shall understand what these instruments are and what they do, but there is a shot in the Albert Hall scene itself[14] in which the camera pans across the empty bars in the cymbalist's score to close in on the single note he has to play. The suspense would undoubtedly be stronger if the audience could actually read the score and understand what the single note implies. For that note is the real killer, the cymbal-player the real agent of death.

The Wrong Man (1957) was based on a real-life story of a New York double-bass player called Manny (Henry Fonda) arrested for crimes he did not commit because of his resemblance to the real criminal. Much of the picture is realistic and quasi-documentary in style and is beset by a grey, gloomy and oppressive atmosphere. This Herrmann took pains to enhance and avoided the upper strings; and the harmonic/instrumental colouration throughout is bare and cold. The scene in the sanatorium is the only one where any degree of 'personalized' emotion is called for, and even here the combination of a solo piccolo against low clarinets and flutes memorably evokes the bleakness and unfeelingness of the Valley of Shadows through which Rose (Vera Miles), Manny's wife, appears to be groping in a misty semi-trance. The only 'strings' which are permitted, in fact, are those of the string basses and their next of kin, the harp. Because Manny is a bass-player Herrmann gives this instrument special prominence throughout, even after the credits which show him at work in his night-club fast-plucking his way through a piece of Latin-American dance music. Thereafter the *pizzicato* double-bass returns in all major sequences: first, to accompany Manny's nightly routine on returning home (checking on his sleeping children, putting the milk in the fridge, joining his wife in their bedroom). Second, when he is arrested outside his house and is driven in the police car to the station wedged between two detectives; here the muted horns in octaves make a cold, pinched and sinister sound, the more so in that they and the basses are the only instruments playing with no supporting cushion of harmony. Once in the police station, these muted horns and trumpets start to answer each other back, first as fingerprints are taken, then — and this is the most frightening scene in the picture, thanks to a virtuoso combination of camera and music — when he is locked up in a tiny sordid cell with the prospect of spending the night there. Manny is a man of few words, a placid individual not given to outbursts either verbal or physical. He settles himself in his cell, and, but for the slightly shocked expression on his face, nothing betrays what is going on inside his mind. Nothing, that is, except the camera and the music. The muted trumpets and horns vie with one another with increasing persistence and a degree of stridency which approaches the unbearable; the camera shows the walls and bars shifting and moving until they are spinning backwards and forwards all around the lonely figure sitting motionless on his stool. The result is an audio-visual nightmare.

Psycho (1959) is perhaps Herrmann's most spectacular

Hitchcock achievement. Since the film was shot in black and white, the composer felt that the strings of the orchestra alone would provide a suitably monochrome aural complement, and the result was the first, and to date the only, film score for strings. It turns a mediocre concoction of colour-supplement psychology and Grand Guignol into a cinematic experience of unforgettable intensity.

One in-depth study of *Psycho* from the musical point of view is the work of Fred Steiner, known in Hollywood as a composer in his own right for films, radio and television, who in 1974 prepared a paper on the score as a special research project for the University of Southern California Cinema Department. In it he asks 'can such a thing (i.e. 'black and white' sound) exist in music? It can when we remember that the string choir of the modern symphony orchestra may have only one basic tone-colour, but it does enjoy certain advantages not possessed by the other instrumental families when isolated from their normal symphonic context. The strings span the largest effective gamut of notes; they have an effective range of dynamics unmatched by the other groups, and within the confines of their basic single tone-colour they can command a great number and variety of special effects: pizzicato, tremolando, harmonics, playing near the bridge, and so on. Because there are so many of them, the strings may be divided in a number of ways: antiphonal writing is possible and facilitates the blending of all the different effects just mentioned within any single string section. In fact, it is safe to say that no amount of ingenious scoring for a standard symphonic ensemble could encompass the same range of expression, gradation of dynamics, or gamut of emotions as a large body of strings. And when the expressive range of the string orchestration is compared to that of black-and-white photography, Herrmann's analogy becomes perfectly clear. Both have the capability — within the limits of one basic colour — of covering an enormous range of expression and of producing a great variety of dramatic and emotional effects, with all the gradations in between.'

The tone is set by the main title music, whose function is to inform the audience that something traumatic is going to happen. This is particularly necessary here since nothing traumatic *does* happen for the first fifteen minutes or so. But the title music's message has registered with the audience, and they keep to their seats — although they should know with Hitchcock that they are on safe ground anyway. In this connection it is relevant to quote from an article by Brian de Palma, the young director of *Sisters*, who approached Herrmann to score his picture. He gives this account of their preliminary discussions:

> I launched into an eager 10 minute explanation of why I didn't want any title music. The first scene in *Sisters* is a long set-up shot from a hidden camera in a bathhouse changing room. The partition separating the women's room from the men's has been removed. Over the scene of a blind girl undressing I wanted to fade in and fade out four titles with the primary screen credits . . . to make the credits short without any dramatic music. After I finished, Herrmann exploded.
>
> "No title music? Nothing horrible happens in your picture for the first half an hour. You need something to scare them right away. The way you do it, they'll walk out."
>
> "But in *Psycho* the murder doesn't happen until 40. . ."
>
> "You are not Hitchcock! He can make his movies as slow as he wants in the beginning! And do you know why?"
>
> I shook my head.
>
> "Because he is Hitchcock and they will wait! They know that something terrible is going to happen and they'll wait until it does. They'll watch your movie for 10 minutes and then they'll go home to their televisions."
>
> Herrmann was brutal and, of course, right.
>
> "What do you think we should do?" I asked.
>
> "I will write you one title cue, one minute and 20 seconds long. It will keep them in their seats until your murder scene."
>
> He did, and it did.

Hitchcock makes no particular effort to speed *Psycho* on its way. We open with a panoramic view of the big city (Phoenix) but close in slowly on the open window of a dowdy hotel room. Inside the room Marion Crane (Janet Leigh) and her lover Sam (John Gavin) are in bed together. The time is 2.43 pm. The conventional musical response to the opening shot would have been the conventional clatter of big-city music, complete with Gershwin-like xylophone. But Herrmann goes straight to the heart of the matter. He knows that in a few seconds the camera will take us from public daylight into private near-darkness, and he prepares us: a lethargic procession of high string chords suggests both the oppressive heat of the early afternoon sun, and the tension-fraught atmosphere in the upper room where the two lovers have been snatching a clandestine hour together.

The title music returns after Marion has stolen the $40,000 and is fleeing from Phoenix by car. It begins immediately after her employer has spotted her leaving town. Her face and general demeanour betray nothing of the risk she is taking; she cannot afford to permit them to. She might be an ordinary young woman on her way home or to the supermarket. Only the music reveals the true nature of the venture she has embarked upon. It drops out for the scene when she is questioned by the road patrol policeman, but returns with renewed vigour as she drives on through the black wet night; here it so blends with the rain streaming down the windscreen, the wipers dancing frenziedly from side to side and flashes and darts of light from unspecified sources, as to produce a paroxysm of terror in our minds: the music so fuses sight and sound as to put us momentarily in the protagonist's place. By telescoping her inner agitation with the turmoil raging about her, as in the opera sequence in *Kane*, Herrmann enables us to identify with the heroine (or anti-heroine).

The most remarkable music is connected with the activities of Norman Bates (Anthony Perkins), a schizophrenic who is also a homicidal maniac. He has an obsession with birds, and when Marion first notices the unnerving collection of stuffed birds in his office, violas quietly begin a soft jabbing motion.

This persists as she remarks to him that he eats like a bird and recurs first when she leaves him alone in his office and we sense that he is aroused by her, and when she accidently knocks the bird picture off the wall of her cabin. Then comes the celebrated shower murder. Many thought that Herrmann had used some electronic device to underscore both this scene, the murder of Arbogast and the *dénouement* which reveals Norman and his 'mother' as one and the same person. One suggestion was that the sounds were achieved by the electronic processing and amplification of actual bird noises. This, or something like it, was actually reserved for *The Birds* itself, on which Herrmann worked as a sound-consultant. But in *Psycho* the composer's simple expedient was to make the violins play *glissando* upwards in short, sharp spurts to create a bird-like pecking: a screeching, stabbing sound-motion of extraordinary viciousness. The sound was recorded very close to the microphone and in a harsh acoustic, the result being almost physically painful. We seem actually to feel in the music the blows of the murderer's knife, to hear in it the terrified screams of his victim: and the music links in our minds, whether consciously or not, Norman's pathological obsession with *birds* and with *murders*. It tells us in advance who the murderer is, anticipating the psychoanalyst's account, in the final scene, of Norman's mother-complex. In this way the motivic threads are subtly woven together in the music, which in the murder-scenes is also called upon, as in the opening sequence of *Kane*, to negate the audience's time-sense. But whereas in the latter the music speeded up the action, here it slows it down. The shower murder takes in reality only some 45 seconds; watching it, it seems interminable. The music so heightens and exacerbates our responses as to protract the emotional resonance much longer. The extraordinary fact is that Hitchcock's original intention was to play the scene without music. Later, when he became dissatisfied, Herrmann prevailed upon him to try it *with* music. Of course the scene was changed out of all recognition: whereupon the composer reminded the director of his original ruling. 'Improper suggestion', came the reply.

In a sense the cleverest music has yet to come. After the murder we move outside the Bates' motel with the huge period mansion looming atop the hill. We hear Norman's voice berating his 'mother' and then see him come hurtling down from the house to the motel, evidently in a state of panic. The music which comes hurtling down with him is a compression, a verticalization, of the music already heard 'horizontally' i.e. through the longer period of a half-a-minute or so in the murder scene. Not content with giving us clues *before* the event, Herrmann now leaves us in no doubt as to the murderer's identity *after* it.

North by Northwest (1959) demanded a totally different type of score. Here the overture is the mainspring of the musical action. Saul Bass' title design of intersecting lines horizontal and oblique opens eventually on to a Washington cityscape, and the studio wanted Herrmann to do the familiar Gershwin city thing. Instead he built the roars of Leo the Lion into the opening of what he described as a 'kaleidoscopic orchestral fandango designed to kick off the exciting route which follows': not a conventional cityscape but 'the crazy dance about to take place between Cary Grant and the world'. The fandango is a Spanish dance possibly of South American origin in alternating 3/4 and 6/8 time, but Herrmann employs it not for any nationalist overtones (the entire action takes place in North America), but for its lithe propulsive rhythm which accords well with Grant's occasionally Astaire-like agility; the music flashes and bites with a quicksilver wit. If *North by Northwest* is to be classified as a comedy thriller, unusually larger-than-life even by Hitch-cockian standards, in musical terms the comedy lies in the elasticity of the dance rhythm, the thrills and chills in the harsh brilliance of the orchestral sonority.

This fantastic dance is a recurrent musical symbol. After the credits it returns first for Cary Grant's crazy-drunk drive along the cliff-edge, swerving and skidding right and left, narrowly missing trees and other cars, all but plummeting over the side, and ending in a three-car pile-up. Then, after apparent evidence has conspired to divest Grant's story of every shred of credibility, we hear a crestfallen, grotesquely-scored version of the dance. Later, snatches are cued in to throw all into confusion the moment after Townsend's assassination, and after Cary Grant has successfully thwarted *his* would-be assassins piloting the crop-dusting aeroplane on the prairie wasteland. This nail-biting sequence itself is played without music, since the latter would have interfered with the contrast between the vast empty silence of the prairie and the sudden spurts of sound from the aeroplane as it comes swooping towards Grant.

The most elaborately-choreographed scene is the pursuit and the fight to the death on top of the National Monument on Mount Rushmore, South Dakota, which begins in the gathering dusk; and here the dance initially assumes an appropriately black-veiled character in the scoring. But as the pace quickens it soon reverts to type and energizes the *dénouement* in its brazen and glittering main title guise. Nor must we forget the short, triumphantly sardonic burst of dance which boots the picture off the screen as the train carrying Cary Grant and Eva Marie Saint (now happily re-united) is swallowed up in the (very Freudian) tunnel.

A side-issue is the rather unorthodox romance which develops between Grant and Saint, and at one point this induces an interesting *rapprochement* between realistic and commentative music. For when Grant is first shown Saint's table in the restaurant car, realistic music in piped form is going on, the usual synthetic smoochy string syrup.[15] But as a relationship between them begins to form, the musical background subtly changes to Herrmann's own commentative music with an expressive clarinet solo, until it is no longer 'background' at all but part of the scene.

In 1966 Herrmann began an association with François Truffaut, a Hitchcock admirer of long standing. In his second film with Herrmann, *The Bride Wore Black* (1967), he avowedly attempted — and succeeded in — a reconciliation of Renoir and Hitchcock, the *film de situation* and the *film de personnages*.

Herrmann's way of allowing the rhythm and texture of a

film to determine the character of his music so that the one may enhance and complement the other is nowhere more apparent than here. Much of the feeling of airy grace and fluidity, of effortless flow and glide, is achieved through the interweaving of camera movement and music; the effect is almost literally a dance in which camera and music combine, the one adapting itself to the needs of the other. This is particularly noticeable in the tracking shots which introduce every episode — the first, for example, as Julie appears in the guise of a fairy princess in white outside the block of flats where Bliss (her first victim) lives, and the third, when the camera stalks the little Morane boy and his mother walking unsuspectingly home from school. The music joins forces with the camera deliberately to allay the audience's suspicions by transporting them now into a fantasy, now into sunny childhood. The orchestra dispenses throughout with violins, establishing a pastel tone-quality.

Another unifying device is a motto theme, namely the Mendelssohn *Wedding March*, in employing which Herrmann blends quasi-realistic and commentative music in an almost surrealistic manner. In the main title, the fanfares which always introduce the march are played not on the organ but by the orchestra; the full organ then enters with the march itself which at this point we hear *in toto*. When Julie is disposing of her second victim, Coral, we are given the first of several flash-backs to the fatal moment when the bridal couple appear on the church steps and David, the bridegroom, is shot down from an upstairs window opposite. An obvious cue for the organ again: but it is not used in true realistic fashion since we do not hear it as from inside the church but *fortissimo* in the foreground, and it cuts out the second the shot rings out.

The third murder, that of Morane who is suffocated in the cupboard under the stairs in his house, is the occasion of an even longer flashback, in which the train of events in the upper room immediately prior to the shooting is re-enacted in dumbshow. Here the organ does not play at all. Instead the orchestra has a series of sardonic variations on the *Wedding*

March, culminating in the fatal shot fired accidentally and the five friends' panic-stricken flight from the house.

We learn from Morane that these five had only two things in common — their passion for hunting, and for women. Hence the suggestion of hunting horns at the beginning of the sequence, rather in the manner of the murder-hunt in *On Dangerous Ground*. Yet again we witness the scene on the church steps as it passes through Julie's mind's eye — 'pour vous c'est une vieille histoire . . . pour moi ça recommence toutes les nuits. . .' but this time as the groom crumples and falls the organ does not cut out but overlaps with a dissonant orchestral outburst. Then finally as she murders the fifth and last member of the party off-stage in a prison cell the account is paid in full and the whole *Wedding March* peals out *fortissimo* and uninterrupted to bring the picture to an ironically triumphant conclusion.

The treatment of the individual murders themselves is no less original. A bitter-sweet waltz[16] reminiscent of Ravel hovers around Bliss' wedding reception, rather like some elusive perfume. It enhances the aura of unreality surrounding the white-clad Julie who is greeted by a wondering Bliss and his friend Delvaux as an 'apparition'. This waltz is another recurrent musical motif; it stops suddenly as Julie, on the balcony, pours the water Delvaux has brought her into the shrub-pot, and in so doing helps to brand the incident (very necessarily) in our memories. Julie asks Bliss to rescue her scarf which she has allowed to entangle itself on a nearby branch. As he climbs over the balcony and reaches out towards the branch, the music starts again, picking up the first phase of the waltz and reiterating it with increasing animation until the whole orchestra is gyrating madly with it — the climax being reached, after a long crescendo, as Julie pushes Bliss off the balcony to his death a hundred stories below.

The camera now returns to the scarf and follows it as it floats away over the Mediterranean landscape to the lilting accompaniment of some equally Mediterranean mandolin music. The latter, we know, comes from a 45 rpm record which Julie evidently associates with David in some way, since she plays it wherever she goes (we have already seen it playing on her record player before the murder of Bliss). Like the organ, it is in fact used here in a quasi-surrealistic *mélange* of commentative and realistic music. Julie asks Coral to put the record on his player so that she may dance to it. As she does so the 'realistic' mandolins become inextricably interlinked with a waltz in the 'commentative' orchestra based on none other than our old friend from *Citizen Kane*, the *Dies Irae*. It is a true *danse macabre*, in fact, not unlike the death-waltz in *The Devil and Daniel Webster*. Slowly, too, Coral is drawn towards his death, and the dance is brought to a head as Julie reveals her purpose and the occasion of the earlier 'meeting'.

Coral is the first of the two of Julie's victims for whom the director, supported by his composer, intends us to feel some sympathy. Coral is shown as an unattractive middle-aged man, balding and overweight, living by himself in a seedy bed-sitter. He has obviously failed in all the important issues of life, and himself confesses to having had very little success with women. He is an object of pity, not of contempt like Bliss and Morane: accordingly the music for the pathetic scene in which, just before Julie's arrival, he tries to make both himself and his room as presentable as possible, fairly overflows with sympathy. A serene and beautiful string melody, with solo oboe punctuations, makes no reference whatever to the impending tragedy; but when Julie arrives the waltz theme from the *first* murder sequence is cleverly adjusted to fit the rhythmic pattern of this string melody. The musical continuity thus remains unbroken even though the mood and inflexion have been modified.

We are also intended to feel sympathy for the penultimate victim, Fergus, the painter, though in a different way and for a different reason. Julie and Fergus fall in love. This becomes abundantly clear in the beautiful sequence — sculpture in music and moving image — showing Fergus preparing Julie in her pose as Diana, Goddess of the Hunt — (the 'hunt' symbol is, of course, carried over from the Morane episode).

The music intensifies both the contained eroticism of the scene and the couple's increasing emotional involvement, Fergus' awareness and the faltering of Julie's resolution. On two occasions this music — a tender love-theme — erupts in a volcano of passion. First, when Fergus is left alone in his apartment after his first session; as he feverishly starts work on the mural, the music transmits the powerful feeling ulie has awakened in him. Second, after Fergus has thrown his weekly gathering of friends and admirers out of his studio and we watch them from the window trooping across the courtyard. The music points to the fact that this apparently insignificant shot is really the climax of the episode: for when we next see Fergus he is lying dead on the floor with Julie's arrow in his back. His friend Delvaux is too late to save him: as he idly pours a glass of water into a shrub-pot, the waltz-like flute music from the first episode tells us that the action has rung a bell in his mind, and now he knows where and when he has seen Julie Kohler before.

Herrmann was angered by musical discrepancies between the French and English versions of *The Bride Wore Black* — a result of Truffaut's well-known tendency to tinker with his films even after they had passed the definitive cutting stage. The above discussion reflects the composer's original intentions as clearly as can be ascertained. However, from the composer's point of view at least, *Fahrenheit 451* (1966) was the more successful of the two Truffaut collaborations.

The film is set in an unspecified totalitarian state at an unspecified time in the future, and Herrmann was curious to know why Truffaut had declined to commission one of the French avant-garde composers to prepare a 'futuristic' score. But Truffaut revealed that he, like Herrmann, felt that the music of the future, of the 21st century and beyond, would revert to classical concepts of order and beauty: that the Apollonian element would supersede the Dionysian. Truffaut was convinced that Herrmann could create such a music. The film's focal point is not those brainwashed into unthinking acceptance of the regime, but those who oppose it — the 'Bookmen' who commit great literature to memory before it is burned by the authorities. In particular it is the story of Montag, the misguided fireman (Oskar Werner) who rather resembles Hans Castorp in Thomas Mann's *Magic Mountain* — an ordinary young man who is at first a willing tool in the hands of the Establishment. But his stifled sensitivity is gradually reactivated, he loses himself to contemplation and discovery until he achieves a complete *volte face* of thought and feeling and allies his fate to that of the 'Bookmen'. If, therefore, the music in its early stages must reflect something of the savourless texture of life in the 21st century, thereafter it must help us share in Montag's gradually sharpening perception of the world about him. This is why it progresses from a nadir of non-humanity and non-feeling in the prelude to a zenith of humanity and feeling in the finale. Herrmann scores for the classical string orchestra with some assistance from two harps and three light percussion — xylophone, glockenspiel and marimba — a combination which can easily sound clean, cold and hygenic. The credits are tersely spoken by a woman announcer over a series of zooms on a parade of television aerials: in the film television has completely usurped the place of literature and no written words appear on the screen until the end. This music is the most de-humanized of all — it is akin to the 'outer space' main title music in *The Day the Earth Stood Still*, with the same ice-cold beauty, the same cut-diamond hardness. No less impassive, though different, is the music which accompanies the bright-red fire engine on each of its book-burning expeditions. It is an authoritative, march-like movement for 'black and white' strings with an occasional clatter of marimbas, emotionally quite dead. This deliberate greyness and emotional neutrality should itself alert us to something suspicious — for real firemen in a real fire-engine would surely have drawn a more positive response from the music: urgency, impatience, apprehension, or whatever, but not mere soulless efficiency. This music recurs whenever the fire-engine goes on its rounds and is a powerful symbol. Again, as we watch Montag seek out a cache of books and burn them, the music emphasizes the unthinking, automaton-like nature of his actions. It inspires in us no feeling of resentment or sympathy, it simply distils the spirit of hopelessness in a world drained of the values of living. The first sign of a breakthrough comes at the time of Montag's meeting with Clarisse (Julie Christie) on the monorail. This meeting is framed at the start and at the finish by music of such lyrical warmth and sweetness that the contrast with the preceding scenes is immediately striking. From then on the music forces the emotional temperature steadily upwards. The scenes where Montag first chances upon *David Copperfield* and is forced to watch the martyrdom of the bookwoman among her books are particularly significant, the music expressing wonderment in the one case, compassion in the other. Finally, after Montag has been denounced to the Fire Service by his wife, he witnesses the destruction of his own books before turning the flamethrower on the Captain; and the music voices what can only be described as a kind of cosmic despair, with harp *glissandi* shooting madly in all directions like the flames.

This is the turning point for Montag. He is forced to abandon civilization and seek the wilderness where the outcasts, the bookpeople, live. Here they learn books by rote, recite them, pass them on, in anticipation of the Age of Darkness. On arrival he is welcomed by *The Life of Henri Brulard* and introduced to a polyglot assortment of comrades. Then he sees Clarisse coming from the distance reciting Saint-Simon's memoirs in French. This is the climax of the picture, for at last she and Montag can meet and talk on equal terms without fear or restraint. Herrmann therefore releases all his strings in a full streaming song of humanity. But Truffaut was anxious to avoid any suggestion of the conventional Happy Ending. As we move away from the boy reciting Stevenson's *Weir of Hermiston* and are lost in the multilingual murmur of voices — among them Montag's who is starting to learn Poe's *Tales of Mystery and Imagination* — the icy harp figurations which envelop the string theme may be related visually to the snowfall, but they also bring *ipso facto* a reminiscence of the 'outer space' main title music; and Herrmann ends his score, not on the familiar 'happy' major chord or 'unhappy' minor, but on one poised equivocally in between.

By the time Herrmann came to write his last scores, Brian de Palma's *Obsession* and Martin Scorsese's *Taxi Driver* — both in 1975 — he was an ailing man, a fact to which neither score bears any testimony. In *Obsession* the musical protagonists are a chorus of female voices (wordless) and pipe organ, supported by an orchestra of strings and brass. There is an interesting association of ideas here: the combination of organ and voices was evidently suggested in the first instance because the dramatic crux — Cliff Robertson's encounter with the girl who appears to be the reincarnation of his dead wife, Geneviève Bujold — takes place in a church in Florence. But because this 'reincarnation' is ultimately expressed as a fraud whose objective was to destroy Robertson, we may suppose that Herrmann had Debussy's 'Sirènes' at the back of his mind here. Debussy in No 3 of the *Nocturnes* used the wordless female chorus in the same remote, impersonal way: and Bujold is literally a 'siren' whose beauty lures Robertson to his doom. Herrmann does not restrict his use of organ and voices to the scenes in the church: they are the focal point of his colour scheme as a whole: and if anyone doubts what a splendidly dramatic sonic entity the organ can be once freed of its ecclesiastical connotations, let him listen especially to the scene where Robertson journeys by ferry to deliver the ransom money.

The scene of *Taxi Driver* is contemporary New York, a 'city of dreadful night', and Herrmann in his unique way creates a poetry of the modern metropolis, a music which reflects and comments sympathetically on the mental torment of 'God's lonely man' (Robert de Niro) as he journeys to the end of his night — 'sympathetically' in that the music is here obliged to 'soften' both character and situation, whereas normally it is called upon to harden them. The score evolved unpremeditatedly out of the bluesy alto-saxophone melody at once sensuous and acrid, originally written separately (as I earlier explained) as a piece of source music. This eventually became the recurrent theme of de Niro's introspection, and Herrmann constantly reverts to it in its original realistic format and instrumentation (alto sax solo with accompaniment of strings, piano, bass and drums) generally effecting the transitions through a blur of vibraphones. Apart from these repeated literal references, the theme is an all-pervasive influence on the rest of the score: e.g. it returns hair-raisingly in the scene of the great bloodbath which forms the climax of the film, this time *fortissimo* in the horns at the top of their compass. Another stratagem is to isolate the harmonic support of the first phrase of the melody — four chords, or the first two of them — and to settle them on the brass (deprived of their melody), in a different musical environment altogether. In fact the film begins and ends in this way.[17]

Taxi Driver was set in New York, the scene of Herrmann's greatest conducting triumphs and where he laid the foundations of his career. It was recorded in Hollywood where he achieved world renown as a composer, having been written in London which, I feel, he always regarded as his spiritual home. In fact, as at the end of *Kane*, the pieces all fit together; and *Taxi Driver* is dedicated by Scorsese — in the film's final caption — 'in gratitude and admiration to the memory of Bernard Herrmann.'

POSTSCRIPT

No account of Herrmann's film career would be complete without some mention of his one film score which was never used: Hitchcock's *Torn Curtain*. Although thanks to Elmer Bernstein's *Film Music Collection* we are at last able to hear it, the film itself will of course always be shown with the second score composed by John Addison, which is as unlike Herrmann's as could be.

Herrmann, as we know, was a man who found compromise difficult if not impossible. His music demonstrated time and again, in all manner of contexts, a rare ability both to enhance the accomplishments of his collaborators and to mask their incompetence; so renowned was he for the soundness of his dramatic instinct that, in 99 cases out of 100, directors and producers deferred to his judgement. The hundreth case was *Torn Curtain*. In all his earlier Hitchcock collaborations Herrmann had been given a free hand: and his was a hand that rarely pointed of its own accord, nor could be persuaded to point, in the direction of the commercial exploitation of music. In his eyes the first and only responsibility of music in a film was to the drama; as he put it in one of his most striking metaphors, 'You're grateful enough to a doctor for making you well. You don't also expect him to make you rich'.

But *Torn Curtain* went into production in the mid-1960s, by which time directors were being urged on all fronts to take advantage of the money-making potential of scores in the form of hit-tunes and theme-songs. Hitchcock, it seems, was no exception — though Herrmann always maintained that he could and should have made himself one. But in asking Herrmann for a 'theme' in *Torn Curtain*, it is possible that Hitchcock was also indicating obliquely the kind of score he wanted for the kind of picture he had made. But Herrmann, as was his practice, remained steadfast in his own conception. Small wonder that when Hitchcock walked on to the Universal sound-stage and saw the amazing orchestra that Herrmann had assembled — 12 flutes, 16 horns, 9 trombones, 2 tubas, 2 sets of timpani, 8 cellos, 8 basses — he wondered where his 'theme' was going to come from. This time he expressed his misgivings to the composer in no uncertain terms: and that, suddenly, was the end of their ten year-long relationship. It was a rupture that was to have profound consequences for both men. Herrmann never returned to Hollywood to work permanently, although he did come back to record *Taxi Driver*. As for Hitchcock, many feel that none of his films after 1966 are the equal in quality to those made during the golden decade of 1955–65 when Herrmann was his composer and both men were stretched to the limits of their capacities.

The *Torn Curtain* orchestra is not an exercise in megalomania. The 'curtain' that is 'torn' is the Iron Curtain; and that one word — 'iron' — seems to have governed the composer's conception. Here he created an all-pervading sense of hopelessness, a spirit of negation. His aim was evidently a music of 1984–ish totalitarian futility. In this respect the real musical *dramatis personae* are the 12 flutes, all of whom are required to double on piccolos, alto flutes and bass flutes. 'The sound of 12 flutes', exclaimed Herrmann to his friend and colleague Laurie Johnson with a characteristic gesture, 'is TERRIFYING'. Strange epithet to apply to the instrument which conjures up the Arcadian dreamworld of Debussy's faun; but then how different is the life-denying effect of the alto flute solo which opens Alex North's score for *Death of a Salesman*! Herrmann's use of 12 flutes is founded on the latter premise. Theirs is a flesh-creeping sound, almost literally sick unto death. Nobody could live with such a sound over an extended period and retain his sanity. This of course was precisely Herrmann's intention. The flutes' theme is a sequence of four 'dead' chords that may be taken as representing the grey world behind the Iron Curtain.

It is worth noting that not one of Herrmann's 16 horns or 9 trombones can be dispensed with without leaving a 'hole' in the texture. We notice too the absence of any high, brilliant sonorities (trumpets, violins) — with the calculated exception of the piccolos which squeal like rats. The scene of Paul Newman's escape through the corridors of Leipzig University is a kind of zanily choreographed dance movement for trombones divided into 3 groups of 3 (open, straight-muted, cup-muted) and for alternating stopped and open horns. For concentrated ferocity of sound Herrmann never surpassed the scene of the murder of Gromek; as if to emphasize that this is the turning-point of the film he introduces here a new motif founded on an age-old musical formula for striking terror: the interval of the minor third. (Interestingly, in the film as it was eventually released, both this scene and that of the formula and blackboard are played without music). On only two occasions does Herrmann attempt to mellow the austerity of his sound world. The first is a little piece of source-music for a handful of strings, a 'Valse Lente', which Herrmann himself described as 'apologetic' — a kind of frayed reminiscence of a dim-and-distant past. The other is the scene of the reconciliation between Michael (Paul Newman) and Sarah (Julie Andrews). Here the music aspires tentatively to some degree of human emotion; but the naturally drawn, tense sound of the cellos in their high register precludes any effect of full-blooded expressiveness. The entire score remains hung in a limbo which, forgetting the film, we perhaps do best to regard as Herrmann's personal vision of a dehumanized Orwellian future.

NOTES

1 In conversation with Elmer Bernstein.

2 I think of this characteristic of Herrmann and of Hitchcock every time I see, in *Marnie*, the moment when Tippi Hedren emerges from the washbasin a blonde. It is in fact the first time we are shown her face; previously we have seen only a back view of her brown wig. The burst of musical technicolor that accompanies this dazzling, God-like apparition makes it one of the most memorable images in the film, which is not one of Herrmann's or Hitchcock's more significant.

3 For a fuller discussion of *Vertigo*, and for many detailed insights into Herrmann's other Hitchcock scores, see Royal S. Brown, 'Herrmann, Hitchcock and the music of the irrational', *Cinema Journal*, Spring 1982.

4 A motif that has haunted composers through the ages. Herrmann himself returns to it in the third movement of his Symphony, in the death waltz of *The Bride Wore Black*, in the hydra's music in *Jason and the Argonauts*, and in *Obsession*.

5 Much of the 'period' music both from *Citizen Kane* and *The Magnificent Ambersons* is to be found freely developed in Herrmann's popular orchestral suite *Welles Raises Kane*.

6 In a lecture given at Rochester in October 1973 as part of a symposium on the 'Coming of Sound to the American Film' Herrmann stressed the importance of music in a montage: 'You can cut a scene ABA, or CBA, or BCA — any way you like. But if you gun-run music from one point to the next there is no alternative, it has to stay that one fixed way. It's a kind of binding veneer holding the scene together, and hence it's particularly valuable in a montage. It's really the only thing that seals a most primitive form. Did you ever see a newsreel without music? Well, try it!'

7 In *The Films of Orson Welles*, California 1970.

8 It has been alleged that the original intention was to use an excerpt from Massenet's *Thais* but that financial considerations intervened. This is effectively disproved by a telegram from Welles to Herrmann dated July 18th, 1940, just a few days before shooting began on *Kane*:

'To: Mr Benny Herrmann
      Columbia Broadcasting System
      New York City, New York.
. . . opera sequence is early in shooting so must have fully orchestrated recorded track before shooting. Susie sings as curtain goes up in first act and I believe there is no opera of importance where soprano leads like this. Therefore suggest it be original . . . suggest *Salammbo* which gives us phony production scene of Ancient Rome and Carthage, and Susie can dress like Grand Opera neoclassic courtesan. . . Here is chance for you to something witty and amusing — and now is the time for you to do it. I love you dearly.
(Quoted in Peter Bogdanovich: 'The Kane Mutiny', *Esquire*, October 1972.)

9 A creative orchestrator–arranger of the first rank, the man responsible more than anyone else for giving the MGM musicals of the 40s and 50s their individual sound.

10 Op. cit.

11 As is generally known, the film's ending as we are familiar with it bears no relation to Welles's original conception. Studio officials substituted a conventional lachrymose Hollywood finale in the form of two scenes directed by Robert Wise with music by Roy Webb. Musically as in every other way, this tacked-on 'cadence' is out of character with the rest of the film.

12 Herrmann's use of 'Springfield Mountain' pre-dates that of Copland in *Lincoln Portrait* which was composed in 1942. Other New Hampshire folk melodies employed by Herrmann are 'Lady McLeod's Reel' (for the sleigh-ride) and 'Devil's Dream' (in the barn dance).

13 By the same token *King of the Khyber Rifles*, also written in 1953, is a concerto for drums — five large timpani, five small, five timbales. Reinforced by a large bass contingent and organ pedals they charge the Rifles' attack on the enemy's mountain stronghold with great conviction and enthusiasm.

14   This Albert Hall sequence is one of Hitch's most spectacular, and marvellously cut to Benjamin's music: the irony being, of course, that the drama inside the music is an unconscious mirror-image of the drama *outside* it. Thus the first intimations of doom in the music coincide with the assassin and his accomplice readying themselves in their box; the *agitato* section with its steady heightening of tension begins just as James Stewart arrives on the scene and we observe his frenzied attempts to impress the officials with the gravity of the situation (all enacted in pantomime: the Cantata here has the effect of a silent-film-like musical commentary); the cymbal-clash at the climax is, as we know, pre-empted by Doris Day's scream; and even the very last chord is made to accentuate the bump of the assassin's body falling on the floor of the Hall.

15   Actually a piece of realistic music by André Previn called 'Fashion Show'.

16   Judging by the number of occasions on which a waltz occurs as symbol of a particularly strong emotion (*Citizen Kane, The Magnificent Ambersons, The Snows of Kilimanjaro* and — most explicitly and eloquently of all — in *Obsession*, one may surmise that this particular dance-form lay at a crucial point in Herrmann's musical nervous system. Its source, no doubt, is to be found in his fondness for late-19th century comic opera, and we are reminded of Constant Lambert's description of Debussy as a composer 'who in his capacity for investing an apparently insignificant and light-hearted tune with an almost tragic significance, stands very close to Mozart.'

17   Although in fact the last sounds we hear — Herrmann's last music — consist of a motif from *Psycho*, which Herrmann inscribed in my score with the words, 'This is the real *Psycho* theme.' Royal S. Brown notes that it is always associated in *Psycho* with madness, and we last hear it in the latter when the mummified face of Norman's mother is superimposed on a shot of Marion's car being dragged up from the swamp. The unexpected reappearance of this motif at the end of *Taxi Driver* may suggest that Herrmann viewed the hero, de Niro, as a madman; or it may be that the motif was, for Herrmann, a musical synonym for mortality. If that is so Herrmann wrote his own musical epitaph. Consciously or unconsciously? We should never forget that a true artist — and Herrmann was one — sees and knows in a way that often transcends normal faculties.

ALEX NORTH,
ELMER BERNSTEIN
AND LEONARD ROSENMAN:
END OF AN ERA

On September 30 1955, James Dean was killed in a car crash on his way to Salinas in California, at the age of twenty-four. He made three feature films which still play to packed houses all over the world: *East of Eden, Rebel Without a Cause* and *Giant.* His best work is generally considered to be the first two, but what few people realize is that the composer, Leonard Rosenman, contrived in them to create what may be described as a James Dean sound. This 'sound' was of major significance in respect of Hollywood film history, for it advanced a process which had been gathering momentum since the early fifties: the gradual loosening of the 19th century romantic stranglehold. In the main, three composers were responsible: Alex North, Elmer Bernstein and Leonard Rosenman. Their approach was not totally without precedent: some of the music David Raksin was writing in the 1940s was idiomatically more advanced than that of his colleagues, and his score for Abraham Polonsky's *Force of Evil* (1949) in particular, with its dislocated, elliptical, quasi-expressionist phraseology, anticipates the Rosenman 'sound'. In 1947 Hugo Friedhofer successfully leavened the 20th Century Fox house-style with Copland in his celebrated *Best Years of our*

Lives. But, of those composers immediately accepted by Hollywood and allowed to contribute on a regular basis, Alex North was the first whose roots lay not in late 19th century Europe but in the immediate past of his own country; though he so absorbed his influences that the extent of any stylistic debt to Copland, for example, with whom he studied, is difficult to gauge.

Elia Kazan launched North's film career. The two had met in 1948 when Arthur Miller asked North to score the Broadway production of *Death of a Salesman* which Kazan was directing; and when Kazan later went to Hollywood to make the 1951 film version he took North with him as his composer.[1] North made a name quickly in Hollywood, not so much with *Death of a Salesman* as with Kazan's film version of Tennessee Williams's *Streetcar Named Desire* (1951). This was the first jazz-based functional score ever written for a feature picture and it paved the way for Elmer Bernstein (*Walk on the Wild Side*, 1955), Johnny Mandel (*I want to Live*, 1958) and Leonard Rosenman (*The Chapman Report*, 1962).[2] There was good reason for the novelty of North's approach. The play is set in a sleazy area of New Orleans and, as Williams explains in his stage directions, 'In this part of town you are practically always just around the corner, or a few doors down the street, from a tinny piano being played with the infatuated fluency of brown fingers. This "blue piano" expresses the spirit of life which goes on here.' In the play we are intended to be perpetually aware of this realistic tinkling 'blue piano', generally in the background, sometimes bursting in on the foreground, as when someone leaves the Kowalskis' flat door open. It serves in fact as a kind of scenery. For this piano North substitutes the jazz emanating from the band in the 'Four Deuces' a little way down the street. Why? Because it enables him to grade and ease the necessary transitions from realistic to commentative music inasmuch as the latter is written in a jazz idiom also. The stageplay does not need commentative music and therefore the background 'blue piano' is ideal; the filmed stageplay *does* need commentative music, to which the piano is not suited, and there must be smoothness in the transitions from one music to the other. The jazz band is a happy solution. Sometimes a scene which starts with realistic jazz ends with commentative jazz, the necessary instrumental modifications (chiefly the addition of 'emotive' strings) being made with subtlety and taste, and always within the jazz context. Sometimes even a piece of realistic jazz actually does duty for commentative music — as in the wearily nostalgic blues being played in the 'Four Deuces' after the poker game has ended in violence and uproar; and Stanley, bitterly ashamed of himself, emerges from the bathroom dripping wet and racked with sobs: 'My baby doll's left me!' The scene where Stanley rapes Blanche (thus toppling her over into madness) while his wife is in hospital having her baby, starts nonchalantly enough with a blues which could be coming from the 'Four Deuces'. Gradually it gains in raw sexual violence until the off-screen climax comes with the terrifying sound of glissando horns. The horns' screaming represents Blanche's screaming and make manifest what is (in terms both of dialogue and action) less explicit in the film than in the play.

Themes are used to designate situations rather than people — the theme associated generally with the pathos of Blanche also accompanies Stella as she comes down the stairs from Eunice's room after the fight and takes the contrite Stanley's head in her hands. This theme is not, however, limited to doleful contexts but undergoes a violent transformation on strident trumpets after Blanche has sent Mitch away and breaks down hysterically. She rushes round shutting all the windows in her room, and the music is a kind of demented scherzo with prominent *pizzicato* strings, bitonal harmonies and sharp neurotic rhythms. The most bizarre effect is that produced by the massed *pizzicato* strings. Whether this is because strings are rarely played *pizzicato* at this tempo, and in bitonal harmony, is difficult to determine. Whatever the reason, the music plays its part in telling us that the thread of Blanche's sanity has finally been snapped, and we have been witnessing the process of its snapping in the previous scene. In it Mitch discovers Blanche not only to be a faded, ageing has-been but also riddled with fantasies of glamour and respectability and thus a constitutional liar. At this point a blind Mexican woman in a dark shawl appears, carrying bunches of Mexican tin flowers and calling: '*Flores para los muertos!*': 'Flowers for the dead!' As if to underline the fact that this strange, half-symbolic apparition is a bringer of death, North begins a dirge in the music. Frightening, bass remains imperturbably constant, sliding down four notes and back again. The middle parts descend chromatically in a wail (muted strings) which resembles a wordless keening.[3] Only in the topmost register do trumpets, violins and woodwind force their way higher as Blanche grows increasingly frenzied: the climax comes with a dissonant chord prolonged seemingly forever as Mitch flees from the scene and Blanche starts screaming.

Music is worked even more closely into the drama in the case of the little tune to which Blanche and her young husband danced their last dance — the tune that was cut short by the sound of his shooting himself. This tune recurs on celesta (sometimes superimposed on other music) whenever Blanche's mind returns to the traumatic incident which has played havoc with her emotional constitution. As soon as she reaches the shot the music always stops — except on the one occasion when she is talking to Mitch and the music goes on *after* the sound of the shot, suggesting that the incident has lost coherent shape in her mind. And on one occasion the tune is used quite differently. A beautiful young man appears, collecting for the 'North Star'. The dance-tune tells us that he reminds Blanche of her husband. He is, it seems, not unwilling to be seduced by her, at least to the extent of allowing her to kiss him gently on the lips. In this instance the dance-tune, as if bemused by her fantasy, steps out of its original context and underscores the scene in its own right, to touching effect.

The finale, which ends on a note of happiness and triumph, was criticized by writer-composer Frank Lewin in *Film Music Notes*, whose estimate of the score was otherwise favourable.

Jerome Moross

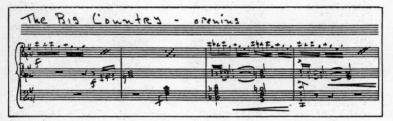

The Big Country: main title sequence

Alex North in the late 1940s

Leonard Rosenman, David Raksin and Elmer Bernstein

He described it as 'pretentious' and 'a great disappointment'. Evidently he felt that North had merely conformed to the bad old Hollywood 'happy-musical-ending-at-all-costs' convention. But is the issue so straightforward? The film deviates from the play in that the latter shows a weeping Stella being soothed and comforted by her husband, whereas in the film she races upstairs to join Eunice, swearing that this time her husband has gone too far and that she will not be reconciled to him. It is at this point that the music swells to end in its exultant G major. Does this imply that life will go on as before, and that despite her grief-crazed vehemence Stella will very soon be back in her husband's arms? The composer himself said of his music for this film, 'I think you may find some of the scoring running counter to the scene because of the attempt to reflect the inner feelings of the personalities rather than the situation'.

Elmer Bernstein's importance in the final phase of Hollywood's film-music history rests on two major achievements, both of them based on earlier, isolated developments. First he followed up North's pioneer use of jazz as a functional medium in *Streetcar*, and second, he supported the stand taken by Copland in 1940 with *Our Town* which showed that in a certain type of picture a score written for fifteen musicians was more dramaturgically appropriate than one written for fifty. Bernstein has always been an advocate of the small orchestra score, and one of the most attractive features of his work is its chamber-music-like concentration and concision of expression. He is in fact essentially a miniaturist, whose warm lyrical gift makes the greater impact for being discreetly exercised.

In 1951 his *Sudden Fear*, a high-grade Joan Crawford thriller set in San Francisco with many real-life locations, was unusual for its time in the economy of its orchestration, viz. prominent use of solo piano, flute, cello in an un-romantic role, and other instruments. The idea of adopting a more cautious, questioning and judicious approach to music — and not just what should play it but whether it should be played at all — set a trend for post-war developments. (It is interesting, for instance, to look at a film like Bernstein's *To Kill a Mockingbird* of 1962 and note the number of music-less scenes which some 15 years before would automatically have been scored).

Bernstein's *The Man with the Golden Arm* (1955) was not a jazz score but a score which made imaginative use of jazz elements; and for good reason. Frankie Machine (Frank Sinatra) is a drug addict who returns to the Chicago slums after a period in jail, apparently cured of his addiction. In prison he has discovered an unsuspected talent for drumming, and his ambition is to join a band and earn a living as a musician. A jazz milieu is therefore central to the plot: and the main title jazz sequence[4] soon reappears as realistic music emanating from no particular source, but just in and around the sleazy saloon frequented by Frankie, Louie Schwiefka the dope pedlar, and others. Throughout the film this music is associated — commentatively — with Frankie's craving for narcotics. Each time he feels the need for a 'fix' the music sets in, telling us first of his struggle against temptation and then, as his resistance breaks, of his despair. Particularly powerful is the scene of the first 'fix' when Frankie, succumbing to intolerable pressures from Zosh, his crippled wife, and Schwiefka, his former boss, allows Louie to minister to him. As Louie plunges the syringe into his arm the camera closes right in on Frankie's face until only his eyes fill the screen: here the music speaks with a voice no actor can project. What makes jazz indispensable in these circumstances is its hysterical, raw-nerved intensity; the earthy frenetic excitement of its rhythmic drive is overlaid by an anguish which almost borders on the masochistic, and the sonorities are knife-edged. In the traumatic scene in Molly's apartment where in the course of a cure Frankie inflicts horrific violence both on himself and the room, this music creates a devastating sense of physical as well as mental torment, the more effective in that for the other characters Bernstein resorts to more conventional scoring — a self-pitying theme for Zosh the 'cripple', a serene and unselfish theme for Molly (Kim Novak), the girl who helps Frankie rebuild his life. This use of jazz as both commentative and realistic material is of the same imaginative order as in *Streetcar*.[5]

A case could almost be made for the main architect of musical reform in Hollywood being not so much any one composer as one director, namely Elia Kazan. As we know, Kazan had North come to Hollywood to write *Streetcar*; but he also allowed himself to be persuaded by James Dean that Leonard Rosenman, a friend of Dean's in his New York days, was the right composer for *East of Eden*. It is unlikely that Dean could have understood much or anything about Rosenman's 'advanced' concert music; but, interestingly, he must have intuitively recognized that it was the right kind of music for *him*. In both this film and *Rebel Without a Cause* Dean plays severely disturbed adolescents reaching out and agitating for love, understanding and security. The films marked the beginnings of the teenagery of the fifties. They were studies in adolescent rebellion and the reasons behind it. So it was appropriate that their musical scores should have been symbols of revolt in themselves — revolt against the still-prevailing romantic temper of Hollywood film music. Nothing resembling *East of Eden* had been heard on a Hollywood soundtrack before; and the result is that this sound is always associated first and foremost with Dean. Rosenman unwittingly gave Dean a musical identity, and it may be that something of Rosenman's personal knowledge of Dean's sensibility and temperament seeped into these scores and helped to make them sound authentic.

Like Herrmann on *Kane*, Rosenman was intimately involved with *East of Eden* from the start. The music was written as the footage was pieced together. Director and composer would confer on those scenes where music was to be a determining factor, and those scenes would then be shot with the projected music in mind. The composer, even when on location, played his sketches to Kazan each day, and by the time the film had reached the rough-cut stage the music was 'rough-cut' too. All that remained was the orchestrating and recording.

The highly complex and dissonant nature of Rosenman's musical style gave rise to something of a friendly disagreement between composer and director. Eventually, a compromise was reached: the children, Cal (Dean), Abra (Julie Harris) and Aron (Richard Davalos) would be scored simply or consonantly, the adults, chiefly Adam Trask (Raymond Massey) and Kate (Jo van Fleet) would be treated more dissonantly. In theory, that was. In practice, dramatic necessity rendered the issue less clear-cut.

First, the principal themes: the protagonists. This is essentially Cal's film. He is on screen almost all the time, and even when he is not (as in the finale when Abra intercedes with the stricken father on behalf of his son) he is never far away and is directly implicated in what is happening. And if the film sees everything and everybody from his vantage-point, so also must the music. Cal's own themes, according to the composer, are conceived not so much in terms of Cal himself as of his relationships to other people. But since Cal is what he is directly as a result of his relationships with other people, the distinction is perhaps rather fine. Thus he has two themes, or rather motivic ideas, both short and pregnant and coloured by circumstance. The one is a dissonant pile-up of fourths and thirds, declamatory in nature and suggestive of Cal's latent hysterical violence, the other a disconsolate woodwind motif of intense loneliness. 'Violence' is of course, psychologically speaking, merely the outward manifestation of 'loneliness', and because these are the two aspects of Cal's character which have a bearing on everything that happens in the film, these two thematic ideas are central to the harmonic and polyphonic thinking of the entire score.

Another theme is associated with Cal's father, Adam. Again, according to the composer, not so much Cal's father as he is, but as Cal would like their relationship to be. In fact, the theme does reflect something of Adam's own personality, objectively viewed: it is plain and austere but also gentle and even lyrical in a mildly astringent way. Its modal character has the ring of much of Copland's 'endless prairie' music, as in *Appalachian Spring* and *The Tender Land*.

There is also the love theme for Cal and Abra, simple and beautiful, with no trace of sentimentality. As heard in the

Main Title, it has an almost folksong-like freshness, but recurs in this form on only two subsequent occasions.

After the main title music (the three main themes), silence reigns as the camera focusses on the as yet unidentified figure of Kate Trask on her way to the bank in Monterey. Then for the first time we see Cal crouching by the roadside. There is no dialogue and no immediately visible reaction on Cal's part except to look up. Only one thing can tell us of the chaos of bitterness, resentment and frustration thronging his mind; the music. 'Violence' raises its head. It is always a danger signal — in fact it almost has a fanfare-like quality. It always announces some violent manifestation of Cal's disturbed state of mind, and in this case the climax is the stone he hurls through Kate Trask's window. This red light flashes again — its most dramatic appearance — shortly before the end when Cal emerges from beneath the weeping willows (after his father's birthday party has ended in disaster) bent on taking revenge on Aron by revealing to him his mother's whereabouts and disreputable status. 'Violence' sounds menacingly just before Cal asks 'How'd you like to go somewhere with me, Aron?' and continues through the scene where the two boys meet their mother in her room at the burlesque house.

The theme of Cal's loneliness of spirit is the most pervasive. Rosenman resorts to various technical devices to increase its omnipresence: turning it upside down, developing and varying it in every conceivable manner. It comments on the unintended wounds Cal receives to his pride from his father. He tries to infect him with some of his enthusiasm for beangrowing and its profits, but all Adam can find to say is, 'But I'm not particularly interested in making a profit'. The plaintive theme of loneliness enable us to feel Cal's disappointment the more keenly. When Cal makes his first attempt to contact his mother in the bawdyhouse, he passes into the darkened corridor leading from the saloon and the music assumes a strange quality of stillness, a slow procession of consonant chords. Then 'loneliness' is superimposed, (on the oboe); and the music follows Cal as he discovers his mother half-conscious in a drunken stupor, tentatively edges his way into her room, crouches down and looks at her pleadingly. Slowly she comes to herself, recognizes her son, and the music swells on a dissonant chord just *before* she screams and throws the place into an uproar — a classic example of how music may provide a split-second anticipation of a violent action, enhancing its impact. The mind resents being taken by surprise.

Rosenman has Adam Trask introduce his own theme — he hums it to himself as he exults at the success of his iced lettuce experiments, with Cal (unbeknown to him) listening at the window outside. Cal is determined to win his father's affection, and throws himself heart and soul into the business of preparing the lettuces for their journey in refrigerated railway cars. In the scenes in the lettuce-fields (with the coal-chute) the music is based solely on Adam's theme, reminding us all the time of Cal's concern for his father. At the same time, by allowing the pastoral flavour of this theme to assert itself Rosenman enhances the beauty of the scene: green fields in summer, the Santa Lucia mountains a stern and rugged outline against the blue Californian sky.

Through bad luck Adam's lettuce experiment is a failure, and Cal sets out to repair the damage by growing and investing in beans. Again, the music must concentrate on his idealized relationship with his father, and so for the scene in the beanfields when Cal dances and cavorts about for joy, Adam's theme, assisted by the bright-toned piccolo, is turned into a rollicking scherzo.

Like Adam, Abra introduces her theme herself — she hums it during the love scene with Aron in the ice-house, and he takes it up in unison with her. It is a rather awkward moment; the tune comes in self-consciously, more so than Adam's. There is, however, a nice irony in that although the song is here hummed by Abra and Aron, it eventually becomes the love theme for Abra and Cal. Apart from brief references, we do not hear it again in full until the scene in the funfair. Here the pair are both embarrassedly struggling against their feelings for one another, and it voices the emotions they dare not express themselves. Finally, as they kiss, the love theme casts off the slough of discordancy and appears in the radiant C major of its main title statement. The music reinforces the idea of some enclave of bliss, however momentary, discovered in the midst of turmoil. In the bar scene which follows the fight between Cal and Aron, Abra attempts to extract some assurance from Cal that what had happened in the funfair was devoid of real significance. Cal, despairing over the violent scene with his brother, asks, 'But why did I hit him so hard?' The music alone answers in the form of the love theme. He hit him so hard because of his unacknowledged, unfulfilled love for Abra. In this scene too, as in the following scene at Abra's window at night (scored in the manner of a nocturne), the themes of violence, loneliness and love are contrapuntally combined and developed. They are also combined in this way in the finale: Cal's repentance and final reconciliation with his now invalid father, effected by Abra. This cue is a large-scale symphonic synthesis of all the themes, lasting a full ten minutes, one of the longest in films. The difference between the clarity of the contrapuntal *mélange* in the finale and the complexity of other sequences which also involve aggregations of themes is that in the former Rosenman is at pains to insist on a definite key centre, corresponding to the new feelings of security and mutual understanding which now begin to permeate the lives of the protagonists. Earlier when all was insecurity and misunderstanding, Rosenman cast his themes adrift on a sea of indefinite and confusing tonalites, thus complementing in his music what we felt to be happening on the screen. The finale-music starts when Cal and Abra enter Adam's sickroom and throw out the nurse. The conflicts are gradually resolved: the tone of the music is austere, 'classical,' perhaps in its dignified beauty. Magically, the breakthrough between Cal and his father, as Adam asks his son to get rid of the detestable nurse, is marked by a soft upward harp *glissando*. The music's natural culmination, the point towards which all its tensions and relaxations have been aspiring, is carefully graded: the recrudescence of the love theme in its pristine, guileless C major, as in the titles. It is almost upon this note — but not quite — that the picture ends. For the last word is actually had by the fanfare-like 'danger' motif; but this, though still dissonant, is now so firmly enveloped in the C major diatonic stability of the love theme that its aggressive demeanour is annulled, and it simply adds a touch of fire and exultation to the apotheosis.

Two individual sequences, not related in any way to the main themes, call for comment. The first is when a group of townspeople, inflamed by anti-German propaganda, run riot in front of Mr Albrecht's garden. Rosenman's intention here is to depict the townspeople not as a group of unprincipled savages but as ordinary decent men and women roused in the heat of the moment to senseless violence. So he builds the music around the brutish, unthinking repetition of a commonplace tune which starts off amiably enough but ends up embedded in an orchestral texture of almost phantasmagorical character, its rhythm and all its constituent intervals distorted. Not only does the music comment on *what* is happening on the screen, but it also tells us *why* it is happening, what the real facts of the matter are as opposed to what they appear to be. Rosenman has always been conscious of this special responsibility of film music:

> Reality is, in films, an interpretation of naturalism. The image of the film, vastly larger than life, is by itself not real. It is often the musical statement in the film that gives it its reality. This is somewhat paradoxical because music is, within the filmic frame of reference, its most unnaturalistic element . . . film music has the power to change naturalism into reality. Ideally, the musical contribution should be to create a *supra-reality*, a condition wherein the elements of literary naturalism are perceptually altered. In this way the audience can have insight into different aspects of behaviour and motivation not possible under the aegis of naturalism.

The mob-scene in *East of Eden* shows the theory being put into practice.

Secondly, Rosenman paid particular attention to the relationship between music and voices in the dialogue scenes:

> I took into account that Julie Harris was a soprano, James Dean a tenor and Raymond Massey a bass-baritone. The design of the instrumentation and of the thematic material itself was influenced by these vocal ranges and qualities. Often 'holes' were left in the scoring for the voice to be utilized as a sort of speaking instrument. Sometimes in moments of high tension or concentrated dialogue music was not used at all, and entered later for punctuation in quiet reactive moments'.

This is apparent in the scene when Cal and his new-found mother conclude their business deal, and when Cal and Abra talk in the fields and she tells him how much better she had felt on one occasion when she had been able to forgive her father for some supposed injustice. Only at this point does music enter with a clouded transformation of Adam's theme telling of and pointing out Cal's reaction to what he has just heard. Normally, of course, the device of pitching music under actors' voices is one we are only conscious of when it goes wrong: when there is conflict between the tone-quality of the voice and the timbre of the music. But in the scene between Cal and Sam (Burl Ives) in the car, when Sam talks of Adam and of Cal's mother, the voices are almost scored as if they were singers in an opera; they spin the missing strands into a composite texture. Rosenman evidently took note also that Burl Ives was a high tenor and balanced his orchestral tone colours accordingly. The music is nocturnal in character — a dialogue between melodic winds (mostly dry, mellow clarinets) and soft chordal strings — and, therefore, complements on its own terms the conversation between Cal and Sam.

Rebel Without a Cause (1955) lacks the thematic and contrapuntal complexity of *East of Eden*, no doubt because the character relationships and emotional issues are less involved. Unlike *East of Eden*, too, *Rebel Without a Cause* contains a number of important 'set-pieces' which are greatly dependent on music for their rhythm and continuity.

The Warner Brothers shield comes up over aerial shots of Los Angeles at night. It is accompanied by an aggressive, rhythmic motif which gives way to an alcoholic saxophone as Dean collapses in a drunken stupor outside the police station. Most of the movie takes place at night, and the score is a kind of symphonic nocturne. The main title now comes up to the two main themes which represents Jim's relations with the world. The second is a glorious melody which represents Jim as he really is: not the violent, embittered young tearaway the *world* thinks he is.

This theme is mainly used to characterize the love which develops between Jim and Judy (Natalie Wood). We can follow its slow burgeoning in the music. The first time we hear it after the credits is in the police station where the three juvenile protagonists are assembled, all for different infractions of the law, and all still unknown to one another. It is the music's job to establish some connection between them, and a flute with the love-theme is the first to link Jim and Judy as the latter is taken in to be interviewed by the friendly sergeant, Jim's 'father-confessor'[6]. The main theme is then heard for the first time since the titles as Jim offers his jacket to Plato (Sal Mineo) and is followed immediately by the love-theme — on strings this time — as we pan to Judy. In other words the music helps to edge and ease together these three unrelated characters in our minds, simply by causing us unconsciously to assimilate the melodic threads which link them as a trio. It is necessary that the harmonic environment of the Jim/Judy theme be as yet unformed, even hostile, for the relationship itself is still unformed; but the music has made the initial move.

Next day, when Jim meets Judy on their way to school, the theme is heard again as he remembers dimly having seen her before; but it is still unsure of itself, still searching for a congenial harmonic envelopment. So too just before the 'chicken-run' when Jim asks Judy to give him some dirt to rub on his hands as she has just done for Buz, her nominal boyfriend; but here it comes closer to finding what it seeks. After Buz's death in the 'chicken run', the fear-crazed gang flee the scene, leaving Jim and Judy alone together. They look at each other and Jim holds out his hands to Judy: the theme sounds clearly on strings this time, no conflicting harmony or counterpoint, no harmony or counterpoint at all, but obviously searching, questioning, appealing. As her hand touches his, the long-awaited climax is reached and the love-theme is at last arrayed in the harmony which reveals it in its essential warmth and beauty. Now it has found it, it is never going to lose it — neither in the first nocturne in which Jim and Judy talk intimately together (after Jim's big row with his parents), in the second, in the old house — a sensitively acted scene when the couple declare their love for each other for the first time and kiss tenderly but passionately.

The first of the big 'set-pieces' is the planetarium scene. The main theme immediately establishes Jim's sympathy for lonely, neurotic young Plato, but is soon caught up in the stampede of students into the lecture theatre. Curiously, the music's function here is twofold. It begins by observing not the reactions or behaviour of the student audience during the demonstration, but rather the demonstration itself, reflecting the eternal rhythm of the stars and constellations. The climax is a vivid representation of the destruction of planet Earth in a burst of blue gas and flame; and here the music both matches the fictional cataclysm and intensifies the terror it strikes into the impressionable Plato.

The next set-piece is the knife-fight outside the observatory which follows the planetarium show. This is intricately choreographed to the music, which starts as Buz and his boys arrive on the scene just in time to prevent Jim leaving with Plato. As the gang saunters towards the two with menacing nonchalance, a solo saxophone blows a remarkable anticipation of the Sharks/Jets music in Leonard Bernstein's *West Side Story*.[7] In the first part the music enhances the interplay of tension between Jim on the upper level and the gang down below on the parapets letting the air out of Jim's car tyres. A momentary respite is broken when the gang's ribald 'chicken' clucking goads Jim — and the music — to action. A long-sustained trill, which recurs later in a similar context, preludes the knife-fight as it begins in earnest — again triggered off by the taunt of 'chicken'. References to the main theme constantly inject themselves, and a repeated note figure on muted brass imitates both the lethal clucking sound that so maddens Jim and also the picking motion of a knife. The climax — another trill — comes as Jim knocks the knife out of Buz's hand and the 'poop-heads' intervene, fearful of bloodshed.

The trills recur in the 'chicken-run' scene which culminates in Buz's car plunging over the cliff edge and being dashed to pieces on the rocks below. Alone together before the start of the run, Buz and Jim have taken a liking to each other. The main theme indicates a rapport, but the dry, cold, all-woodwind sonority underlines the pointlessness of the venture: 'Why do we do this?' 'We've gotta do *somethin*!' The cataclysmic trill begins when the gang turn their headlights on the two waiting competitors. Starting in the upper reaches of the orchestra, strand is added to trilling strand to bloodcurdling effect. This persists as the cars move along the runway, gathering speed. Somewhere in the shuddering morass of sound Jim's theme can be heard in its agony and bloody sweat. Only as Buz's car goes hurtling over the edge — Jim has jumped clear of his — is the tension finally shattered.

The last set-piece overlaps with the love scene in the old house described earlier, coinciding as it does with the brusque awakening of the sleeping Plato by the gang. Again, the first part — the gang chasing Plato through the derelict house, in and out of the empty swimming pool — is almost balletically organized in its interweaving of music and movement. With Plato's flight after the shooting, a panic-stricken string *ostinato* in a lunging rhythm breaks loose, complete with burly muted brass interjections and crazily whooping *glissando* horns. Inside the planetarium, the dialogue between Jim and the demented Plato brings reminiscences of the earlier planetarium scene in varied scoring, its impassive nocturnal tranquillity belying the potential explosiveness of the situation. During the perilous transit to the exterior the music insists throughout on the calm that Jim is trying at all costs to maintain in Plato's mind.

Jim fails, and Plato is shot down by the police; but Jim and Judy together have now gained sufficient maturity to be able to present a united front to the world. As Jim introduces Judy to his parents, the two main themes are symbolically joined in counterpoint. The music's dissonant last word, however, dismisses any idea of a conventional happy ending. It ensures that the taste of tragedy and all that it implies is left like brine upon the lips: this has been a 'problem' picture about real people, and the problems are still there, waiting to be solved.[8]

Finally a tribute to a composer who in a classic Western — Wyler's 1958 *The Big Country* — emancipated Hollywood Western–American music from Europe once and for all. Jerome Moross was born in Brooklyn in 1913, and graduated from New York University in 1932. During the early 'thirties he supported himself by writing music for dancers and for the theatre and by playing the piano in theatre pits. Through Oscar Levant he came to know Gershwin, whose *Porgy and Bess* was at that time (1936) nearing the end of its New York run. Gershwin suggested that Moross should take over the piano in the pit and go out with the show for a six-week tour. When plans were finalized for the West Coast production he was engaged as pianist and assistant conductor, and in 1940 he came to Hollywood to try to establish himself as a composer for films.

He failed. All through the 'thirties he had been composing furiously, and, independently of his friend Copland, sought to develop an authentically American nationalist idiom which was not exclusively jazz-orientated but drew nourishment from a great variety of American folk and popular music cultures — musical comedy, vaudeville, folksong of the Appalachian mountain variety, spirituals, blues, rags and stomps. He grew up with this music around him: he loved it, so there was nothing contrived about his composing vernacular. His reputation as an individualist was established before he set foot in Hollywood; yet, ironically, it was this very reputation and individuality which prevented him from finding employment as a composer there. The supposedly 'radical' nature of his style placed him in the 'Carnegie Hall' category, and nobody dared engage him to do an original score. Yet ironically again, when in 1940 Copland, a *bona fide* 'Carnegie composer', was brought out to Hollywood by Sam Wood to score *Our Town*, time pressed as always, and an orchestrator was needed. Moross was offered the job; at least he could do no harm there. He accepted, and made in a sense a fatal mistake. For he found himself pegged down in the Hollywood hierarchy as an orchestrator. Moross, one of the foremost of America's new composers, spent the next ten years or so doing commercial orchestration (his credits included Friedhofer's *Best Years of our Lives*). I suspect he never wanted desperately to become a Hollywood composer. He was not a careerist. He wanted to spend his life writing music, not for money or fame but for the sheer joy of doing it. He valued the movies because they offered him the means to earn a living and practice his technique at the same time; but he never truly committed himself, never became a full-time resident of California ('I commuted when I needed money' he told me) and eventually gave up films altogether. He felt he had other work to do and up to the end was shuttling back and forth between different projects, theatrical and non-theatrical. However, in earlier days it was at least an achievement to be able to give up orchestrating other people's film scores and compose his own. The first was a 'quickie' made in New York entitled *Close-up*. Others included *Captive City* (1952), the ballet 'The Little Mermaid' (based on music by Liszt) in the Frank Loesser/ Danny Kaye musical *Hans Christian Andersen* (1952), one-third of the Cinerama *Seven Wonders of the World* (1955), and Samuel Goldwyn Jr's *Proud Rebel* (1957). Then came 1958 and *The Big Country*. *The Big Country* is the score of a lifetime, in the sense that it was the score Moross had been waiting a lifetime to write. The very first bars of the title — one of the most electrifying in film music — are inspired. I pressed the composer for an explanation: 'I was shown the film before I saw the script and I remember that as it opened with the horses and stagecoach hurtling across the Great Plains, I had the feeling of going back more than twenty-one years to the first time I had seen the West. I travelled by bus from Chicago to Los Angeles and as we hit the plains I got so excited that I stopped off in Albuquerque, at that time a small town of about 35,000 people. The next day I got to the edge of the town and then walked out on to the flatland with a marvellous feeling of being alone in the vastness with the mountains cutting off the horizon. When I came to do the main title of the film I set down the string figure and opening theme almost without thinking about them.' (letter to the author dated March 22 1973).

What distinguishes Moross's *Big Country* music from the 'Western' scores of Steiner, Tiomkin or Victor Young (*Shane*) is that whereas theirs is 'American' music written by expatriate Europeans looking in from outside, his is authentic music of America by an American on the inside. All Moross's music is intimately related to the American scene — the ballets *Frankie and Johnny* and *The Last Judgement*, the First Symphony, and those theatre works whose originality lies in their hybrid or experimental forms, in this skilful mating of 'pop' and 'art' — the *Ballet Ballads* (four one-act ballet-operas) and his two two-act operas, *Gentlemen be Seated!* (a portrait of the Civil War in the form of a minstrel show), and *The Golden Apple*, a kind of folksy American burlesque of the Homeric epics. Moross breathes new life into worn-out conventions of Americana — e.g. the old cowboy-song style of the *Big Country's* main theme — not selfconsciously, flippantly or pedantically, but because these tunes form an integral, vital part of his musical language. It is as natural for him to write a tune in the style of *The Big Country* as it was for Steiner to write a Viennese waltz. The basic elements of Americana are those employed by the old European guard: only the frame of reference has been changed to secure not only keener-pointed orchestral sonorities but above all else a much stronger emphasis on rhythm. These rhythms — sturdy, muscular, rugged (the Hannasseys' 'welcoming' of McKay, the gathering of the war party to kidnap Judy Maragon, McKay in Blanco Canyon where the battle between the rival factions takes place) — seem sprung of the native soil, of rock, plain, sun, sand and sky, the way Western Americans talk, walk, dance and ride. Moross's musical language — its tunes, its chords, its rhythms, its structure — is basically very simple; it is also personal to Moross. A few bars identify it. Because it is so felt, so meant, so spontaneously melodic, because its substance is so distinguished, it can do things; take liberties, and be basic (e.g. repeating phrases or sentences *ad infinitum*) which in other contexts would sound simplistic or crude. It is a remarkable 20th century achievement. The *Big Country* music has a plainness that not only supports the drama but adds gritty authenticity to the film as a whole; and, in its own right, offers a sequence of sound impressions of the grandeur and beauty of the Big Country (much enhanced by the Cinemascope screen). The authenticity is perhaps the grittier for the paradoxical fact that Moross is not, in fact, a 'country' composer like Roy Harris. His music has this in common with Copland's, Gershwin's, Ellington's and Leonard Bernstein's; that it pits the skyscraper against the prairie. It is essentially *town* music, city music written by composers born and bred in the metropolis. Even when they sing of the country — as in *The Big Country* — they are always homesick for the city. Hence the needle-sharp perspective — we see most clearly when we view from a distance — and also the nostalgia which is quite different from that voiced by, say, Tiomkin in *Red River* or *Night Passage*. Tiomkin's is nostalgia for a never-never land, voiced by a Russian-in-exile in America, the nostalgia of the Wandering Jew with nowhere to wander. Moross's is nostalgia for urban America voiced by an urban American in rural America. He finds the urban isolation of the skyscraper reflected in the empty spaces of the prairie. It is a kind of nostalgia so personal and so American that it cannot adapt itself successfully to many varieties of film, so soaked is it in

American urban and related folk cultures; but it does have *identity*, a quality not lavished so indiscriminately among composers that we can afford to neglect those who possess it in the way we neglected Moross. *The Big Country* revolutionized the scoring of Westerns.[9] There could be no going back to the old way, and the blaze and magnificence of Elmer Bernstein's Westerns (*The Magnificent Seven*, *Sons of Katie Elder*, *True Grit*, *The Comancheros*) are a musical debt repaid with interest. Moross's place in film music history is assured, thanks to *The Big Country*. Almost every episode contains something to admire — when McKay (Gregory Peck) rides the unrideable stallion with no one watching him except the Mexican stable-hand, Moross turns the scene into a full ringside spectacular with musical implications of big bands playing and thousands of spectators cheering themselves hoarse; the music provides the missing audience. (This music is not in the film). A charming country-style waltz and polka for the Terrills' party — clearly Moross loved writing in this vein — lies at the opposite end of the emotional spectrum from the bone-hard, dust-biting elegy or funeral march for Buck Hannassey, killed by his own father; and a sequence of great dramatic force is the slow, lumbering rhythmic phrase which reiterates itself over and over, ever gaining in volume, weight and intensity as Major Terrill (Charles Bickford) and Rufus Hannassey (Burl Ives) approach from opposite ends of the sand-white canyon for the climactic confrontation which finally dissolves the feud between them. When McKay rides into the canyon the music deals in pregnant silences and echo effects, as if in harmony with the landscape; and the Major's self-righteous and foolhardy stubbornness in going it alone results in what is perhaps the most moving musical moment. He sets off to a pseudo-*religioso* chorale, Moross' intention being to suggest — and, in this context to mock — the idea of an early Christian walking to martyrdom in the arena. However, as his foreman Leech (Charlton Heston) and his men — who had earlier defied the Major — ride up to join him, the music becomes genuinely noble, genuinely heroic. The tempo changes are also interesting: slow and majestic at first, then a gradual *accelerando* to *Allegro eroico* as the men ride up, finally a drastic *ritenuto* — holding back — as the party presses on into the canyon, implying a nemesis at hand. In this case the film is dependent on the music not only for its emotion but also for its pace and rhythm. The tone of this music, like all Moross, is unfailingly positive, a celebration of the joy of being alive. As long ago as 1936 Copland wrote an article lauding the then 23-year-old composer as one of the most gifted of the rising generation and commented on the quality of 'sheer physicalness' to be found in his work: the effect it produces is uniformly tonic. Moross's music for whatever medium is a triumphant vindication of his own credo: 'I feel that a composer should write not only to put down on paper what he feels, but in such a way that his audience experiences his emotions anew. Down with Obscurantism!'[10]

NOTES

1   It is surely significant that one of Kazan's protégés was Nicholas Ray, who directed the second Dean picture, *Rebel Without a Cause*; and that the scores for some of Ray's earlier films are by Hollywood irregulars like Bernard Herrmann (*On Dangerous Ground*) and particularly George Antheil, who provided some powerful musical support for the two marvellous Bogart vehicles *In a Lonely Place* and *Knock on any Door*. Leigh Harline's titles sequence for *They Live by Night* — another of Ray's anthems for doomed youth, like *Knock on any Door* and *Rebel* — is as atypically Hollywood as Antheil's expressionistic *noir*-ishness and astringent though passionate romanticism. Common to all these scores, though, is an almost total avoidance of jazz idioms in the underscoring, regardless of their world of night and crime.

2   As a young man, North studied at the Curtis Institute in Philadelphia and later at Juilliard, and went to Moscow on a scholarship. It was homesickness brought on by hearing Duke Ellington's 'Mood Indigo' which brought him back in 1934, and Ellington's influence can surely be sensed on more than one occasion in *Streetcar*. The alto sax solos in 'Four Deuces' and 'Blanche', to use the album track titles for convenience, might almost have been written with Johnny Hodges in mind; and the solo violin writing in 'Belle Rive' and 'Della Robbia Blue' strongly suggest Ray Nance. So central are these warm, rich, sweet colours to the conception of the music that one can really make sense of the printed piano suite only through the instrumental sound of the original.

3   A sequence in which North claimed to be trying to evoke, via non-electronic means, 'the wail of all women suffering, the women of the world'.

4   Played, as are all the jazz episodes in the picture, by the Shorty Rogers Band with Shelly Manne (drums) who also coached Sinatra in drum technique.

5   Another influential jazz score was Leith Stevens' for the *Wild One* (with Marlon Brando; 1954). For Fred Steiner's detailed analysis see Elmer Bernstein's Film Music Notebook, Vol 2 nos 2 and 3. Of the older generation only Waxman (drawing no doubt on his early experiences with the Weintraub Syncopators) successfully essayed jazz-in-movies in *Crime in the Streets* (1955). Here, as in Rosenman's Dean scores, we can see the gradual taking-shape of a 'teenage' musical idiom which was to reach its popular apogee in Leonard Bernstein's *West Side Story* of 1956. Inasmuch as *Crime in the Streets* is about rival knife gangs who bring havoc to tenement dwellers, it may be viewed as a predecessor of the world-famous musical both musically and otherwise. See also my remarks on *Rebel Without a Cause* (note 8) and note the curious coincidence that Sal Mineo was in the cast both of *Rebel* and of *Crime in the Streets*. Incidentally, Waxman's score for Hitchcock's *Rear Window* (1954) is interesting in that it employs only naturalistic music — jazz, pop, whatever is going on around the apartment block in which James Stewart is marooned with his leg in plaster — and diverts it to 'commentative' purposes as required.

6   In connection with this scene, Rosenman described how the addition of music at one point made all the difference. When the detective at whom Jim has swung a punch tells him to 'take it out on the desk', Jim takes him literally, slamming his fists into the wood so violently that the first preview audience laughed:

> It wasn't, of course, what we intended, and we couldn't cut the scene because it was crucial. So I added about five seconds of music, and when the scene came on the audience started to laugh, but as soon as they heard the music they shut up. It was as if the music was a second voice saying, 'Wait a minute, take another look at this scene. It isn't funny. . . ' And that's the only function of music in that scene — to keep the audience from laughing.

(David Dalton, *James Dean*, London 1975, pp. 237–8)

7   If in *East of Eden* Rosenman created a musical identity for the adolescent solitary, in *Rebel* he had to do the same for a collective teenage mentality. In the latter director Nicholas Ray wanted to do a kind of *Romeo and Juliet* in a contemporary urban environment; other ingredients were teenage gang warfare or at least anti-social aggression, and Natalie Wood as heroine. Mention these three elements out of context to a movie buff and you would be sure to get

the reply: *West Side Story*. David Dalton has remarked that when Jim tells Judy that 'there's a place' where they can hide (the old mansion Plato has pointed out from the Observatory steps) he is foretelling the star-crossed lovers' great song in *West Side Story*, 'There's a Place for us'. Dare I suggest that Lenny Bernstein might have picked up an idea or two from Lenny Rosenman? (*Rebel* was composed in 1955, *West Side Story* soon afterwards.)

8   In 1977 Rosenman had an interesting opportunity compositionally to review *East of Eden* and *Rebel* for *9/30/55*, a James Bridges film in which Richard Thomas plays an adolescent profoundly affected by the life and death of his idol Dean.

9   In an essay on Copland, Wilfrid Mellers relates his rhythms and textures, with their free air and white light and high, fierce, forward sonorities, 'to the rectangularity of early American architecture where we can see the influence of the hard, sharp American light, with deep shadows and clear angles; and we can trace the relationship between the flat elevation and the open plane on the one hand, and the razorblade edge of sawn wood on the other . . . the texture of [Copland's] music has points in common with the painting of a nineteenth century Master such as J.S. Copley who gave so sharply linear a reinterpretation to baroque flamboyance or rococo prettiness, even when he was painting portraits'. In the same way we can say that Moross in *The Big Country* gave a 'sharply linear reinterpretation' to the 'flamboyance or prettiness' endemic in the 'Western' music of earlier Hollywood composers.

10   Moross died in New York July 25 1983.

EPILOGUE

Hollywood was a wonderful place when I first went there
. . . it was a bright dream about a beautiful democracy in a
world under the shadow of tyranny. I suppose there were
fakers and phonies but I can't help thinking there was an
innocence which has now vanished. Once Hollywood
forgot the dreams and got down to reality it failed . . .

Dimitri Tiomkin.[1] He was right, of course. We have just seen
the process of 'getting down to reality' beginning and with it,
the end of an era. Its root causes are complex and far-reaching
— the war was a major motive-force — but as far as film
scoring is concerned, the long-term result was that the need
for the 'escapist' romantic music in the grand old European
manner ceased to be so vital a part of the scheme of things.
The old 'dream factory' Hollywood was a creation of the
studio system. Once the cracks, such as early television, began
to show in the foundations of that system, the factory began to
show a marked decline in profits. It has never, even to this
day, been forced to shut down completely, but its productivity
is sporadic and of variable quality. The Second World War
changed the world in every imaginable particular. In the

entertainment world it (metaphorically) killed off the Stars.

Miklós Rózsa in his 80s is the sole survivor of the Old Guard, those whose achievements I have been discussing, and he is no longer active in films. Of the next generation Elmer Bernstein, John Williams and Jerry Goldsmith all started their careers under the aegis of the studio system, but developed independently of it. They had to adapt, for once films were cast adrift on the ever-expanding waters of free enterprise they changed out of all recognition; and the music, of course, had to change with them. In the mid- and late sixties the symphonic score disappeared almost completely; rock and pop was the norm. Now the use of synthesizers is increasingly widespread, largely on economic grounds: it is clearly preferable from a budgetary point of view to have an active score performed by one musician rather than by 50, 60 or more. Yet I doubt whether the live-orchestra score will ever become completely extinct. If we ever reach a point when everybody prefers sham or substitute living to the real thing, we shall have far more basic worries to engage us than the nature or quality of our film music.

The party's over; all we can do is look at the photographs. We turn from a world of shams and substitutes and second- and third-raters in every artistic sphere, a world in which showmen and buccaneers have been replaced by lawyers and accountants, to look back at Hollywood as it was in the thirties and forties. Let us view it for a moment in its ever-receding distance. Let us view it for a moment in its wider context. Think of who came there and what they achieved. Here, secluded in beach houses, hillside cottages and luxurious hotel bungalows were to be found an astonishing plethora of the world's great artists, seduced by the sun, by filmdom's Mephistophelean bargains, by something in the atmosphere which makes it — or made it — a place one wanted to be. Success breeds success, and an increasing concentration of talent nurtured creativity. There were performing artists like Bruno Walter, who conducted in the Hollywood Bowl and who, in his autobiographical *Theme and Variations*, wrote of the splendour of the *nox Californiensis*, the Californian night: "stunned by so much beauty, I felt overcome by a mood of happy exaltation, renewed at every future visit to the magic valley".[2] Jascha Heifetz, Gregor Piatigorsky and Artur Rubinstein, Vladimir Horowitz, Josef Szigeti, all settled and flourished in Southern California. Rachmaninov chose to end his days in Beverly Hills. The roster of composers is dazzling: Schoenberg, Stravinsky, Weill, the Gershwins, Vernon Duke, Copland, Leonard Bernstein are among the better-known who lived in, died in or merely visited Hollywood to compose. Prokofiev's tour of the film studios in 1937 led to his composing back in Russia one of the finest of all film-scores, *Alexander Nevsky*. In André Previn the 'magic valley' produced a studio prodigy who went on to become a conductor of international stature.

Then there were lesser-known musicians of the calibre of Mario Castelnuovo-Tedesco, Alexandre Tansman, Hanns Eisler, Ernst Toch, Albert Coates, Anthony Collins, Oscar Levant, George Antheil, Robert Russell Bennett. There were artist-songwriters like Harry Warren, Jerome Kern, Irving Berlin, Frederick Loewe, Vincent Youmans, Arthur Schwartz, Hugh Martin, Burton Lane, Victor Young and Gene de Paul; and artist-arrangers like Conrad Salinger, the great unsung hero of the MGM musicals, the like of whom no other studio could boast and whose influence on the Previn-Williams generation was enormous. Ferde Grofé, orchestrator of the *Rhapsody in Blue* and composer of the *Grand Canyon Suite*, settled in Santa Monica. Aldous Huxley and Christopher Isherwood were among the expatriate Englishmen. Thomas Mann bought a house in Pacific Palisades and wrote *Doktor Faustus* there. Other refugees from Europe included Franz Werfel (and his wife Alma Mahler), Heinrich Mann, Bertolt Brecht. Edgar Wallace and Somerset Maugham were just two of the many first-class popular writers brought (and bought) in by the studios. As for the galaxy of great stars, directors and film technicians, either home-grown or imported from Europe and Russia: merely to list them would require a chapter to itself. Is it any wonder that great movie music was created in such a milieu? Previn once said that those who maligned Hollywood were generally those who had never lived there. It is/was scarcely necessary to spend much time in the company of men like Herrmann, Rózsa and Elmer Bernstein in order to appreciate the distinction of their minds, their wide-ranging knowledge and understanding both inside music and outside.

Some of the composers whose work I have discussed were actually made (in every sense) by Hollywood; others were permanently changed. It brought out the best in some, the worst in others, or more often than not the best *and* the worst: for the best of Hollywood *is* very good, the worst *is* very bad. There is an enduring ambivalence about Hollywood. There is something in it which appeals to all of us; some find it too hot to handle, others a measure of self-fulfilment, yet others are alternately attracted and repelled. In a sense it is a part of the growing-up of us all, for we have all grown up with Hollywood movies. One thing is certain: at its best the Hollywood community was one of the most remarkable and variegated cultures, and at its most accomplished Hollywood musicianship was non-pareil. That is one good reason why, whatever it is that draws us to Hollywood, we should not be ashamed of it.

NOTES

1   *The Courier Journal and Times*, 18 March 1973.
2   *Theme and Variations*, New York 1946, p. 281.

APPENDICES

SELECT BIBLIOGRAPHY

G. Antheil: *Bad Boy of Music* (New York 1945)

G. Antheil: 'New Tendencies in Composing for Films', *Film Culture*, i/4 (1955), p. 16

W. Alwyn: 'How Not to Write Film Music', *British Film Academy Journal* (1954), autumn, p. 7

W. Alwyn: 'Composing for the Screen', *Films and Filming*, v/6 (1959), pp. 9, 34

I. Bazelon: *Knowing the Score: Notes on Film Music* (New York, 1975)

E. Bernstein (ed): 'An interview with Hugo Friedhofer', *Filmmusic Notebook* i (1974) pp 12–21

E. Bernstein: 'On Film Music', Journal of the University Film Association xxviii/4 (1976) p. 7

E. Bernstein (ed): 'A Conversation with Leo Shuken', *Filmmusic Notebook* spring 1975, p. 14

M. Bookspan and R. Yockey: *André Previn* (New York and London, 1981)

K. Cameron: *Sound and the Documentary Film* (London, 1947)

J. Caps: 'Interview with Jerome Moross', *Cue Sheet* v/3, 4 (1988)

B. Carroll: *Erich Wolfgang Korngold 1897–1957. His Life and Works* (Paisley, Scotland 1984)

K. Darby: 'Alfred Newman Biography and Filmography', *Filmmusic Notebook* ii (1976) pp 5–13

A. Deutsch: 'Collaboration Between the Screen Writer and the Composer', *Proceedings of the Writers' Congress* (Los Angeles, 1944)

D. Elley (ed): 'Dimitri Tiomkin: The Man and His Music', *National Film Dossier No. 1* (1986)

M. Evans: *Soundtrack: The Music of the Movies* (New York, 1975)

Film Music Notes (1941–57)

R.R. Faulkner: *Hollywood Studio Musicians* (Chicago, 1971)

C. Frater: *Sound Recording for Motion Pictures* (Cranbury, NJ, 1975)

M. Freedland (ed): *Composed and Conducted by Walter Scharf* (London and New Jersey, 1988)

K. Gough-Yates and M. Tarratt: *The Film Music Book: a Guide to Film composers* (New Rochelle, 1978)

E. Hagen (ed): *Scoring for Films* (Hollywood, Calif., 1971)

B. Herrmann: 'Score for a Film', *Focus on Citizen Kane*, ed R. Gottesman (Englewood Cliffs, 1971), p. 69

B. Herrmann: 'The Colour of the Music', *Sight and Sound*, xli (1972), p. 36 [interview]

A. Hopkins and L. Morton: 'Film Music Orchestration', *Sight and Sound*, xx (1951), p. 21

J. Huntley: *British Film Music* (London, 1947)

J. Huntley and R. Manvell: *The Technique of Film Music* (London and New York, 1957, rev, 2/1974)

E. Irving: 'Film Music', *Proceedings of the Royal Musical Association*, lxxvi (1949–50), p. 35

J. Jacobs: 'Alfred Newman', *Films in Review* x (1959) no 7, pp 403–14

H. Keller: 'Film Music: Some Objections', *Sight and Sound*, xv (1946), p. 136

H. Keller: 'Hollywood Music: Another View', *Sight and Sound*, xvi (1948), p. 168

L. Korngold: *Erich Wolfgang Korngold* (Vienna 1967)

O. Levant: *A Smattering of Ignorance* (New York, 1959)

L. Levy: *Music for the Movies* (London, 1948)

J.L. Limbacher, (ed): *Film Music* (Metuchen, NJ, 1974)

K. London: *Film Music* (London, 1936)

C. McCarty: *Film Composers in America: A Checklist of their work* (Glendale, Calif., 1953)

C. McCarty (ed): *Film Music* 1 (London and New York, 1989)

D. Meeker: *Jazz in the Movies* (London, 1972) [index]

L. Murray: *Musician – A Hollywood Journal* (New Jersey and Ontario, 1987)

La musica nel film: Firenze 1950 [see also A. Hopkins: 'Film Music Conference at Florence', *Sight and Sound*, xix (1950), p. 243]

R.U. Nelson: 'The Craft of the Film Score', *Pacific Spectator*, i (1947), p. 435

R.U. Nelson: 'Film Music: Colour or Line?', *Hollywood Quarterly*, ii (1946), Oct. 57

A. North: 'Composing for Films', *Motion Picture Herald* (1965), no. 23, p. 12

C. Palmer: *Dimitri Tiomkin: A Portrait* (London 1984)

R.M. Prendergast: *A Neglected Art: A Critical Study of Music in Films* (New York, 1977)

L. Rosenman: 'Notes from a Sub-culture', *PNM*, vii/1 (1968), p. 122

M. Rózsa: *Double Life* (London, 1982 and New York, 1989)

L. Sabaneyev: *Music for Films* (London, 1935)

F. Skinner: *Underscore* (New York, 1960) [textbook on film scoring]

F. Steiner: *The Making of an American Film Composer: A study of Alfred Newman's Music in the First Decade of the Sound Era* (1981: unpublished dissertation)

M. Steiner: 'Scoring the Film', *We Make the Movies*, ed. N. Naumberg (London, 1938), p. 216

F.W. Sternfeld: 'Music and the Feature Films', *Musical Quarterly*, xxxiii (1947), p. 517 (analysis of Hugo Friedhofer's *Best Years of our Lives*)

T. Thomas: *Music for the Movies* (London, 1973)

T. Thomas (ed): *Film Score: The View from the Podium* (New Jersey and London, 1979)

V. Thomson: *The State of Music* (New York), 1939/R1974), 174ff

D. Tiomkin: 'Composing for Films', *Films in Review*, ii/9 (1951), p. 16

D. Tiomkin and P. Buranelli: *Please Don't Hate Me* (New York, 1959)

R. Vaughan Williams: 'Composing for the Films', *Some Thoughts on Beethoven's Choral Symphony and other Musical Subjects* (London, 1953)

J. Wagner: 'Music in the Western: Variations on the Folksong', *Image et son* (1972), no. 248, p. 41

INDEX OF FILMS

INDEX OF NAMES

FILM BOOKS FROM
MARION BOYARS PUBLISHERS

Ingmar Bergman

Ingmar Bergman's ability to combine the greatest universality with the most delicate intimacy of situation and characterization gives his films something of the power of myth. The quality of his writing is such that the scripts are almost as rewarding to read as the films are to watch. The volumes are illustrated with stills from the films.

A Film Trilogy

Ingmar Bergman's theme in this great trilogy of films is the obsession with God; that strange, compelling search for guidance which is, perhaps, doomed by the very contingency from which it springs. Bergman calls his treatment a 'reduction':

Through a Glass Darkly — certainty achieved

The Communicants — certainty unmasked

The Silence — God's silence — the negative impression

Persona & Shame

Persona totally involves the spectator in the action: he is forced to participate in the erosion of the distinction between the personalities of the two main characters: Elisabeth, an actress who has suffered a nervous breakdown and Alma, her apparently well-balanced and extrovert nurse. The relationship turns into a bewildering reversal and substitution of their respective identities.

Shame has, seemingly, a more straightforward and clearly defined plot. In it we watch Jan's progress from artist to survivor/murderer in a war-torn society. The progressive breakdown of all civilized standards of behaviour have completely brutalized the hero, and his culture and morality are shown to be only superficial attributes, annihilated by the unconcern of an arbitrary and amoral universe.

INGMAR BERGMAN
The Cinema as Mistress
Philip Mosley

Philip Mosley's study is primarily a critical history of Bergman's films dating from his earliest work as a writer/director in the late 'forties right up to *Autumn Sonata* and his first projects outside of his native Sweden. The author traces the development of Bergman's highly individual techniques, dialogues and his disjointed use of time and space in the narrative. Mosley sees Bergman's cinematic innovations as a product of his own sense of identity as a Scandinavian artist. He stresses the importance of Bergman's personal biography, especially his early life and experiences in Sweden as the son of a Lutheran Minister.

A useful and provocative companion to Bergman's films, this book includes many stills from Bergman's more famous films.

Other Bergman film scripts available:
Face to Face, Scenes from a Marriage, and *The Serpent's Egg.*

ALFRED HITCHCOCK
AND THE MAKING OF PSYCHO
Stephen Rebello

Here, for the first time, is the complete inside story of the making of *Psycho*. The author takes us behind the scenes to witness the creation of one of cinema's boldest and most influential films. From Hitchcock's private files, in-depth interviews with the stars, writers and technical crew, we get a unique picture of the master at work.

Psycho came close to not being produced. The reader's report said, 'impossible to film'. Paramount refused to produce the film. However, Hitchcock personally bought the film rights to Robert Bloch's novel. He then decided to finance the picture himself, but with no blockbuster stars, no exotic locales, no top screen wriiters, no big budget — and to film it himself in black and white.

Using newly-discovered material, the author shows how Hitchcock overcame studio politics, censorship and feisty collaborators. Along with other unique insights — including an account of Bernard Herrmann's breathtaking film score — the author gives a day-by-day inside view of the master director at work, creating one of cinema's most daring, ground-breaking and dark thrillers.

Stephen Rebello is a film journalist and the author of *Reel Art-Great Posters from the Golden Age of the Silver Screen* and several screenplays. The book contains 16 pages of photographs highlighting dramatic scenes from *Psycho*.

Pauline Kael
Film Writings

'The thing that makes her special — makes her a critic in fact —
is the way her work accumulates into a living body of writing
from which a robust aesthetic can be derived ... a body of
criticism which can be compared with Shaw's criticism of music
and theatre.'   *The Times Literary Supplement*

Kiss Kiss Bang Bang

America's most celebrated film critic gives us what amounts to an
informal history of cinema. Her reviews (of some 300 films) are as
cogent, entertaining and informative as we have come to expect. As
well as these there are essays on westerns, big Hollywood films, camp
films and spoofs, art films, fad films, films for children and films on
television. There are thoughtful analyses of the careers of Marlon
Brando, Orson Welles and Stanley Kramer and a fascinating day-by-day
account of how Mary McCarthy's novel *The Group* was turned into a
film.

Taking It All In

Taking It All In runs from June 1980 to June 1983, and discusses some
150 films as varied as *The Chant of Jimmy Blacksmith* — 'a dreamlike
Requiem Mass for a nation's lost honour,' *Tootsie* — 'marvellous fun'
and 'Richard Pryor is the only great poet satirist among out comics.'

State of the Art

The title of this collection of reviews from June 1983–July 1985 is a
caveat to those who think that technological whizzkiddery and ever
more extraordinary special effects are as important as a good script and
a good cast. The collection itself is Kael at her inimitable best:
entertaining, provocative, uncompromising — unique.

Hooked

Hooked runs from July 1985 to June 1988 and discusses over 100 films
from *Mona Lisa* to *Robocop* and from *Beetlejuice* to *The Unbearable
Lightness of Being*.

Other collections of Pauline Kael's film writing:
Deeper into Movies, Reeling, and *When the Lights go Down.*